INDIA:

ITS NATIVES AND MISSIONS

INDIA:

ITS NATIVES AND MISSIONS

REV. GEORGE TREVOR, M. A.

GYAN

Published by

Gyan Publishing House
5, Ansari Road
Daryaganj, New Delhi-110002
Phone: 011-47034999, 9811692060
E-mail: books@gyanbooks.com

Distribution Network
gyanbooks.com
India, USA, Canada, UK, Australia, France

ISBN: 978-81-212-8804-0 (PB)
First Published, 1799

2nd Impression 2023

Printed at: Gyan Press, Delhi.

INDIA: ITS NATIVES AND MISSIONS
Author: George Trevor

INDIA:

ITS NATIVES AND MISSIONS.

INDIA:

ITS NATIVES AND MISSIONS.

BY THE

REV. GEORGE TREVOR, M.A.,

CANON OF YORK; LATE CHAPLAIN ON THE MADRAS ESTABLISHMENT;
AUTHOR OF "INDIA: AN HISTORICAL SKETCH."

LONDON:

THE RELIGIOUS TRACT SOCIETY:

Instituted 1799.

56, PATERNOSTER ROW; 65, ST. PAUL'S CHURCHYARD;
AND 164, PICCADILLY.

CONTENTS.

CHAPTER V.

MOHAMMEDANISM.

CHAPTER VI.

POLITICAL GOVERNMENT.

CHAPTER VII.

PRIVATE LIFE.

CHAPTER VIII.

STATE OF KNOWLEDGE AND EDUCATION.

CHAPTER IX.

CHRISTIANITY—EARLY EFFORTS.

CHAPTER X.

CHRISTIANITY—EXISTING MISSIONS.

PREFACE.

The contents of the following pages were originally designed to form part of a publication which has already appeared under the title of "India: an Historical Sketch." In determining to issue them as independent works, some trifling repetition has been rendered unavoidable. Each is now complete in itself: while taken together, they form as full an account of the ancient and modern state of India as the author was able to condense into the prescribed limits.

In a work of this description, it has not been thought advisable to encumber the pages with too many references. Nothing has been stated as a fact which the author has not verified, either from personal experience or from authorities universally admitted. The works of which most frequent use has been made, are, Elphinstone's History of India; Professor H. H. Wilson's Translation of the Rig-Veda Sanhita; Mr. Muir's Sanscrit Texts; Mr. Caldwell's Comparative Grammar of Dravidian Languages; Dr. Macbride's Mohammedan Religion Explained; The *Qanoon-e-Islâm*, or Customs of Mussulmans in India, by Jaffur Shurreef; Dr. Allen's India, Ancient and Modern, (published at Boston); Thornton's Gazetteer; and the Reports of the Religious Societies.

For the opinions and suggestions which will be

found interspersed, the author alone is responsible. He is not content simply to re-echo the conclusions of other minds; but, in submitting each question to the review of a judgment which can lay no claim to the submission of others, he has endeavoured briefly to assign the reasons which have convinced himself.

If the reader shall derive from his labours some more definite conceptions, than are generally entertained, of the extent and nature of the dominion which a gracious Providence has intrusted to the British Crown in India, may the result be to augment the efforts for the subjugation of its vast and varied population to the sceptre of CHRIST. No political or financial reforms can be compared in urgency with this indispensable obligation; nor will any be successful, save in proportion as the higher object is faithfully kept in view.

It is not to the political government, but to the heart of the British Christian, that India sends her cry for the gospel. The author is anxious, indeed, to see the great questions of *caste*, and the *position of the Bible in native education*—happily all that now remain of the long controversy with Indian statesmen—entertained in a broader and loftier spirit, than seems as yet to have been inherited by the Ministers of the day. But this will follow when the British public shall be in earnest for the conversion of the natives, and testify their zeal by multiplying a thousandfold the men and the means for the direct preaching of GOSPEL TRUTH among them.

GLOSSARY.

A, Arabic; C, Canarese; M, Mahratta; H, Hindustanee; S, Sanscrit; T, Tamil.

Ab (H), water; *e.g.*, *Doab*, two waters; *Trimab*, three waters; *Punjab*, five waters.

Abad (H), dwelling or city, as Allahabad (God's house).

Adawlut (H), court of justice.

Aeen (H), laws or regulations by secular authority, in distinction to those of the Koran or sacred tradition.

Ameen (H), a native judge.

Ameer or *Amir* (H), noble or chief.

Amil and *amildar* (H), a native collector of revenue.

Aswamedha (S), Horse sacrifice, which, performed a hundred times, raises the sacrificer to the rank of Indra.

Aum (S), the mystic monosyllable secretly uttered before all prayer, supposed to typify the three Vedas, or Brahma, Siva, and Vishnu.

Avatara (S), descent or incarnation of a deity.

Ayeen (H), see *Aeen*.

Bagh (H), a garden; also a tiger.

Bahadur (H), title of rank.

Bajra (H), a kind of millet (*panicum spicatum*).

Begum (H), a princess (Mohammedan).

Bhang (H), an intoxicating preparation of hemp.

Brahm (S), the Divine essence.

Brahma (S), the personal Creator.

Brahmin or *Brahman* (H), the first of the four Hindu castes.

Bund (H), a dyke or bank.

Byragees (H), *lit.*, one devoid of passion; a religious mendicant, properly a worshipper of Vishnu.

Caliph or *Khalifa* (H), the successors of Mohammed.

Cazee or *Kazee* (A), Mohammedan judge, formerly presiding in towns, now chiefly employed as advisers to the British Court.

Chowt or *chouth* (H), a fourth part of the government collections, demanded by the Mahrattas as the price of forbearing to ravage the country.

Circar (H), a district.

Cooly (T), daily hire; a day labourer.

Cot and *cottah* (H), a fort.

Crore (H), ten millions, a hundred lakhs.

Deccan (H), the south.

Deen or *din* (H), religion, especially the Mohammedan.

Desmook (M), a hereditary native officer of police and revenue.

Dewan (H), a royal court (*divan*); the head financial minister; the head of a department.

Dewannee (H), the office of Dewan; also used for the territory from which the revenue was receivable.

Dharma (S), law divine.

——— *Shastra*, the Hindu code.

Doab (H), "two waters;" a tract of land between two rivers.

Droog (H), a hill fort.

Durbar (H), the royal court or levee.

Dwarpar Yug (S), the third age of the world.

Emir, corruption of ameer.

Enam (H), a grant of land rent free, varying in right according to the authority of the grantor.

Faquir (H), an indigent person, generally a Mohammedan religious mendicant.

Fateeha (H), *lit.*, opening or commencement; the first sura or chapter of the Koran; prayers for the dead.

Firman (H), a mandate; grant or patent.

Florikin, a small species of the bustard.

Ghât (H), a mountain pass; also a landing place or flight of steps on a river.

Gosayen or *Gossain* (S), *lit.*, one who restrains his passions; a religious mendicant, worshipping Mahadeo (or Siva), and wearing yellow or orange, his emblematical colour; the term is also applied to vagrants in general.

Guru (S), *lit.*, heavy; a person of weight; a spiritual teacher or guide.

Haj (A), the pilgrimage to Mecca.

Haji or *Hadgi* (H), a Mohammedan who has performed the pilgrimage to Mecca.

Harem or *Haram* (H), sacred; the women's apartments.

Havildar (H), *lit.*, an office-bearer; in the army equivalent to a sergeant.

Hegira (A), the flight of Mohammed from Medina.

Islam (H and A), the Mohammedan religion.

Istan (H), a termination signifying country, as Affghanistan, the country of the Affghans.

Jaghire (H), a fief or grant of the revenue and government of a district for a time or for life; sometimes renewable to the heir on payment of a fine.

Jemadar (H), a native subaltern officer; a leader; a lieutenant.

Jin (A), a genie or goblin.

Jowar (H), a kind of millet (*holcus sorghum*).

Jummabundy (H), a revenue settlement.

Kali Yug (S), the fourth, or present age of the world.

Kalpa (S), the day or period for which Brahm assigns the universe to the sacred triad.

Kanoon (H), rule or regulation.

Khan (H), a title borne by Mohammedans of Persian or Patan descent.

Koran, properly *Kuran* (A), sacred book of the Mohammedans.

Kshettriya (S), the second or military caste of the Hindus.

Lakh or *lac* (H), a hundred thousand.

Lingam (S), *lit.*, a mark or sign, the symbol of Siva.

Miras (H), inheritance, whence

Mirasdar or *Meerasdar*, the holder of hereditary lands or office in a village.

Meer or *Mir* (H), a chief, head of a department; also a title borne by the Syeds.

Mofussil (H), "separate;" a district or jurisdiction; the provinces as opposed to the town, or Sudr.

Mohurrum (H), "sacred;" the first month of the Mohammedan year, in which it is unlawful to make war; the feast held in this month.

Monsoon, the trade wind; also the period for which it continues.

Moolla Mulla (H), a Mohammedan lawyer or learned man; a judge, the deputy of a Kazee; also applied to village schoolmasters.

Moonsiff (H), "equitable;" a judge; under British government a native civil judge of the lowest rank.

Moslem, *Mussulman*, *Musliman*, *Muslim* (H), a believer in Islam or Mohammedanism.

Moulvie or *Mufti* (H), a Mohammedan law officer, whose duty was to expound the law for the Kazee to execute.

Muntra (S), a prayer; a magical formula.

Musjid or *Mosque*, Mohammedan place of worship.

Musnud, a throne.

Nabob, English corruption of nawab.

Naib (H), deputy or viceroy.

Namaz (H), prayer (Mohammedan).

Nautch or *Nách* (H), dancing or acting.

Nawab (H), plural of naib; used honorifically as a title of rank (Mohammedan).

Nazim or *Nizam* (H), viceroy, or chief administrator of criminal laws (Mohammedan).

Nuggur (H), a town.

Nullah (H), a watercourse, rivulet, or ravine.

Oordu or *Urdu* (H), a camp; the Hindustani language, spoken by the Mohammedans generally throughout India.

Omrah (H), plural of ameer; *ameer-ul-omrah*, chief of the nobles; sometimes "commander-in-chief."

Padishah or *Padshah* (H), a king (Mohammedan); title of Mogul emperors.

Padre (Portuguese), common term in India for a Christian clergyman.

Pagoda, Portuguese word for heathen temple.

Patan, a term applied to the old *Affghan* Mohammedans, as distinguished from the *Moguls*.

Peishwah (M), chief minister of the Mahratta court.

Pergunnah (H), a district or province; less than a zillah.

Perwanah (H), a permit or pass.

Polian or *Pulayan*, caste of slaves in Malabar.

Pollar (T), caste of shoemakers.

Poojah or *Puja* (S), worship.

Polygar (C), a petty chieftain, formerly independent, now a landholder.

Prusad or *Prasad* (S), "favour or kindness;" term applied to food or sweetmeats offered to an idol, and then distributed among the worshippers. May be eaten by all castes.

Punchayet or *Punchayat* (H), a native court of arbitration, consisting properly of *five* members.

Pundit (S), a Brahman learned in the Vedas and other Shastras.

Pur, *poor*, or *pore* (S), a town or city, mostly used in composition, as *Sirram-pur*, vulgarly *Serampore*.

Purana (S), old; the especial designation of the eighteen books of Hindu traditions and legends, which are really more modern than the Vedas.

Raggi (H), a grain extensively cultivated in the south of India (the *cynosurus corocanus*).

Raja and *Rai* (H), a king, a prince (Hindu); given as a title by Mohammedan governments.

Rana (H), corruption of raja.

Ranee (H), feminine of raja.

Rig (S), a stanza; whence

Rig-Veda, the first or principal Veda.

Rupee (H), a silver coin, worth about two shillings, formerly bearing the impress of the emperor Shah Alum and other native authorities; but in 1835 the "Company's rupee" was issued and made current throughout British India, bearing the effigy of the British sovereign.

Ryot or *Rayat* (H), a cultivator, farmer, or peasant, whence

Ryotwar, settlement; a land assessment levied direct from the cultivators.

Sastra or *Shastra* (S), scripture.

Satya Yug (S), the first age of the world.

Sepoy or *Sipahi* (H), a soldier.

Shah (H), a king, a prince (Mohammedan); used as a title.

Shahzada (H), son of the king.

Shastra (S), Hindu scripture.

Shastree, a Brahman learned in the Shastras.

Sheikh (H), "an old man;" elder; given to Mohammedan saints; head of an Arab tribe; also used to designate the descendants of Mohammed, of Abubeker, and of Omar.

Shias or *Shiites* (H), one of the great Mohammedan sects; "followers" of Ali, the son-in-law of the prophet, and esteeming the three caliphs, Abubeker, Omar, and Osman as usurpers. To this sect belong the Persians generally, the royal family of Oude, and most of the lower orders of Mussulmans in India.

Shradh (S), a funeral ceremony, in which food and water are offered to the deceased ancestors.

Sirdar (H), a chief.

Sirdeshmooki (M), the claim of the desmook, ten per cent. on the revenue exacted in addition to the chout.

Sirkar (H), the state or government.

Soonnees (H), the orthodox Mussulman party, who maintain the lawful succession of the three caliphs before Ali, and pay great deference to the "traditions" of Islam. The Arabs, Turks, Affghans, and most of the educated Mussulmans of India are of this class, and style themselves *orthodox*, the Shias being regarded as heretics.

Stan, see *Istan*.

Subah (H), a province or government; hence

Subadar, a governor or viceroy; also a captain in the army.

Suddur (H), chief, supreme, as *sudder adawlut*, the Company's supreme court of justice.

Sudra (S), the fourth, or servile caste of the Hindus ; now vaguely applied also to all the mixed castes.

Sultan (H), a sovereign prince (Mohammedan); also a title borne by the younger members of the royal family, especially Delhi.

Sunnud (H), a grant or diploma.

Swami or *Sami* (S), a master or lord; title given to idols.

Syed or *Said* (H), a lord; designation of the descendants of Ali.

Taboot (H), a coffin or bier, carried in the procession of the Mohurrum.

Tahsildar (H), a native collector of revenue.

Talook (H), an estate usually smaller than a zemindarry, but in North-West provinces presents various peculiarities.

Tank, a term applied in India to an artificial lake or reservoir, large or small.

Tazzia (H), model of the tomb of Hussan and Hussein.

Thug (H), a cheat, a knave; latterly a robber or assassin.

Treta Yug (S), the second age of the world.

Tulwar, a sword.

Vaishya (S), the third of the Hindu castes.

Vakeel, a proxy or advocate.

Veda (S), "the book," or the Hindu sacred scriptures; properly four, or some say three, but the term is extended to other works.

Vedanta (S), a system of pantheistic philosophy, founded on scattered texts of the Vedas.

Vizier (H), the principal minister in a Mohammedan sovereignty.

Vizierut (H), the office of vizier.

Yogi (S), a religious mendicant.

Zeearut (H), pilgrimage to a grave.

Zemin or *Zamin* (H), the earth; whence

Zemindar, a landholder; and

Zemindary, the district or estate of a zemindar.

Zillah (H), a large district.

THE NATIVES OF INDIA.

CHAPTER I.

RACE, AND LANGUAGE.

Diversities of origin—Peopling of India—Aboriginal—Dravidian—Dasyus—Hindus or Aryans—Caucasian race—Existing variety of feature—Languages—Northern and southern families—Hindustani—Sanscrit—Tamil—Scythian elements—Sudras anciently independent—Reduced to serfdom—Superior grade in the Deccan—Modifications in Brahmanism—Mohammedan invasion—Foreign element—National diversities of Hindus and Mohammedans—Punjab—Sindh—Guzerat—Hindustan East and West—Bengal—Orissa—Goondwana—Maharashtra—Telingana—Carnata Drawed, or Tamil country—Malabar—Travancore—Neilgherries—Tinnevelly—Mohammedans of different origin—Four clans—Parsees.

To form a just conception of the natives of India, the first thing requisite is to abandon the idea, that they consist of one people, or even one race of mankind. India itself is not a national or indigenous appellation. It is a geographical term of foreign origin and use, extending over a region as large as that included between the Baltic and the Mediterranean seas, and which, from the earliest antiquity, has been partitioned into states, more numerous and more diversified than those of Europe. Like Europeans, the natives of India have mostly embraced a common religion; their governments have repeatedly succumbed to foreign empire, as those of Europe once acknowledged the mastery of Rome; but the populations of India never parted with their distinctive peculiarities, which remain as strongly marked at this day as in the nations of the west. The natives of the Punjab and of Bengal, of Northern and Southern India, of Guzerat and the coast of Coromandel, differ in language, blood, and sentiment, greatly more than the Englishman differs from the Italian, or the German from the Portuguese. The mountains and forests are tenanted by fragments of races obviously older than those which cultivate the fields and occupy the cities. Traditions of race and ancestry, and a wide diversity of language, still separate those whom religious institutions have endeavoured to unite. In fact, the various portions of the heterogeneous mass own a stronger sympathy and much closer relations with the European and Christian power which holds them all in subjection, than have at any time subsisted between themselves.

The natives of India are commonly divided into Hindus and Mohammedans; these, however, are religious designations, implying no community of language or blood. Both Hindus and Mohammedans entered India as invaders. The former have extended their name and institutions to more than five-sixths of the population, but without obliterating the previous distinctions of nationality: the Mussulmans are few in number, and scattered as aliens among the indigenous masses: while sixteen millions of an earlier race than either still inhabit the mountains and forests, strangers to civilization of any kind.

The peopling of India has been regulated, as in other regions, by the conformation of the country and the attractions of soil and climate. These are the earliest means employed by Divine Providence for the dissemination of the human family through the appointed "bounds of their habitation."* The wanderers from Babel would easily find their way, through the passes of the mountainous region on the north-west, to the banks of the Indus, and thence across the river to the well-watered valleys of the Punjab, and the spacious plains of the Ganges. Spreading southward, their course was arrested by the deep valley of the Nerbudda, which crosses the entire continent, and has in all periods formed one of its great natural divisions. The tide of migration was stayed here long enough to render "*the South*" the designation of an unknown country: pressed at last by new accessions in the rear, the human wave rolled over this barrier, and spread itself to the next great natural boundary, the Kistna. With another impulse this also was surmounted, and the population advanced to the furthest cape. The whole was occupied from a period anterior to any vestiges of history; but the population still exhibits the relics of the successive races which, hurled upon one another, have left their remains like geological formations, stratified or in fragments, in the different localities.

The aboriginal people—at least the earliest that can now be distinguished—is represented by the wild denizens of the jungle and hills, who are found under different names, and at great distances, in India, with sufficient resemblance in feature, speech, and habits, to justify the opinion that all are descended from one original stock. The *Kols* of Orissa, the *Bheels* who roam the mountains of Central India, the *Coolies* and *Dunjas*

* Acts xvii. 26.

of Guzerat, the *Sontals*, *Doms*, and other fragments of a people clearly more ancient than the Hindu, seem to be relics of a race once spread throughout the continent, and whose features still exhibit decided evidences of a *Scythian* origin. They are usually smaller and darker than the inhabitants of the more cultivated parts, slender but extremely active, with a quick restless eye, broad flat features, large ears, and cheek-bones imparting somewhat of a square or lozenge-shape to the face. They exhibit an indomitable love of hunting, wear but little clothing, and are armed with bows and arrows. They usually live in a state of warfare with their more civilized neighbours, subsisting themselves by hunting and thieving. When attacked, they retreat into the rocks and jungle, whence the pursuer is overwhelmed by showers of arrows from an invisible foe. Their agriculture is scanty and imperfect, and their habits migratory. They seem indeed to be natural denizens of the forest, receding into its depths as cultivation advances upon the outskirts, and again taking their revenge by devastations so extensive that the jungle has recovered its dominion, and the ruins of villages are seen among the haunts of wild beasts.

Nearly a tenth of the existing population of India are still in this savage condition, acknowledging no laws but the will of their local chief, and no institutions but those of the desert. Others of the same race are found in the villages, where they have taken service as hunters and watchmen, and constitute a rude but efficient rural police. They remain, however, entirely distinct from the Hindu population, and are easily recognised by the peculiar features and habits of their race, no less than by their straw huts invariably reared *outside* the wall of the village they belong to.

This portion of the natives are altogether strangers to the civil and religious institutions of the Hindus. There are larger and more civilized divisions of the same, or a kindred, race, who, in adopting the Brahmanical rites, have retained no less distinctly the traces of a separate origin. The Brahmanical or true Hindu population had its seat in the plains of the Ganges, thence called by the Mohammedans *Hindustan.* The *Deccan,* or country south of the Nerbudda, was peopled by quite another race, to whom the name *Dravidian* has been applied, from *Drawed,* the native appellation of the most southern division of India. Of this race upwards of thirty millions are still settled in the Deccan, who, from their resemblance in many particulars, are supposed by some to be of the same stock with the wild aboriginals. Others, however, with greater probability, consider the Dravidian immigration to have been posterior to the aboriginal settlement; and while issuing, like the other, out of Scythia, to have consisted of tribes in a more advanced state of civilization. On this theory the aboriginals were first subdued or expelled by the Dravidians, as the latter were in turn compelled to yield, at a much later date, to the Hindus.

Some writers find indications of a *third* population from Scythia, intervening between the Dravidian and the Hindu, and constituting the *Dasyus,* whom the latter found in possession of Northern India. By these it is conjectured the Dravidians had been previously compelled to retreat into the south, where they form the bulk of the population at this day. These migrations, occurring long before the period of history, are all of course involved in considerable doubt; but the distinctions of race and language still existing, are facts which cannot be overlooked.

The first Hindus, termed in their own ancient writings *Aryas*,* seem to have been comparatively few in number, though, from a superior physical and mental organization, they became the dominant race throughout India. They were taller and fairer than the natives whom they found in possession, and who had probably been darkened and enervated by exposure to the Indian sun. Hence the Vedas say that Indra, when he cast out the Dasyus, "divided the fields with his white-complexioned friends." They were distinguished also by the Caucasian features, a thin straight aquiline nose, full but not projecting lips, oval face, and long silky hair with a tendency to curl. Their language (Sanscrit) enters largely into the composition of Greek and Latin, with all the southern languages of Europe, as well as into all the Sclavonic and Teutonic dialects, from Russian to Anglo-Saxon. The true Hindus, therefore, were of the same stock with those who, at a distance of thirty centuries, have succeeded to the supremacy over their posterity, together with the country they subdued.

The existing Hindu population derives no little variety in colour and feature from the extensive admixture of races, aided by the effects of climate and social insti-

* In later language, the word *Arya* signifies a respectable man, and *Dasyu*, a thief or robber; but in the Vedas the two terms are invariably contrasted as expressions of religious and political antagonism (see Professor H. H. Wilson's Introduction to the Rig Veda). Sir W. Jones thought the Aryas came from a part of the old Iranian empire, which preceded the Persian, and the limits of which are lost in fable.

tutions of a particular kind. The higher castes, representing most closely the primitive Aryans, are usually tall and well proportioned; in many instances not darker than some of the inhabitants of Europe, and still retaining a distinctly Caucasian physiognomy. Casts may be seen at the East India House, taken from the faces of Brahmans and Rajpoots, which it would be hard to distinguish from Europeans; in others the Caucasian is plainly mixed with the Scythian feature. This mixture is most perceptible among the lower classes, and more in the south than in the north.

Similar conclusions are attained from a comparison of the languages still spoken and written in India. Omitting the ruder jargons of the jungle, and the numerous local dialects (which would swell the list to many scores), not less than *twenty-two* distinct languages have been grammatically compared and classified. They are distributed into two, or perhaps three, distinct families, of which the first is seated in the north, the second in the south, and the third is more faintly indicated among the scattered fragments of the earliest population in central India. The first family consists of the Sanscrit and its eight derivatives,—Bengali, Hindi western (or Canuji), Hindi eastern (or Mithala), Punjabi, Sindhu, Guzerathi, Marathi, and Uriya the language of Orissa. These are the vernaculars of Hindustan and the nearest parts of the Deccan. The rest of the south belongs to the Dravidian family; it includes five cultivated vernaculars,—Tamil, Telugu, Canarese, Malayalam, and Tulu or Tulava (once prevalent in Canara, but now limited to some 150,000 persons in the neighbourhood of Mangalore), with four unpolished tongues, the

Toda and Kota of the Neilgherries, and the Gond and Khond (more properly called Ku), which are found behind the hills of Orissa, in the great jungle of Gondwana. The Kols speak an aboriginal language of another and probably earlier family; two other uncultivated idioms of central India, the Uraon and Rajmahal, seem to be intermediate links between the Kol and the Dravidian family. To all these is to be added the *Hindustani*, which is not the vernacular of any portion of the natives, but simply the *Oordu*, or camp language of the Mussulman invaders, formed from a mixture of Persian and Hindi, and spoken by individuals and classes throughout India.*

Sanscrit, now entirely a dead language, was probably never spoken in the elaborate form used in literature, and termed *pracreet* or perfect. In the Hindu drama a ruder dialect is put into the mouths of the lower orders, which may have been the vernacular of the early Aryans. From Sanscrit are derived all the existing vernaculars of Hindustan, together with those of Maharasthra and Orissa, the two adjacent countries of the Deccan. The other languages of the south exhibit a structure and origin wholly different: they belong to the Dravidian races, and have been traced, like them, to a *Scythian* parentage. Of these the Tamil, lying furthest to the south, and possessing an extensive literature, is at once the most polished, and the freest from Sanscrit admixture. The other dialects are observed to partake of this infusion in the same proportion as they recede from the south and approach the seat of Sanscrit dominion.

* Mr. Caldwell adds, also, the tongues of Cashmere and Nepal as Hindu languages, but those countries are not included in our view of India.

The particulars in which the Dravidian tongues differ from the Sanscrit, and agree with the Scythian, have been traced, with more or less of success, in the dialects of the wilder aboriginals, and also in some elements of the northern vernaculars which seem to belong to an earlier origin than Sanscrit. Similar analogies have been found in the speech of the earliest settlers in Lapland and Siberia; and again, on the other side of the world, in the dialects of Australia; so truly does all investigation confirm the apostle's statement, that "God hath made of one blood all nations of men for to dwell on all the face of the earth." *

The conclusions, which thus agree in pointing at the existence in India of races and nations older than the Hindu, are further confirmed from the ancient writings of the latter people. In their system *Sudra* is the name of the lowest caste, assigned to perpetual servitude; yet mention is made in the Shastras of cities governed by Sudra kings, which Brahmans are exhorted to avoid; and even whole territories are described as inhabited by Sudras, "overwhelmed with atheists and deprived of Brahmans." These expressions evidently refer to communities existing previous to the Aryan invasion. The word *Sudra* has been derived from the name of a tribe in the Punjab, which was one of the first to receive the Brahman yoke. Among the notes which link the Aryan with the European race, general Briggs places their habit of reducing subjugated enemies to a condition of agrestic (not domestic) slavery; a state equivalent to the *serfdom* of Russia, Poland, and Hungary, and which was once universal throughout Europe. It is disputed whether this class existed

* Acts xvii. 26.

among the Aryans themselves; but it seems pretty certain that, after reducing a large portion of the aboriginal and Dravidian races to their obedience, they admitted them into the Hindu community in that inferior position. Others, however, while receiving the Brahmanical religion and civilization, retained their political independence. These, accepting the appellation of Sudra, converted it into a title of distinction; whence it may be remarked that in the Deccan generally, where the Hindu institutions prevailed at a later date, and by persuasion rather than force, the Sudra has always occupied a far higher position than in the north.* The Brahmanical system, as it proceeded southward, and encountered the resistance of previously established rites and customs, underwent many other modifications, and incorporated a great variety of new elements. Hence the existing condition of Hindu society, and even of Hindu religion, differs in different parts, while all have widely diverged from the most ancient standards.

Another great interval of time was succeeded by another immigration of race and religion in the Mohammedan invasion. These invaders, like the Aryans, were comparatively few in number, yet strong enough to impose a dominion by force of arms. They differed, however, in not being able either to drive the natives before them, or to incorporate any considerable portion into their own system. The Hindus remained in possession of the soil, or were only partially removed by slaughter. Their conquerors, though mixing more freely with native

* The Sudra is, in fact, a *high caste* in the south of India at this day, and scarcely inferior in pretension to the Rajpoot of the north. The Mahratta princes and chiefs boast of being Sudras.

blood than the existing rulers, never became amalgamated with the previous inhabitants. They subjugated, but could not occupy, the land; planting military colonies, and wielding the powers of empire, yet remaining ever a foreign element in an uncongenial population. Mohammedanism has been modified by Hinduism, as Hinduism was by local usages of older date; but it never amalgamated with the Brahmanical, as the latter did with aboriginal systems. It could never cease to regard the idolater with a savage scorn, nor to be itself abhorred by the native as an unclean and barbarous intruder.

The distinctions of race which have been mentioned, form the leading, though unequal, features of the existing native population, but they are far from approaching to a national classification. The aboriginal, Dravidian, and Aryan races each probably entered India, not in one body, but (as the Celts and Goths came into Europe) by many successive migrations, each importing its own social distinctions. Certain it is that, from the earliest period of history, India has been partitioned into many different states, waging war with their own race as freely as against the common invader. The existence at this day of distinct civilized languages, must be taken to denote at least as many Hindu *nations*, which were doubtless organized out of a much larger number of anciently independent tribes. The Mussulman population, also, though amounting to only one-fifteenth of the whole, is made up of many heterogeneous elements: a full half consists of Hindu proselytes, and the foreign moiety is descended from several distinct, and even hostile, ancestries. The Arabs, Turks, Patans, Mongols, Persians, and Affghans, though all disciples of the false prophet, acknowledge little other community with each other. The Patan and Mogul dynasties of Delhi, the sultans of Bengal, Malwa, and Guzerat, with the Bahmani empire, and the four shahs of the Deccan, were all Mohammedan powers; but, springing from various origins and guided by antagonistic objects, they never constituted, or attempted to constitute, a Mussulman nation in India. Their remnants are not less diversified in feeling and interest at this day, and are consolidated only by a common subjection to the British sway.

So vast and varied a population manifestly cannot be classed under the common names of Hindu and Mohammedan. It would be as accurate to divide the inhabitants of Europe into Christians and Jews. No doubt, the religious distinction exercises considerable influence in both regions; but the diversities of race and language are not less marked in the one than in the other. Political divisions are, indeed, too unstable in India to create much distinction in social life. The natives accept and part with a government as a mere external accident: but whether under British or native rule, the Mohammedans of that country differ from one another even more than the English Jew from his brother of Moldavia; while Hindu idolatry extends over nations not less dissimilar than the Christians of Greece, Italy, Germany, France, and Britain.

To ascertain their real condition, the several divisions of the population must be considered separately, and in succession. There can be no greater fallacy than to apply the incidents of one locality indiscriminately to the rest. To interpret a "native" usage of the north by another people or class of society in the south, would be often as ridiculous as to explain the habits of the English aristocracy from the daily life of a Russian serf.

To give an idea of the extent and variety of the field, some of the leading features of the principal nations may here be rapidly sketched, following the broad lines afforded us by diversity of language.

Beginning at the north-west frontier, the *Punjab*, or country of the five waters, is inhabited by an aboriginal agricultural race, called *Gujurs*, by two divisions of Hindus (Rajpoots and Jats*), and by Patan Mussulmans. The last are the most numerous, constituting about two-thirds of the entire population, but of these a large portion are of Hindu origin. The most remarkable are the Jats, who formed the nucleus of the Sikh community. They are descended from a monotheistical sect of Hindus, who were driven into the mountains by the persecutions of Aurungzebe. Here they addicted themselves to a martial and predatory life, assuming the Rajpoot appellation of *Sing*, and making it a religious duty to wear steel at all times on their persons. Some sects among them push this peculiarity to a degree of fanaticism bordering on insanity—carrying a drawn sword in each hand, with two others in the belt, a matchlock at their backs, and sharp iron quoits on their turbans. The last they are said to twirl with force and precision enough to cut off the leg of an elephant.

The Sikhs repudiate caste, and eat all kinds of food except beef. They esteem it an impiety to kill kine, and prohibit the use of tobacco. They are more robust in person than other Hindus. The women are

* The word *Jat* or *Zat* means *caste*. It was assumed, apparently, in order to assert a title to the same parentage with the Rajpoots.

renowned for beauty, and the men are valiant, active, and cheerful soldiers. Their dress consists of a jacket, with trousers reaching to the knee, or, among the upper classes, to the ankle: the religious colour is blue. Their language, called *Jatski*, or Punjabi, is one of the Sanscrit family; towards the south it becomes mixed with Sindhu, and in towns gives place to a dialect of Hindustani. They are a rude and illiterate people, but it is remarkable that female education is met with in all parts of the Punjab. The Sikhs are, for the most part, concentrated in the vicinity of the capitals Amritsir and Lahore.

Next in place to the Punjabis are the *Sindians*, now a mixed race of Jats and Beloochis; the latter being of comparatively recent settlement. The former represent those early Hindus with whom Alexander the Great came in contact in this country and the Punjab. The Greek writers give an account of their wealth, courage, veracity, love of liberty, and patriotism, which it would be difficult to parallel from any portion of the Hindu race at the present day. The native annals, also, boast of a powerful kingdom subsisting in Sindh for 2,000 years before the Mohammedan conquest; and the Mussulman accounts present a high idea of the bravery of the men and the beauty of the women. It is difficult not to think that the Hindus of that ancient period were in reality possessed of many virtues and resources, which were gradually trodden out by the long and cruel pressure of Mohammedan rule. Even the face of the country was altogether changed under that usurpation. Populous towns have disappeared; and tracts of land, once waving with the golden harvest, exhibit now an endless waste of sand.

The ancient Sindians were probably, in religion, Bhuddists. The most remarkable deeds of Gottama Buddha were performed on the banks of the Indus, and are said to have been first committed to writing in the Sindhu language, which is still accounted one of the purest dialects of India. About the year of our Lord 622 a Brahman named Chach was elevated to the throne, through a criminal intrigue with the wife of the reigning monarch; and shortly after the storm of Mussulman invasion burst on the country and deluged it in blood. Both from Persia and Arabia the land was entered and spoiled, thousands of its much-admired women being carried into slavery. No part of India suffered more from the violence of the invaders, and in none were more spirited exertions attempted by its chiefs to regain their independence. Their subjection to the thrones of Ghizni and Delhi was often, and for long periods, nearly nominal; and after their transfer to Nadir Shah, to whom the fallen Mogul ceded this province, they reasserted their independence upon his death, and practically maintained it till the incursion of the Beloochis at the end of the eighteenth century. The population is still among the finest of the Hindu race. The men are tall and well proportioned, though dark in colour, and the women retain their proverbial character for beauty.

The Talpoor tribe of Beloochis, who had previously embraced the tenets of Islam, wrested Sindh from its nominal subjugation to Kabul about the year 1790, and placed it under a military despotism administered by nine sovereign ameers. These Beloochi people are a still finer and more martial race than the Hindus; the latter form the agricultural population, and include a large number of converts to Mohammedanism, the descendants of those who were proselyted during the Mussulman reign, in some instances perhaps by a voluntary choice, in others to save their lands, and in not a few as a punishment for some real or imaginary offence.

Guzerat is another country distinctly characterized by race and language, and not included, in native estimation, either in Hindustan or the Deccan. Of aboriginal races it contains the *Dunjas*, a small but well-knit active breed of foresters, who live upon wild fruits and the produce of the chase; and the *Bheel* tribe, existing in much larger numbers in the north and north-eastern part of the country, whence they extend into the jungles and hilly district of Malwa. The latter seem to have been possessed of no little degree of civilization till subdued by the Rajpoots and Mussulmans. They were till lately robbers and thieves by profession, but have been found to make excellent soldiers to the British Government: some also have been induced to adopt settled abodes, and devote themselves to agriculture. The *Coolies* are another aboriginal people, who have adopted the Brahmanical faith, but eat flesh, particularly the buffalo. They are a robust, hardy race, often living by plunder, yet faithful when hired as guides or convoys. They form the bulk of the population along the north-western frontier. The Hindu population is largely composed of Brahmans and Rajpoots, but the Mahrattas, who only claim to be Sudras, are the predominant nation. Mussulmans abound, but chiefly in the towns, which contain also many Parsees. The peninsula has taken the name of *Kattywar*, from the Katties, a Hindu race, whose fair hair, blue eyes, and lofty stature, still remarkably attest their northern origin. It contains also a tribe from the coast of Africa, called *Seedras,* and these alone are said to encounter with impunity the deadly climate of the wild tracts they inhabit.

Hindustan, as before stated, has long been the principal seat of the proper Hindu race, which has here almost entirely supplanted the aboriginals. It is here, of course, that the characteristic features of their central-Asian origin are most conspicuous. They are in general tall, well-proportioned, and of a martial disposition. Their colour has been darkened since the day when Indra gave the lands to his white-complexioned friends, but they are still perceptibly fairer than the natives of Bengal and the Deccan, and the upper classes are not darker than the inhabitants of the south of Europe. The general tint is a yellowish olive deepening to a dull copper brown when exposed to the sun and air: the most striking contrast to the European complexion is the universal want of *red,* even on the cheeks of the fairest women.

A general similarity marks the population, from the Punjab to the borders of Bengal. The eastern portions, however, still attest, by a diversity of language, the ancient existence of two great divisions of Hindustan. Over the North-west Provinces and Oude the vernacular is *Hindi,* the language of the ancient empire of Canouj, but the province of Bahar retains another dialect called *Mithila,* the last lingering witness of that great kingdom of Magadha, which, according to the Puranas, existed for above 2,000 years, and extended its dominion over all India. Under the Mohammedan rule, also, frequent revolts, and at one time a regular kingdom "in the east," betrayed the existence of much national diversity from the natives of the west. It was always to the east that the Patan Mussulmans fled from the Moguls, and from the same quarter Shere Shah returned to expel the successor of Baber, and reunite his conquests under a Patan dynasty.

Many other national distinctions formerly subsisted among the natives of Hindustan. Malwa, long an independent kingdom under Mussulman rule;—Rajpootana, where the spirit of Hindu independence has never been extinguished;—Oude, and the vicinity of Delhi and Agra, where Mussulman domination was most entire,—exhibit corresponding varieties in the character and spirit of the population.

Hindustan, being the principal seat of the Affghan and Mogul invasions, still contains, also, the largest portions of those races, settled among and upon the Hindus. The nations have intermingled to some extent in blood, and still more in manners. The Hindustanis have adopted the turban and dress of the Mohammedans, and the *Oordu* language prevails more generally than in other parts of India. Even their religious usages have yielded in some degree to the persecutions and influence of the unscrupulous victor. On the other hand, Mussulman observances have felt the spirit of the people among whom they were planted, and the prejudices of caste, with many of the idolatrous practices of Hinduism, are participated, to a considerable extent, by the modern Islamites.

Bengal presents another section of the population, which, though in religion, habits, and manners, one with that of Hindustan, has been so altered by the effects of climate and occupation, and perhaps by mixture with the aboriginal race, as to be now quite.

another nation. The Bengalis are small, dark, and effeminate in appearance and spirit. They are remarkable for superstition and timidity, no less than for subtlety and art. The houses of Hindustan are built of mud and unbaked bricks, covered with tiles, and ranked in compact villages or towns in the open country; but the villages of Bengal, hid in woods of bamboo and palm, are composed of scattered cottages, which, with their cane walls and trim curved roof of thatch, make the prettiest dwellings in India. The Bengalis retain the old Hindu dress, formed of two cloths or scarfs; one wrapped round the waist, and falling to the knee, the other thrown about the shoulders, and occasionally drawn over the head. By rubbing their skins with oil after bathing (a practice unknown in Hindustan), they acquire a sleek, glossy appearance, and are, at the same time, protected from the effects of the damp climate. They live almost entirely on rice, while the Hindustanis mostly eat wheat and other dry-growing grains. The language of each is unintelligible to the other, though the idioms are in fact more nearly allied than English with German.

The religious ceremonies and festivals of Bengal exhibit likewise great diversity from those of Upper India, and have doubtless been largely corrupted by admixture with the savage rites of the earlier inhabitants.

Orissa, receiving its name from the Oriyas or Odras, a branch of the Hindu immigration which occupies its western plains, is still largely populated by aboriginals. The Kols are in the north; the Khonds occupy the east; and the Saurias the south. The Kols have approximated the nearest to Brahmanical observances, but are honourably distinguished from the false and crafty Bengalis by a truthful and ingenuous disposition. The Khonds have little in common with the Hindus, save the worship of Kali, who, however, may perhaps be considered as their own aboriginal deity under a Hindu appellation. They are muscular, robust, and active, with expanded foreheads, prominent cheek-bones, full lips, and large mouths; the physiognomy exhibiting intelligence and determination blended with good humour. Brave, hospitable, and industrious, they are also, like other children of the forest and hills, irascible, vindictive, and sadly addicted to drunkenness. Their religious rites, as will be shown in another place, are of the most barbarous and sanguinary description, yet they are adhered to with a ferocity which it is difficult to overcome. The Saurias are still more uncivilized, and said to be altogether destitute of the moral sense.

Notwithstanding this large retention of the barbarian element, Orissa is regarded with peculiar veneration by the Hindu population. Its whole extent is declared to be one place of pilgrimage. Its sacred rivers, lofty temples, and vast crowds of Brahmans, struck the armies of Akbar with astonishment, and it still enjoys the highest renown for sanctity among the natives of the other parts of India. The language (Uriya) is ranked by Mr. Elphinstone in the Tamilian (or Dravidian) family, but it is so largely mixed with Sanscrit as closely to resemble Bengali, and is therefore assigned by other grammarians to the Northern division.

To the north and east of Orissa lies *Gondwana*, the country of the Gonds, who seem to be somewhat more advanced in civilization than their kinsmen the Khonds. This country stretches from Cuttack throughout Berar, and the Saugor territory. Its many leagues of jungle, occasionally interrupted by patches of cultivation, still present a lively image of the state of the Deccan from the Nerbudda to the Godavery, at the time when Rama traversed the forest, and raised the auxiliary troops which the legend has converted into monkeys.

Next to Gondwana is *Maharashtra* "the great country," reaching from the Nerbudda to the boundaries of the Telugu and Canarese languages, and including the greater part of the Bombay Presidency. The Mahrattas, who have been long seated in this broad and fertile region, are either a portion of the population from Hindustan, or early assimilated to it by adopting the Brahmanical institutions. Their language is of the Sanscrit family, and their attachment to Hinduism fierce and bigoted. Though pretending to no higher caste than the Sudra, they afforded a second home to their religion, when Brahmans and Rajpoots could no longer protect it in the plains of the Ganges; and it was their armies which, at a later period, re-crossed the Nerbudda and avenged its wrongs in the overthrow of the Mohammedan empire. Still, both the physical type and social peculiarities of the Mahrattas are strongly distinguished from those of Hindustan.

Further south the Hindu element becomes weaker and more diffused. To the east the Telugu language marks the ancient kingdom of *Telingana*, the natives of which (termed also *Gentoos*)* constitute the handsomest and most numerous nation of Southern India. Their language has been called the Italian of the East,

* A Portuguese corruption, meaning "Gentile."

an appellation not more due to the mellifluence of its sounds, than to the fine air and manners of those who speak it. They are reckoned at fourteen millions of souls.

The Canarese tongue, extending over the great table-land above the ghâts, with a portion of the western coast, indicates the former kingdom of *Carnata*, from which the English have borrowed their appellations of *Carnatic* and *Canara*, though strangely enough both terms are applied to level districts, on either coast, which lie beyond the limits of the language. The Canarese above the ghâts, enjoying great advantages of soil and climate, exhibit a hardier and manlier appearance than the natives of the plain. They are also better clothed, and somewhat lighter in complexion. Like the people of Hindustan, they suffered the full weight of Mohammedan misrule under the nizam of Hyderabad, and the usurper of Mysore. It is little wonder, therefore, that they are described as deceitful and inconstant beyond the average of Hindus. Yet they are allowed to be courteous, patient, and contented, and to these merits, since they have been transferred to British administration, may be added those of industry and order. No part of British India exhibits evidences of greater prosperity than the Mysore territories; delivered from the dread of Mohammedan exactions, the people are no longer afraid to exhibit their rural wealth, and in many districts regular homesteads impart an almost English aspect to the landscape. Canarese is the language of about five millions of natives.

The Tamil language occupies the southern extremity of India, extending from Cape Comorin to a little above Madras, on the east coast, and to

Trevandrum on the west. This is the territory anciently called *Drawed*, and once the seat of the most powerful kingdom of the south. It is believed to have reached a high state of civilization 1,000 years before the Christian era, a date which combines with the evidence of language to attest an origin anterior to the Brahmanical. The natives are among the darkest in India, and the climate would be intolerable to Europeans if it were not for the extensive influence of the sea-breezes. Yet in arts and literature this sultry region bears comparison with the most favoured portions of the Indian continent. It contains some of the finest monuments of native architecture; and the gay and ingenious population is still distinguished for expertness in mechanical and manufacturing processes. Literature is held in high esteem: the wandering Tamil poet, like the troubadour of old, is sure of an intelligent audience and a hearty welcome in every village. The majority of the Hindus in the Eastern Archipelago, and of the emigrants to the West Indies, are Tamilians. They have been called "the Greeks or Scotch of the East," and (according to Mr. Caldwell) are "certainly the least scrupulous and superstitious, and the most enterprising and persevering race of Hindus." They are estimated at ten millions in number.

The Tamil language and nation, though mostly found on the coast of Coromandel, have, strangely enough, received from the English in India the name of *Malabar*, which occasions some confusion to the geographical student, who finds that appellation still properly affixed to the opposite or western coast. The natives of the latter are commonly distinguished as *Malayalam;* they are a branch of the Tamil population, but with so much diversity of speech and habit as to justify their being ranked as a distinct people. The Malayalam is even written in a different character from the Tamil (though doubtless derived from it), and rejoices yet more in poetical power. The Brahmans of Malabar, denominated *Namburis*, consider themselves the aboriginal proprietors of the soil, which they pretend was called out of the sea expressly for their enjoyment. Next to them in rank are the *Nairs*, the descendants of the ancient indigenous chiefs, who are accounted *Sudras* in the Hindu system, but are probably the true aboriginal aristocracy. Of this race was the Tamuri raja (or the Zamorin, as the Europeans write it), whom the Portuguese found occupying the throne upon their first arrival at Calicut: the family of this prince is still extant, and the descent carefully preserved. In common, however, with the other Nairs, it is regulated in a manner which seems to confirm the supposition of a pre-Hindu origin: the succession goes in the *female* instead of the male line, the son of the sister succeeding as heir, in disregard, or rather in ignorance, of the deceased's own offspring. This peculiar custom results from the absence of the marriage tie among the Nairs, the men and women living in a state of promiscuous union, which makes it impossible to determine the father. Usages so contrary to Hindu customs in other parts can only be retained from some earlier state of society. Another and more numerous class in Malabar, called *Poliar Chermar*, were found by the British in a state of slavery, to which they had probably been reduced by the Nairs and Brahmans: they may be supposed to represent the bulk of the aboriginal population, of whom the more secluded mountains contain the wilder and more savage fragments.

The limited population of Malabar is further diversified by a variety of foreign elements. The Mapilas, or Moplahs, are Mussulmans, descended, it is supposed, from the Arab traders of early days;* in the neighbourhood of Calicut they are said to outnumber the rest of the population, but are among the most ignorant and most ferocious of the disciples of Mohammed. No small portion of the population is Christian, divided among the Syrian, Syro-Roman, Roman Catholic, and English communions; while two colonies of Jews, black and white, have been settled (the former from time immemorial) in and near Cochin. The kingdom of Travancore, the one remaining specimen of the numerous native states into which the south of India was once divided, belongs partly to the Tamil and partly to the Malayalam.

The several divisions of Southern India, as well as the North, were all thoroughly Brahmanized before the date of the earliest historical records, and the bulk of the inhabitants are now accordingly accounted Hindus. Yet, as they retain distinct traces of a pre-existing language and literature, so the Brahmanical system is far weaker here than in the north. In Tinnevelly, for example, an open country in the south-eastern corner, containing large tracts of sandy waste only used for the cultivation of palm trees, the population retains the aboriginal or Dravidian character almost unchanged. The Brahmans have little or no influence in society, and the majority of the people are strangers to Hindu rites and caste.

Nowhere within so limited a space is the diversity of population so conspicuous as on the *Neilgherry* hills, which form the southern boundary of the table-land of

* *Mahapilla* is "child of Mocha."

Mysore, and connect the eastern and western ghâts. Into these heights (only lately laid open to British inspection from the accidental discovery of their salubrious climate), fragments of various tribes have successively retreated, and still remain living illustrations of a history which can never be written. The rounded knolls, into which the crest of the range is broken, are crowned with cairns, or barrows, whose resemblance to those in Europe mark them at once for Druidical remains. Similar monuments of a more advanced order, and in better preservation, exist in great numbers on the hills to the south of the great gap of Coimbatore, and they have been discovered on other mountain ranges of the Deccan and Western India. By whom they were erected is a question still involved in the deepest mystery. They are the burial-places of a race of whom no other traces have yet been discovered. They have been frequently opened on the Neilgherries, but none of the existing natives acknowledge either tradition or interest in connexion with them. They were found to contain ashes and fragments of pottery, with spear or arrow heads of iron. The pottery was *glazed*, which is an art unknown to the modern Hindus. *Bronze* vessels also have been discovered, and, in one or two instances, a bell of the same metal.*

The present proprietors of these hills are the Todas, or Todawars, a scanty people, whose language belongs to the Dravidian family, but who in appearance are so dissimilar from other natives, that the first discoverers conjectured them to be the remains of a colony of Jews or Romans. They

* A Roman gold coin is said to have been found, but Mr. Caldwell was unable to verify the fact.

certainly resemble the latter people both in form and feature; and the idea suggested by an athletic frame, aquiline nose, and long flowing locks, is confirmed by a costume which, though mean in material, closely resembles in shape the ancient toga and tunic. The women are fairer than the men, with fine teeth, sparkling eyes, and well-formed feet: some of them wear bangles or bracelets of brass, weighing six or seven pounds. This singular people dwell in hamlets called *munds*, each however containing but one family, among whom the practice of female infanticide has resulted in a kind of polygamy more revolting than usual. The brothers take a single wife among them, a degrading usage, which may seem to link these hill people with the Nairs of Malabar and the natives of Coorg,* where a similar species of polygamy obtains.

The Todas are wholly without history or tradition. A vague story represents their ancestors to have been the palanquin-bearers of Runga Swami, a Hindu deity, but they know nothing of Hindu worship, and the story is probably a modern invention of other natives. Remains of former habitations show that they were once in possession of all the hills, and some of the most picturesque spots are still regarded with veneration; but whether on ancestral or religious grounds cannot be discovered. Offerings of milk and fruit are supposed to be made to their god *Ravel* annually, and it has been thought that a portion of the dairy is deemed sacred; but no images or other

* This was till very lately an independent state of great antiquity and distinct nationality. The natives are tall and well looking, allied to the Nairs, and speaking an idiom which has been generally considered an ancient dialect of Canarese, but later authorities incline to class it with the Tamil or Malayalam. The country is an elevated region of great beauty, enjoying an European atmosphere, and abounding in magnificent forests, tenanted by the elephant, bison, and elk, as well as by the usual beasts of prey, and numerous packs of *wild dogs*.

religious rites exist; and they can only doubtfully be said to have any idea of God. Their occupation is entirely pastoral; large herds of buffaloes are reared, but the flesh is seldom if ever eaten.

Another race on these hills are the *Kotas*, distinguished from the Todas by several marked particulars, and equally ignorant of their origin and descent. These eat the flesh of their herds, but *never milk them.* They work in leather (which is unclean to the Hindu), and also in metals, wood, and pottery, and are at once the artisans and the musicians of the hills. Low and degraded in many ordinary customs, they have a higher sense of morality and domestic purity than the Todas. They exhibit also some more distinct acts of worship, having both priests and swami houses; but they are in utter ignorance of the god to whom the service is paid, and acknowledge no connexion with the Hindu system. Their language is of the Dravidian family.

A third race, not less distinct, is called *Buddagur*, or Burghur. These may be considered the husbandmen of the Neilgherries, cultivating the higher lands, with the country immediately below. They are of Canarese origin, and by profession Hindus, having a caste of Brahmans, called Auroovurs, and another of Lingaits similar to those in the plains; yet they retain many social and religious usages wholly distinct. They worship gods which are unknown in the low country, and employ the services of another hill tribe, called *Koorumburs*, to consecrate the opening of their agricultural labours. A sheep or kid is sacrificed by the Koorumbur to propitiate the god; he is also required to cast the first seed, hold the first plough, and thrust in the first sickle.

These Koorumburs are a wild and savage race, supposed by some to be the true aboriginals of the Neilgherries. Other savage tribes are found on the sides and at the foot of the mountains, bearing the names of *Erulars* and *Mulcers*.

So extensive a collection of fragments within a narrow area, indicates the diversified character of the population once inhabiting the plains, and successively retiring, in the convulsions of society, to seek an asylum in the forest and mountain. Many more such remnants are, doubtless, still hidden in the yet unexplored recesses of India. The enumeration here attempted is not even a proximate sketch of the national distinctions subsisting among the so-called Hindu population. Difference of nation is, of course, implied in difference of language, but it may co-exist, also, to a great extent, with community of speech, as is the case in Italy and Germany, and other parts of Europe. Taking further into account the various grades of civilization found among those who speak the same tongue, it must be felt that the word "Hindu" is but a vague appellation for a vast congeries of nations and states, including, perhaps, more forms of society than any other region of equal extent.

The Mohammedans of India are composed of two classes, about equal in number;—the descendants of the foreign invaders, and the native proselytes, acquired during seven centuries of an intolerant usurpation. They are found in all parts of India, and among all classes of society, the proselytes differing only from their fellow-countrymen in having adopted the costume, with the civil and religious institutions, of their conquerors. The Mohammedans of foreign descent preserve the features of their race in the stronger forms and haughtier bearing which still distinguish them from the Hindus. Mohammedans of rank, and females in general, being secluded from exposure to the climate, retain the fair complexion of their northern extraction, but in the lower ranks of society little difference in colour can be traced from the Hindu. The Mussulman, however, may everywhere be distinguished by his flowing beard.

The language in general use among all the Mohammedans is *Hindustani*, which is a mixture of Persian, the language of the first invaders, and of Hindi, the vernacular of Hindustan. Hindustani is also the most common medium of intercourse between Europeans and natives of all kinds: it is spoken throughout the native armies, and by all government officials, but combining easily with all the northern vernaculars, it varies considerably in different parts of India. The Mohammedans are most numerous in the northern parts of India, where they are derived chiefly from the Persian and Affghan immigrations, and conform to the peculiarities of their respective origins.* They are less powerful in the Deccan, where the colonies from Arabia, retaining the more primitive forms of Islam, engaged in fierce contentions with the Moguls of Hindustan. At a later date, the nizam of Hyderabad, the nabob of the Carnatic, and the sultan of Mysore, were all powerful Mohammedan rulers, and their territories still retain large masses of Mussulman population. But the nizam's is now the only Mohammedan court in the south, and in some

* The term *Patan* was applied to the old Affghan dynasties, while *Mogul* was used to designate the fairer Mussulmans of the north.

districts of Madras the disciples of Islam are not more than one in thirty of the whole population.

The Mussulmans of India mark their diversity of origin by four surnames, which may be said to distinguish as many clans or castes. The patronymic of the Moguls is *Beg*, of the Patans *Khan*, and of the Arabs *Sheikh*, while the descendants of the Prophet by his favourite daughter are designated *Syuds*. One or other of these appellations is almost invariably found among the names of every Mohammedan.

Throughout India, Mohammedans, in spite of their professed hatred and contempt of idolatry, have assimilated themselves in many respects to Hindu usages, and obtained a corresponding raṇk in Hindu estimation. According to Brahmanical theory, they are inferior to even a low-caste Hindu, but practically they occupy a much higher place in native society; so that a Hindu of low-caste who embraces Mohammedanism, actually rises in general respectability by the apostasy. The social advantages so acquired make it remarkable that so little progress has been made by Mohammedanism since the decline of its political power. Some judicious observers, however, think it not improbable that, in the opening of the native mind which must result from the decay of idolatry and caste, a larger extension may be given to the faith of Mohammed, before the heralds of the gospel have afforded a better refuge to the inquiring multitudes.

Another interesting, though not numerous, race of foreigners in India are the *Parsees*, a colony of ancient Persians who emigrated to India on the overthrow of the Sassanian monarchy by the Mohammedans, A.D. 651. Arriving first at Diu, they proceeded to Guzerat, where they were kindly received by the Hindus, and obtained the protection of a raja of Sanjan. Here they assisted 300 years later in the unavailing struggle of the Hindus against the Mohammedan arms. Ultimately they gained the favour of the Mogul authorities by ability in mercantile and financial affairs, and so became possessed of considerable wealth and influence in Surat and other towns of Western India. They made their appearance in Bombay about the time of its transfer to the English, and have ever since formed a leading class in the community of that Presidency.*

The Parsees, preserving strictly the purity of their lineage, retain the features and fair complexion of their Persian ancestors. They wear a high turban, and a costume which at once distinguishes them from the natives. Being often wealthy, and almost always in respectable circumstances, their apparel is good and abundant, comprising shirt, waistcoat of cloth or chintz, and a loose upper tunic, which on highdays is exchanged for a flowing robe girded with a voluminous waistcloth. The rich wear silk trousers, stockings, and English shoes. Their mode of life is half European and half Hindu. They repudiate polygamy, and allow a more honourable position to the female sex than other Asiatics, though the custom of eating apart is generally retained; many of the Parsees, however, have adopted European ideas in this respect also. Their leading members are great patrons of education and of all agricultural improvements. They have always abounded in alms-giving. They are proud of their loyalty to the throne, and

* The Bombay Dockyard was founded by one of this race in 1735, and the post of master-builder has continued in his family to the present day.

often boast that they alone, of the natives of India, properly appreciate the excellencies of British rule, and approximate the closest to British feeling. The Parsees do not exceed 150,000 persons in all.*

Her Majesty has conferred on a member of this race an English baronetcy, an honour without precedent or parallel in the case of any native of the East. Sir Jamsetjee Jeejeebhoy, the individual so distinguished, has lately terminated a useful career, amid the lamentations of society, after expending above £200,000 in donations to charities and public objects in Bombay. The Parsee law recognising no right of primogeniture in the distribution of property, the deceased baronet invested £10,000 per annum (with the paternal mansion) for the perpetual support of the title which has now descended to his son.†

* The numbers of the different races in India are estimated in round numbers as follows :—

Aboriginal races	16,000,000
Dravidian races	32,000,000
Mohammedans	10,000,000
Other foreigners	1,000,000
Leaving a Hindu population of	121,000,000
Total	180,000,000

† The following description of the native baronet's "armorial bearings" is from a Parsee pen. "Sir Jamsetjee Jeejeebhoy's 'coat of arms' consists of a handsome shield in the form of the shields used by the Knights of St. John at the defence of Malta, beautifully emblazoned by scrolls of gold. At the lower part of the shield is a landscape scene in India, intended to represent a part of the island of Bombay, with the islands of Salsette and Elephanta in the distance. The sun is seen rising from behind Salsette, to denote industry, and is diffusing its light and heat, displaying liberality. The upper part of the shield has a white ground, to denote integrity and purity, on which are placed two bees, representing industry and perseverance. The shield is surmounted by a crest, consisting of a beautiful peacock, denoting wealth, grandeur, and magnificence; and in its mouth is placed an ear of paddy, denoting beneficence. Below the shield is a white pennant folded, on which is inscribed the words, 'Industry and Liberality,' which is sir Jamsetjee's motto."

CHAPTER II.

RELIGION—ABORIGINAL AND BRAHMANICAL.

Religion the chief bond among men—Aboriginal and Dravidian views—Demonolatry—Resemblance to Obi men and Indian sorcerers—Objects of invocation—Absence of caste—Shanars of Tinnevelly—Devil worship—Description of a devil dance—And of a sacrifice—Khond rites—Meriah sacrifice—Todas—Singular ceremony—Brahmanical or Hindu religion—Shastras incongruous—Three classes—Vedas—Four editions—Compilation of different parts inconsistent and contradictory—Translation of Rig Veda—Polytheistic views—Contradiction to modern creed—Rites, simple and domestic—Animal sacrifices—Human victim—Aswamedha—Rishis—Hymns to Agni—Indra, etc.—Primitive Aryans—Brahmana—Philosophical doctrine—Supreme Deity—Institutes of Manu—Brahmanical system—Gayatri—Ôm—Cosmogony—Five sacraments—Exclusion of Sudras—Metempsychosis—Doctrine of Egypt—Pythagoras—Jews—Brahmans—Paradises—Purgatory—Transmigration—Absorption—Descriptions of heaven and hell—Penance—Ceremonial merit—Doctrine of faith—Puranas—Incarnate gods—Heroes—Adoption of indigenous rites—Siva—Vishnu—Rivals to Brahma—Epic poems—Specimen—Parallel with corruptions of Christianity.

The human family, divided by numerous peculiarities of social and political growth, is held together by the ties of religion. The last thing that any section parts with is the tradition of its ancestral worship. The gift it most readily welcomes from a stranger is the rekindling of faith and hope where the ideas of God and immortality have died out. Thus the power which re-unites the soul to its Maker, further earns its name* by binding again in one the isolated or discordant fragments of humanity. With the

* *Religio*, from *religo*, to "bind again."

corrupt nature fear is a more common stimulus than love: the memory is more tenacious of evil than of good: the heart remembers its fall when it has forgotten the promise of restoration. Hence the worship of many early religions is invested with terror and gloom: it employs itself in deprecating the Divine wrath, but seldom implores the Divine bounty. Such appears to have been the distinguishing feature of the aboriginal and Dravidian religions in India. They consisted of a number of local and traditionary rites, exhibiting little system, and altogether discordant from Brahmanism.

The faith and worship of the uncivilized mountaineers are still the same, though in some parts the name of a Hindu divinity has been imposed on the local object of reverence, without essentially affecting the nature of the observance.* The leading feature of the rites still prevailing in the forests and mountains, and among the lowest tribes of the south, is *demonolatry*, or the worship of evil spirits.† There is no regular priesthood; ordinarily the head of the village or family performs the office; but any one, either male or female, may volunteer for the awful privilege, and become for the time the prophet of the demon. These persons resemble the Obi men of Africa, or the sorcerers of the North American

* In Tinnevelly, Rama, the great hero-god of the Hindus, is worshipped as a demon, with all the ceremonies of a superstition of which he was the enemy and destroyer.

† It is not to be understood that the gods of the country are styled devils by the missionaries and other Christians, but they are such in the esteem of their own worshippers. So far as these people have any notion of God, they consider him just and good: they speak, also, of good spirits or gods. These, however, are not the objects of their sacrifices, which are avowedly offered to the evil spirits or devils; and these are worshipped expressly *because* of their malignity and power.

Indians; they have no idea, however, of the Supreme Being at all worthy to be compared with the Great Spirit-Father of men, imagined by the Red Indian.

Besides demons or evil spirits, other objects are served, denoting *power* in its baneful operations upon men. Ghosts, wild beasts, serpents, and even deadly diseases are invoked and deprecated. The oblations are sanguinary; blood and intoxicating liquors being indispensable. Human sacrifices, once frequent, are still only held in check by the influence of other religions. The general idea of the worship appears to be to propitiate the divinity by gratifying its evil passions.

No notion of the immortality of the soul, or of a future state of rewards and punishments, seems to exist among the aboriginals. It might be thought that the worship of ghosts, or the spirits of departed men, would of itself imply a belief in a future state of existence. But these objects of superstitious dread are not conceived of simply as disembodied spirits, nor is every man supposed to exist in a disembodied state after death. It is when some sudden or remarkable death occurs, especially of a man notorious for crime or violence, that his spirit is supposed to haunt the neighbourhood, and demands to be appeased by sacrifice. The notion is that the deceased becomes a *demon* rather than a ghost, and in fact the majority of the demons worshipped in Tinnevelly are supposed to have been once human beings, male or female. The worship they require is the gratification of their old malignant tempers in an aggravated degree. A singular instance of this sort occurred in the case of an English officer who fell in the Travancore war (A.D. 1809), and was actually worshipped as a demon, being propitiated by oblations of brandy and cheroots.* Such transformations, however, are exceptional; the general idea of death, among the aboriginal nations, is that of entire annihilation. There is no trace of *metempsychosis*, the favourite creed of all Hindus.

Caste is also unknown to this system, and its absence is one of the notes of aboriginal descent. It is not unusual, however, with tribes who have Brahmans living amongst them, so far to admit their pretensions as to intrust them with the direction of their religious ceremonies. The aboriginal worship will be more particularly understood from some examples, taken from different localities.

The Shanars of Tinnevelly are a portion of the Tamil population, who are still strangers to the Brahmanical religion. The higher and wealthier classes are in a slight degree affected by the system which has become predominant in India, and some few Brahmanical feasts and ceremonies are occasionally observed. But among the bulk of the population (whose ordinary employment is the cultivation of the palmyra tree) the aboriginal demonolatry reigns undisturbed. These demons, it seems, differ in taste. One prefers the sacrifice of a goat; another of a hog; a third of a cock; while those of Pariar origin always insist upon ardent spirits. They reside in trees, or wander in waste lands, or skulk in the thickets. Sometimes a rude temple, called *pecoil*, or devil-house, is erected for their abode. At others they are supposed to take possession of a human being: diseases are attributed to such possession; and exorcisms and incantations are resorted to for the cure. The usual

* The Tinnevelly Shanars. By Rev. R. Caldwell.

emblem is a rude pyramid of earth adorned with whitewash and red ochre; when built of brick, and stuccoed, it assumes the shape of an obelisk, the angles corresponding with the four cardinal points. Its height is rarely more than eight feet, and generally below five. Occasionally temples and idols are used, roughly imitated from their Brahmanical neighbours; and in such cases the idol accords with the monstrous shapes which orthodox Hindus assign to the enemies of the gods, or with the terrific forms of Siva or Durga.

Two particulars, it seems, are essential features in all demon-worship—devil-dancing and bloody sacrifices. The former is thus described by an eye-witness:—

"The officiating priest, whoever he may happen to be, is dressed for the occasion in the vestments and ornaments appropriate to the particular devil worshipped. The object in view, in donning the demon's insignia, is to strike terror into the imagination of the beholders. But the party-coloured dress and grotesque ornaments, the cap and trident and jingling bells of the performer, bear so close a resemblance to the usual adjuncts of a pantomime, that an European would find it difficult to look grave. The musical instruments, or rather the instruments of noise, chiefly used in the devil-dance, are the tom-tom, or ordinary Indian drum, and the horn, with occasionally the addition of a clarionet, when the parties can afford it. But the favourite instrument, because the noisiest, is that which is called 'the bow.' A series of bells of various sizes is fastened to the frame of a gigantic bow; the strings are tightened so as to emit a musical note when struck; and the bow rests on a large empty brazen pot. The instrument is played on by a plectrum, and several musicians join in the performance. One strikes the string of the bow with the plectrum, another produces the bass by striking the brazen pot with his hand, and the third keeps time and improves the harmony by a pair of cymbals. As each musician kindles in his work, and strives to outstrip his neighbour in the rapidity of his flourishes, and in the loudness of the tone with which he sings the accompaniment, the result is a tumult of frightful sounds, such as may be supposed to delight even a demon's ear.

"When the preparations are completed, and the devil-dance is about to commence, the music is at first comparatively slow, and the dancer seems impassive and sullen; and he either stands still or moves about in gloomy silence. Gradually, as the music becomes quicker and louder, his excitement begins to rise. Sometimes, to help him to work himself up into a frenzy, he uses medicated draughts, cuts and lacerates his flesh till the blood flows, lashes himself with a huge whip, presses a burning torch to his breast, drinks the blood which flows from his own wounds, or drinks the blood of the sacrifice, putting the throat of the decapitated goat to his mouth. Then, as if he had acquired new life, he begins to brandish his staff of bells, and dance with a quick but wild unsteady step. Suddenly the *afflatus* descends. There is no mistaking that glare, or those frantic leaps. He snorts, he stares, he gyrates. The demon has now taken bodily possession of him; and though he retains the power of utterance and of motion, both are under the demon's control, and his separate consciousness is in abeyance. The bystanders signalize the event by raising a long shout, attended with a peculiar vibratory noise, caused by the motion of the hand and tongue, or the tongue alone. The devil-dancer is now worshipped as a present deity, and every bystander consults him respecting his disease, his wants, the welfare of his absent relatives, the offerings to be made for the accomplishment of his wishes, and, in short, respecting everything for which superhuman knowledge is supposed to be available. As the devil-dancer acts to admiration the part of a maniac, it requires some experience to enable a person to interpret his dubious and unmeaning replies, his muttered voices, and uncouth gestures; but the wishes of the parties who consult him help them greatly to interpret his meaning.

"Sometimes the devil-dance and the demoniacal *clairvoyance* are extemporized, especially where the mass of the people are peculiarly addicted to devil-worship, and perfectly familiar with the various stages of the process. In such cases, if a person happen to feel the commencement of the shivering fit of an ague, or the vertigo of a bilious headache, his untutored imagination teaches him to think himself possessed. He then sways his head from side to side, fixes his eyes into a stare, puts himself into a posture, and begins the maniac dance; and the bystanders run for flowers and fruit for an offering, or a cock or goat to sacrifice to his honour.

"The night is the time usually devoted to the orgies of devil-dancing; particular nights being appropriated to the worship of particular devils. And as the number of devils worshipped is, in some districts, equal to the number of the worshippers, and as every act of worship is accompanied with the monotonous din of drums and the bray of horns, the stillness of the night, especially during the prevalence of cholera, or any other epidemical disease, is frequently broken by a dismal uproar, more painful to hear on account of the associations connected with it, than on account of its unpleasant effect on the ear and nerves."*

The witness here borne to the fall of man and the subjugation of his faculties to evil, being "taken captive by the devil at his will," is too obvious and affecting to need pointing out. Yet this darkness is not without a witness—broken indeed and obscure—to the True Light of man. The Shanar is far too ignorant to frame for himself the doctrine of a vicarious atonement; yet in the other essential element of his worship, the Christian will not fail to recognise this inborn craving of the guilty heart. The rite of sacrifice is performed in the following manner:—

"The animal, which is to be offered in sacrifice, is led to the altar of the devil-temple adorned with red ochre and garlands of flowers. A pot of water is dashed upon it to test its acceptableness. If it shakes itself, as the astonished creature can scarcely help doing, it is pronounced fit for sacrifice. Ordinarily the animal's head is separated from its body by a single stroke of a bill-hook; the sacrifice being considered unacceptable to the demon if more than one blow is required. The decapitated body is then held up, so that all the blood it contains may flow out upon the demon's altar. The sacrifice being now completed, the animal is cut up on the spot and made into curry; and, with the addition of the boiled rice and fruit offered to the demon on the same occasion, forms a

* The Tinnevelly Shanars. By Rev. R. Caldwell. London, 1850.

sacred meal, of which all who have joined in the sacrifice receive a share.

"The sole object of the sacrifice is the removal of the devil's anger, or of the calamities which his anger brings down. It should be distinctly understood that sacrifices are never offered on account of the sins of the worshippers, and that the devil's anger is not supposed to be excited by any moral offence. The religion of the Shanars, such as it is, has no connexion with morals. The most common motive in sacrificing to the devil is that of obtaining relief in sickness; and in that case at least the *rationale* of the rite is sufficiently clear. It consists in offering the demon life for life, blood for blood. The demon thirsts for the life of his votary, or for that of his child; and by a little ceremony and show of respect, a little music, and a little coaxing, he may be prevailed upon to be content with the life of a goat instead. Accordingly a goat is sacrificed; its blood is poured out upon the demon's altar, and the offerer goes free."*

Another and more frightful form of aboriginal worship is found among the Khonds of the Goomsur territory. The objects of their worship include the moon, the deity of war, and the Hindu goddess Kali. The favourite divinity, however, is the earth, in the cultivation of which this branch of the Dravidian family has attained to considerable proficiency. In order to induce their god to yield them an abundant harvest, a rite called *Meriah* is annually performed, which is no other than a human sacrifice. For this purpose children of both sexes are purchased, or kidnapped, from neighbouring tribes, a foreigner being deemed essential. The intended victims are carefully

* The Tinnevelly Shanars.

reared and guarded in villages appropriated to this use. At the appointed season a feast is held, with drunken and licentious revellings, for two days, during which the victim is indulged with every sensual gratification. On the third he is brought out and bound to a stake or tree, and, at an appointed signal, the savage Khonds rush in with their knives, hack away slices from the yet living body, and hasten to bury them, warm and palpitating, in their fields. Large numbers of wretched captives were formerly immolated in this infamous manner; but the British government having prohibited the practice as murder, the law has been upheld by several military expeditions, in the course of which many young persons of both sexes, destined to this horrible fate, have been discovered and released. The infatuated Khonds, however, adhere to their bloody rite with a ferocious pertinacity; and from the difficulty of gaining access to their fastnesses in the jungle, it may be feared that these atrocities are still occasionally perpetrated.

On the Neilgherries the Todas, like all other aboriginal tribes, are without temples, idols, or priests. A ceremony is performed in their dairies, which is conjectured to be designed to propitiate the *genius loci* by oblations of milk; and a bell, hung up in the same place, is regarded with veneration. They abstain from flesh, using their cattle only for milk, and ordinarily treating them with much kindness. But at certain seasons a general slaughter takes place, which may possibly be an act of worship to the *manes* of their ancestors. On these occasions the Todas assemble their cattle in large herds, and, after a kind of festival, they fall upon the beasts with clubs and beat them to death. The carcasses are left on the spot for other natives to dispose of. This singular ceremony can hardly be called a sacrifice, since it is not known that any notion of a divinity, good or bad, is mixed up with it. But it is not impossible that it may be the lingering memorial of former hecatombs, and be connected with a part of the widespread demonolatry of ancient India. Rites of a similar description were probably observed throughout India, until they were superseded by the more elaborate, though scarcely more enlightened, system of the Brahmans.

This religion professes to be founded on the Vedas and other holy writings, which are popularly supposed to contain one unalterable revelation of the Divine will. In point of fact, however, these works are of various antiquity, and replete with incongruous and even antagonistic sentiments: while the religion of the Vedas has long practically ceased to exist. The Shastras (or Dharma Shastras*) may be divided into three classes;—1. The Vedas; 2. The Institutes of Manu; and 3. The Puranas. All of these are regarded by the Hindus with an indiscriminate reverence, and believed to proceed from the same source. The slightest examination of their contents would prove them to be separated by many centuries in point of date, and, in fact, to belong to different systems of religion.

1. The Vedas are the most ancient and revered, being said to proceed immediately from the four mouths of Brahma: it is even contended that they are literally and truly a part of his essence. They are four in number;

* Equivalent to *Scriptures* or *Holy Scriptures*.

but the last is of inferior authority, and the second and third are largely copied from the first. Perhaps they are rather to be regarded as four editions of one work; the oldest and most authentic is called the *Rig Veda.* All four contain compilations obviously of different dates, which are believed to have been arranged in their present form by one Vyasa, in the fourteenth century before the Christian æra.* This is probably the date of the Aryan immigration, and the Vedas may be supposed to represent the religious views and practices of that race. Being written in Sanscrit—the older portions in a dialect which only a few of the most learned Shastris understand—the Vedas are in fact but very little known to the Brahmans themselves, and it may be doubted whether a single perfect copy exists in Hindustan.

Each Veda consists of two parts: 1, the *Sanhita* or *Muntra*, which is a collection of hymns (called *Suktas*), ranging over a long period of time, and expressing the religious aspirations of the earliest Aryans; and, 2, the *Brahmana*, consisting of rules for the use of the hymns, with ritual directions and comments explanatory of the sacrifices, clearly written long after the hymns themselves were in circulation, and including doctrines and precepts for which little or no foundation appears in their text. The Brahmans, however, consider all as an integral portion of the Veda, and the name is commonly extended to more than fifty mystical and metaphysical works of still

* The Brahmans assign the arrangement of the Veda to the opening of the Kali Yug, 3,000 years B.C. But Mr. Coleridge proves the solstitial points noted in the calendar to coincide with the 14th century B.C.—*Asiatic Researches*, viii. 489.

later date, termed *Upanishads*, and exhibiting "an entirely different state of the Hindu mind from that which the text of the Vedas sprang from and encouraged."*

The Vedas are further encumbered by a cloud of supplementary and dependent works called *Vedangas*, *Sutras*, *Durshans*, etc., whose contents are little known, and "the study of which would furnish occupation for a long and laborious life."† Some of these works are (with little apparent evidence) ascribed to Vyasa; among which is the *Bhagawat Gita*, sometimes called the fifth Veda, which teaches the pantheistical system, termed Vedantism. The contents of these several works are so inconsistent and contradictory, that they can hardly be thought to belong to the same religion; yet all are indiscriminately quoted as "Vedas," and popularly taken to be the foundation of the existing Hindu creed and worship.

The Rig Veda is now in course of publication, edited by professor Max Muller of Oxford, and a portion of its Sanhita, or collection of hymns, has been rendered into English by professor H. H. Wilson. The English reader is thus enabled to examine a large part of this, the primitive and most authentic, Veda; but he will examine it in vain for that which the Brahmans declare to be the fundamental doctrine of their religion, *the unity and spirituality of the supreme God*. Such expressions as "creator of the universe" doubtless occur in some of the hymns, but they are addressed to *different* deities, and the explanation that all the gods are but forms of the Supreme, cannot be admitted with any regard to the clear and uniform language of the text. Fire, air, and the other ele-

* Wilson's Preface to Rig Veda Sanhita. † Ibid.

ments, with their offspring and attendants, are invoked in the language of undisguised polytheism. The greater number of the hymns are in honour of *Agni*, the god of fire, and *Indra*, the god of the air; the former presiding over the rites of religion, the latter fighting the battles of his votaries and destroying their enemies. The sun also is worshipped by the names of *Vishnu*, *Surya*, and *Savitri*, though he is not so prominent an object of adoration as in some other ancient systems of religion. Lesser gods and demigods are introduced, the number of which, according to the ordinary reckoning, is thirty-three. But one passage declares that "three thousand three hundred and thirty-nine divinities have worshipped Agni; they have sprinkled him with melted butter; they have spread for him the sacred grass, and have seated him upon it as their ministrant priest."*

The deities appear to have been worshipped in private dwellings before a sacred fire; on which account Agni is termed the messenger and priest of the gods, the receiver of the sacrificial viands. The usual offerings were clarified butter sprinkled on the fire (or on the sacred grass which strewed the floor), and copious libations of the juice of the acid asclepias, called soma, or the "moon plant," which when fermented, forms a strong spirituous beverage. The residue of the oblations was consumed by the worshippers; and the language in which the gods are urged again and again to "drink the soma juice," indicates no great moderation in the potations of their votaries.

The rites were performed by a band of *hotris*

* Rig Veda Sanhita: Ashtaka 3, Adhyaya 1, S. ix. *Wilson*, iij. 7.

(invokers), varying from seven to sixteen, who presented the offerings and recited the appropriate hymn. On some occasions, animal sacrifices were used, the flesh of which was partaken of by the worshippers. Three hundred buffaloes are mentioned as a holocaust to Indra; and another Sukta specifies the presentation of the fat or marrow to Agni. Animal food was then undoubtedly in use; the flesh of wild cattle is given to the pious who have recourse to Indra for food,* and that of the cow is said to be the chief.† A modern Brahman would explain this of the products of the cow, milk and butter; but professor Wilson understands it literally of beef.

In one passage, distinct mention is made of a *human sacrifice* being contemplated, though not actually perpetrated. The intended victim, when bound to the stake, and about to be immolated by his own father, a Rishi, who had sold his son for the horrid purpose from distress, appeals to the gods in a series of hymns,‡ and is ultimately liberated by Indra. The sacrifice was claimed by *Varuna;* the appeal may intimate the opposition of some of the officiating priests to the inhuman rite.

In two of the Vedic hymns, reference is made to the sacrifice of a *horse,* denominated *Aswamedha;* a rite which has been introduced to the English reader in Southey's "Curse of Kehama." The animal is described as led forth covered with a cloth adorned with golden trappings, and preceded by a goat which is offered to Indra and Pushan (or Agni) as a preliminary rite, announcing the sacrifice to the

* Rig Veda Sanhita: Ashtaka 3, Adhyaya 6, S. xi. *Wilson,* iij. 163.

† Ibid: Ashtaka 4, Adhyaya 7, S. xvi. *W.* iij. 453.

‡ Ibid: Ashtaka 1, Adhyaya 2, Anuvaka 6, S. i—vii. *W.* i. 59.

gods. The horse is led thrice round the sacrificial fire, and then immolated by the blow of an axe, with the exclamation *Vashat.* The carcass is cut up and cooked, partly on the spit, and partly in a cauldron. The dripping, received on the sacred grass and cast into the fire, is said to be "given to the longing gods." The remainder is eaten by the partakers of the rite. Peculiar motives are attached to this rite in some of the later Shastras, one of which forms the subject of Southey's poem. But none of these are countenanced by the Veda, where the supplication is the same with that of other sacrifices. "May this horse bring to us all-sustaining wealth, with abundance of cows, of excellent horses, and of male offspring; may the spirited steed bring us exemption from wickedness; may this horse offered in oblation procure for us bodily vigour."*

The hymns which express these supplications, and which were probably sung during the performance of the sacrifice, are arranged in stanzas, in various metres, and without much connexion. The name of the author is affixed to each, refuting at once the fiction so generally received, that the Vedas proceeded bodily from Brahma, and are a portion of his substance. These authors are termed Rishis and saints, respecting whom many fables were recounted in after-times. The Veda itself attaches to them no peculiar inspiration. A few translations will give the best notion of these celebrated compositions, which, forming in fact the true Veda, are entitled to the highest authority with every Hindu.

1. I glorify Agni, the high-priest of the sacrifice,

* Rig Veda Sanhita: Ashtaka 2, Adhyaya 3, S. vi. *W.* ij. 120.

the divine, the ministrant, who presents the oblation (to the gods), and is the possessor of great wealth.

2. May that Agni, who is to be celebrated by both ancient and modern sages, conduct the gods hither.

3. Through Agni, the worshipper obtains that affluence which increases day by day, which is the source of fame, and the multiplier of mankind.

4. Agni, the unobstructed sacrifice, of which thou art on every side the protector, assuredly reaches the gods.

5. May Agni, the presenter of oblations, the attainer of knowledge, he who is true, renowned, and divine, come hither with the gods.

6. Whatever good thou mayest, Agni, bestow upon the giver (of the oblation), that verily, Angiras, shall revert to thee.

7. We approach thee, Agni, with reverential homage in our thoughts daily, both morning and evening.

8. Thee, the radiant, the protector of sacrifices, the constant illuminator of truth, increasing in thine own dwelling.

9. Agni, be unto us easy of access, as is a father to his son; be ever present with us for our good.*

1. Agni, like patrimonial wealth, is the giver of food; he is a director, like the instructions of one learned in scripture; he rests in the sacrificial chamber like a welcome guest, and, like an officiating priest, he brings prosperity on the house of the worshipper.

2. He who is like the divine Sun, who knows the truth (of things), preserves by his actions (his vota-

* Rig Veda Sanhita: Ashtaka 1, Adhyaya 1, Anuvaka 1, S. i. *W.* i. 1.

ries) in all encounters ; like nature, he is unchangeable; and, like soul, is the source of happiness : he is ever to be cherished.

3. He who, like the divine (Sun), is the supporter of the universe, abides on earth like a prince (surrounded by) faithful friends ; in his presence men sit down like sons in the dwelling of a parent, and (in purity he resembles) an irreproachable and beloved wife.

4. Such as thou art, Agni, men preserve thee constantly kindled in their dwellings, in secure places, and offer upon thee abundant (sacrificial) food. Do thou, in whom is all existence, be the bearer of riches (for our advantage).

5. May thy opulent worshippers, Agni, obtain (abundant) food ; may the learned (who praise thee), and offer thee (oblations), acquire long life ; may we gain in battles booty from our foes, presenting their portion to the gods for (the acquisition of) renown.

6. The cows, loving (Agni who has come to the hall of sacrifice) sharing his splendour, have brought with full udders (their milk), to be drunk. The rivers, soliciting his good will, have flowed from a distance in the vicinity of the mountain.

7. (The gods) who are entitled to worship, soliciting thy good will, have intrusted to thee, resplendent Agni, the (sacrificial) food, and (for the due observance of sacred rites) they have made the night and morning of different colours, or black and purple.

8. May we, mortals, whom thou hast directed (to the performance of sacrifices) for the sake of riches, become opulent : filling heaven and earth, and the firmament (with thy radiance), thou protectest the whole world like a (sheltering) shade.

9. Defended, Agni, by thee, may we destroy the horses (of our enemies) by (our) horses, their men by (our) men, their sons by (our) sons; and may our sons, learned and inheritors of ancestral wealth, live for a hundred winters.*

10. May these our praises, sapient Agni, be grateful to thee, both in mind and heart; may we be competent to detain thy well-supporting wealth, offering upon thee their share of the (sacrificial) food to the gods.†

1. May he, who is the showerer of desires, who is co-dweller with (all) energies, the supreme ruler over the vast heaven and earth, the sender of water, and to be invoked in battles; may Indra, associated with the Maruts,‡ be our protection.

2. May he, whose course, like that of the sun, is not to be overtaken, who in every battle is the slayer of his foes, the witherer (of opponents), who with his swift-moving friends (the winds) is the most bountiful (of givers); may Indra, associated with the Maruts, be our protection.

3. May he, whose rays, powerful and unattainable, issue forth like those of the sun, milking (the clouds); he who is victorious over his adversaries, triumphant by his manly energies; may Indra, associated with the Maruts, be our protection.

4. He is the swiftest among the swift, most bountiful amongst the bountiful, a friend with friends, venerable among those who claim veneration, and pre-eminent among those deserving of praise; may Indra, associated with the Maruts, be our protection.

* These allusions to *horses* and *winters* indicate the northern origin of the Aryans.

† Rig Veda Sanhita: Ashtaka 1, Adhyaya 6, S. ix. *W.* i. 194.

‡ The *Maruts* are the *winds*.

5. Mighty with the Rudras, as if with his sons, victorious in battle over his enemies, and sending down with his co-dwellers (the waters which are productive of) food; Indra, associated with the Maruts, be our protection.

6. May he, the represser of (hostile) wrath, the author of war, the protector of the good, the invoked of many, share with our people on this day, the (light of the) sun; may Indra, associated with the Maruts, be our protection.

7. Him, his allies, the Maruts, animate in battle; him, men regard as the preserver of their property, he alone presides over every act of worship; may Indra, associated with the Maruts, be our protection.

8. To him, a leader (to victory), his worshippers apply in contests of strength for protection and for wealth, as he grants them the light (of conquest) in the bewildering darkness (of battle); may Indra, associated with the Maruts, be our protection.

9. With his left hand he restrains the malignant, with his right he receives the (sacrificial) offerings; he is the giver of riches, (when propitiated) by one who celebrates his praise; may Indra, associated with the Maruts, be our protection.

10. He, along with his attendants, is a benefactor; he is quickly recognised by all men to-day, through his chariots; by his manly energies he is victor over unruly (adversaries); may Indra, associated with the Maruts, be our protection.

11. Invoked by many, he goes to battle with his kinsmen, or with (followers) not of his kindred; he secures the (triumph) of those who trust in him, and of their sons and grandsons; may Indra, associated with the Maruts, be our protection.

12. He is the wielder of the thunderbolt, the slayer of robbers, fearful and fierce: knowing many things, much eulogised and mighty, and, like the soma juice, inspiring the five classes of beings* with vigour; may Indra, associated with the Maruts, be our protection.

13. His thunderbolt draws cries (from his enemies); he is the sender of good waters, brilliant as (the luminary) of heaven, the thunderer, the promoter of beneficent acts; upon him do donations and riches attend; may Indra, associated with the Maruts, be our protection.

14. May he, of whom the excellent measure (of all things) through strength, eternally and everywhere, cherishes heaven and earth, propitiated by our acts, convey us beyond (evil); may Indra, associated with the Maruts, be our protection.

15. Nor gods, nor men, nor waters, have reached the limit of the strength of that beneficent (divinity); for he surpasses both earth and heaven by his foe-consuming (might); may Indra, associated with the Maruts, be our protection.

16. The red and black coursers, long-limbed, well-caparisoned, and celestial, and harnessed, well-pleased, to the yoke of the chariot in which the showerer of benefits is conveyed, for the enrichment of Rijraswa, and is recognized amongst human hosts.

17. Indra, showerer (of benefits), the Varshagiras, Rijraswa and his companions, Ambarisha, Sahadeva, Bhayamana and Suradhas, address to thee this propitiatory praise.

18. Indra, who is invoked by many, attended by the

* The commentator explains this term to denote the four castes, *Brahman*, *Vishahiya*, *Vaisya*, and *Sudra*, and the barbarian or *Nirhada*: but he expresses, of coûrse, the received impressions of his age.—*Professor Wilson's Preface*, p. xliii.

moving (Maruts), having attacked the Dasyus and the Simyus, slew them with his thunderbolt; the thunderer then divided the fields with his white-complexioned friends, and rescued the sun, and set free the water.

19. May Indra be daily our vindicator, and may we, with undiverted course, enjoy (abundant) food; and may Mitra, Varuna, Aditi—ocean, earth, and heaven—preserve it to us.*

1. Day by day we invoke the doer of good works for our protection, as a good milch cow for the milking (is called by the milker).

2. Drinker of the soma juice, come to our (daily) rites, and drink of the libation; the satisfaction of (thee who art) the bestower of riches, is verily (the cause of) the gift of cattle.

3. We recognize thee in the midst of the right-minded, who are nearest to thee: come to us; pass us not by to reveal (thyself to others).

4. Go, worshipper, to the wise and uninjured Indra, who bestows the best (of blessings) on thy friends, and ask him of the (fitness of the) learned (priest who recites his praise).

5. Let our ministers, earnestly performing his worship, exclaim, Depart, ye revilers, from hence and every other place (where he is adored).

6. Destroyer of foes, let our enemies say we are prosperous; let men (congratulate us); may we ever abide in the felicity (derived from the favour) of Indra.

7. Offer to Indra, the pervader (of every rite of libation), the juice that is present (at the three ceremonies), the grace of the sacrifice, the exhilarator of

* Rig Veda Sanhita: Ashtaka 1, Adhyaya 7, S. vii. *W.* i. 255.

mankind, the perfecter of the act, the favourite of (that Indra) who gives happiness (to the offerer).*

8. Having drunk, Satakratu, of this (soma juice), thou becamest the slayer of the Vritras; thou defendest the warrior in battle.

9. We offer to the Satakratu, the mighty in battle, (sacrificial) food for the acquirement, Indra, of riches.

10. Sing unto that Indra, who is the protector of wealth, the mighty, the accomplisher of good deeds, the friend of the offerer of the libation.†

The people whose religious views are represented in these hymns were undoubtedly much in advance of the aboriginal inhabitants of India. They were acquainted with some of the more obvious phenomena of the heavens and the sea, and had attained a higher mental and physical development; but they were as certainly ignorant of the theology and philosophy of the Brahmana. Their religion was a form of the old elemental worship prevalent in the early stages of the general decline from the knowledge of the true God. From this position the reasoning of after-ages was able to re-ascend to the monotheistical idea, and so concluded the other objects of adoration to be manifestations of the Supreme; but as far as the primitive Aryans and their Veda is concerned, there is good reason to doubt if they ever dreamed of any other divinity than the gods to whom their sacrifices were paid and their invocations addressed.

2. A wholly different state of opinion and social organization appears in the second portion of the Veda, called *Brahmana,* and the change is so

* Rig Veda Sanhita: Ashtaka 1, Adhyaya 1 Anuvaka 2, S. i. *W.* i. 11.
† Ibid, Anuvaka 2, S. i. *W.* i. 12.

great as to require a very considerable period of time for its development. A philosophy had now arisen ascribing the creation of the universe, including the divinities popularly adored, to one Supreme Being, who offered himself under various manifestations to the knowledge and worship of the creatures. Without displacing the deities of the ancient hymns, or interfering with the established rites, a new meaning and value were asserted to the existing worship, while a more elaborate ritual invested its ceremonies. To enforce the observance of these religious rites is the main object of the Brahmana. For this purpose detached texts of the earlier hymns are cited, in a way which shows they had been long in possession of the popular reverence, and their meaning is amplified by comments, drawn from argument or tradition, which constitute, in fact, a new theology. It is pretended, indeed, that this portion of the Shastras serves but to embody the oral tradition which always accompanied and explained the primitive hymns. But this dogma, besides overthrowing the position that the written Veda came complete from the mouth of Brahma, and is a part of his substance, is contradicted by internal evidence, which has satisfied European inquirers that the Brahmana has not "the slightest claim to be regarded as the counterpart and contemporary of the Sanhita, or as an integral part of the Veda, understanding by that expression the primitive record of the religious belief and observances and of the archaic institutions of Hindu society."*

The *Institutes of Manu* embody the system elaborated in the Brahmana and Upanishads, in the

* Preface to professor Wilson's Translation of *Rig Veda Sanhita.*

shape of a complete code of civil and religious law. It was compiled about the ninth century before the Christian æra.*

The doctrine of the Supreme Being is here acknowledged as the foundation of all theology. The Deity is described in the most exalted language. He is the "Great God,—the omnipotent, omniscient ONE;—the Lord who goes through all worlds incapable of decay;—the pure *Brahm*,—the mysterious Being in whom the universe perpetually exists, in whom it is absorbed, from whom it issues." "He is perfect truth, perfect happiness, without equal; immortal, absolute unity, whom neither speech can describe, nor mind comprehend; the causing Cause, the Creator, Preserver, Transformer of all things, such is the Great One." The Institutes declare it to be "the principal duty of man to obtain from the Upanishad a true knowledge of the Supreme Being,"† and texts are adduced, as in the Brahmana, from the earlier Suktas to support this position.

A famous example of the mode in which these primitive compositions are made to yield a recondite signification, suited to the genius of the new learning, is seen in the *Gayatri*, a verse which, as it stands in the Veda, is thus simply translated: "We meditate on that desirable light of the divine Savitri, who influences our pious rites."‡ Savitri is the sun, and the passage appears to be an invocation of that luminary to shed his benignant influences on the customary rites; the unsophisticated Hindus still employ the verse, with no

* This is the date arrived at by Mr. Elphinstone: other authorities place it as high as the sixth century.

† Elphinstone, i. 27.

‡ Rig Veda Sanhita: Ashtaka 3, Adhyaya 4, S. ix. *W.* iij. 110.

other signification.* The Brahmans, however, have discovered in this simple aspiration a deep spiritual mystery. It is declared to contain the essence of all religion, and to be an indispensable portion of the daily prayers. Being too sacred to be repeated at length, the mystical syllable *Aum*, or *Om*, has been invented as its substitute, and is pronounced with an extraordinary reverence. This triliteral word, expressing (we are told) the three powers of divinity—creation, preservation, and destruction,—comprehends every deity, for in fact there is only one divinity, the great soul. So great is its power, that "sixteen suppressions of the breath, while the holiest of texts is repeated, with the three mighty words, and the triliteral syllable, absolve even the slayer of a Brahman from his hidden faults."† After all, this mystic syllable, like the Gayatri itself, had reference, according to sir W. Jones, to the sun; the three letters representing the *heat*, *light*, and *flame* of the great luminary of nature.

The theory of Manu is, that the self-existing power called *Brahm* (neuter) with a thought created the waters, in which he placed a productive seed. From this came the *mundane egg*, in which the Supreme Being was himself born as *Brahma*, the masculine impersonation of the godhead: he created the heavens and the earth, and assigned the names and occupations of the several creatures. A number of other deities, with a cloud of inferior spirits, genii, nymphs, and demons, were also created by Brahma. His creation is to endure for a vast period, called *kalpa*, at the close of which Brahma himself is again to be absorbed into the

* Professor Wilson's Preface to Vol. 3.
† Manu, xi. 214.

divine essence ; his whole system will disappear, and another be educed from Brahm.

In this theology care was taken not to interfere with the popular polytheistic worship; the objects of adoration remained as before, Indra, Agni, and Surya, with others from the Suktas; only a few new conceptions were added, as the gods of justice, medicine, etc. The existing worship also was retained and reduced to a stricter observance. Five sacraments are declared to be of daily observance, the first of which is the performance of the oblations, which are the same as of old; the other four are, reading the Vedas, offering to the manes of departed ancestors, giving rice to living creatures, and receiving guests with honour and hospitality. To these are added a daily ablution, with morning and evening prayer, in a solitary place by pure water. These regulations, however, apply only to the three superior castes, who represent the Aryan aristocracy. To read the Vedas, or share the sacrifices with a *Sudra*, is interdicted by the severest penalties. A new aspect, also, was given to society by the institution of a complex system of ceremonial purity, depending on arbitrary rules, of which we find nothing in the Vedas.

It is apparent that this system was a philosophy, not a religion; its knowledge was carefully restrained from the bulk of the community, and in the very moment that the existence of the Supreme Being was announced, care was taken to separate him from the worship of his creatures by providing inferior deities, and perpetuating the popular rites.

The philosophy of the Brahmans had already essayed a flight, and experienced a fall, which later metaphysicians have not altogether avoided. Reasoning from creation to a Creator, and from the Divine attributes to the Being in whom they must inhere, they were not content to rest in the *Person* of God, but would speculate further upon his *Essence*. From Brahma, the active Creator of the universe, they ascended to *Brahm*, the Absolute and Infinite, whom at one moment they found to be everything, at another nothing. With him nothing could be added or diminished: the Absolute and the Infinite could hold no relations with dependent and finite creatures. Creation thus became an impossibility to the Supreme, and Brahma, to whom the work was assigned, was accordingly only a manifestation, an inferior and temporary God. Thus, having reasoned "from nature *up* to nature's God," the presumptuous sages reasoned *down* again from their own conception of God to find he could enter into no relation with themselves or the universe to which they belonged. "The true doctrine of the Vedas (they declared) is that the Supreme Spirit has nothing to do with the creatures, or the creatures with him."* This was the result of seeking to find out God by the light of philosophy instead of revelation. The consequence was to darken rather than illuminate mankind. The True Object of worship was declared to be unattainable; and men were exhorted to address their hopes and fears to the traditional deities as partial manifestations of the inaccessible Supreme. In this teaching lay the fruitful germ of all the subsequent idolatry and debasement of the Hindus.

Another conception developed by Brahmanical philosophy, without being so much as alluded to in the

* These are the words of Kapila, the great native commentator on the Veda.

Vedas, has succeeded in rooting itself in the popular mind, where it forms at this day the most universal article of Hindu belief. This is the tenet of *metempsychosis*, or transmigration of souls, supposed to have taken its rise in Egypt, whence it was imported into Greece by Pythagoras about five centuries before Christ. There is ground for thinking, however, that this tenet originated with the Brahmans in India, from whence it spread into Egypt, and indeed over the larger portion of mankind.

That it was part of the "wisdom of the Egyptians" in the time of Moses, and so passed into the general belief of the children of Israel, has been the opinion of many learned persons. No passage from the inspired Scriptures can be adduced in its support; but in the apocryphal book entitled the Wisdom of Solomon, it appears in unmistakable language, where the author says of himself, that "being a witty child, and having a good spirit, or rather being good, I came into a body undefiled."* The schools of the Pharisees held the same opinion in the time of our Saviour, whom some supposed to be a reappearance of the spirit of Elijah, others of Jeremiah, or one of the prophets.† And that it was a prevalent opinion among the people, would appear from the question of the disciples, "Who did sin, this man, or his parents, that he was born blind?"‡ In short, it appears that while some of the Old Testament saints were unquestionably favoured with *glimpses* of the truth, the nature of the human soul, and of the life to come, was not

* Wisdom of Solomon, viii. 19, 20.

† Matt. xvi. 13, 14.

‡ John ix. 2.

anywhere generally known till revealed by JESUS CHRIST.*

The tenet appears to have been variously modified by the ancient Egyptians, the Rabbinical Jews, and the Indian Brahmans. All agreed that the spirits of men are emanations from the Great Spirit, not called into being as they are successively born into this world, but created all together in the beginning of the universe, and destined to continue their separated conscious existence till again absorbed into the Divine Essence. The Egyptians seem to have first held that this absorption took place at the death of each individual, the vital spark of thought then returning to the source from which it came, and disappearing as a drop of water is dissolved in the ocean. It appearing, however, that this doctrine furnished but an inadequate check on the excesses of men on this side the grave, the defect was supplied by the invention of an intermediate series of transmigrations. The wicked were alarmed by a course of shame and suffering, interposed before the final

* It has often been remarked that the sanctions of a future life, though received by the patriarchs, and frequently alluded to in the Psalms and the Prophets, are nowhere employed in the laws and institutions delivered at Mount Sinai. Bishop Warburton has founded on the omission an argument for the divine legation of Moses, whom he supposes to have designedly suppressed the doctrine of judgment to come, in order to stake the credit of his dispensation on the blessings and curses it could realize in this life. Others, conceiving such a suppression of important truth to be inconsisteht with the character of a teacher inspired by God, account for the omission on the ground that the law was designed for a pattern or miniature of the Divine government in general, and could therefore appeal to no sanctions beyond itself. Some have imagined Moses himself to be but imperfectly informed on the future state: but if the tenet of transmigration was at that time (as many think) generally held by the Israelites, a motive may be suggested for his silence more consistent with the inspiration of the lawgiver. To speak in general terms might be to lend countenance to the prevailing error; while a more particular explanation might anticipate mysteries which were only to be revealed by the Spirit of Christ.

oblivion; and the penitent were encouraged by a succession of probations, to render the polluted spirit more fit for its return to God.

Among the Jews the doctrine was limited to the re-inhabiting of *human* forms, and by some to a return to their own bodies purified for a better life. With them, therefore, transmigration was the lot of those that were eventually to be saved; the utterly wicked being consigned to hopeless perdition. These sentiments contained some dim approaches to the true faith of the resurrection of the body. The Egyptians, on the contrary, held, that on the dissolution of the body the soul entered some other animal, and, after passing through every species of terrestrial, aquatic, and winged creatures, was at last, a second time, united to a human body: the period of these changes was estimated at three thousand years. The pains bestowed on the preservation of *mummies* seem to indicate that it was to their own bodies they expected to return at last, though their faith on this point was far inferior to that of the Jews. These sentiments occasioned them to be content with mean edifices for the living, whom they regarded as sojourning in *tents;* while vast sums were expended on the monuments, which were called the *mansions* of the dead.*

The Brahmanical philosophy has retained all the worst conceits of the Egyptian, together with others of its own. It peoples the unseen world with various heavens, or paradises, called *Swargas*, where the principal gods reign in splendour and feasting. Several hells, or purgatories, are provided on the other hand, replenished with unspeakable tortures. The soul

* Russell's Connexion of Sacred and Profane History, Book i. c. 2.

being conducted after death before *Yama* the judge of the dead, is sentenced by him, according to its deserts, to either one or other of these abodes of bliss or torment. Neither, however, is its eternal portion; but, after remaining a sufficient time to satisfy the surplus merits of its good deeds in the one case, or to atone for some portion of its sins in the other, the spirit returns to renew its probation on earth by being born in another body. The general opinion is, that some millions of such births in other shapes, must be undergone before it is permitted to resume the human form. During this cycle the soul may inhabit the bodies of beasts of prey or other animals, reptiles, birds, fishes, insects, and even trees, minerals, or stones. The rules by which the several conditions are allotted may be judged of by the following extract from the Institutes:—

"Sinners of the first degree, having passed through terrible rigours of torture in hell for a very long period, are condemned to the following births: the slayer of a Brahman to become a dog, boar, ass, camel, bull, goat, sheep, or bird, according to the circumstances of his crime; a Brahman who has drunk spirituous liquors to be a worm, insect, or moth; a man who steals corn to be a rat; if he steals milk, a crow; one who censures his spiritual guide must be born an ass; one who steals the gold of a priest is to pass a thousand times into the bodies of spiders, reptiles, snakes, crocodiles, and *demons living on blood.*"

The highest state in which one can be born again is that of a Brahman. The soul which has attained to the highest Swarga, after enjoying its appointed measure of bliss, must return to earth and complete its probation in this exalted and sacred caste, before it can return to the Divine Essence. It is only as a Brahman that it can attain the perfect knowledge of the Supreme Being, which at once extinguishes the motions and the essence of sin. The spirit then loses all worldly desires and bodily passions, and dying so is at once "reunited to the Deity." This phrase, intended to express the supreme felicity, is still illustrated by the figure of a drop of water falling into the sea and becoming absorbed; or, again, the Brahman will demand, "What have I in my hand? It is air: I open my fingers, where is it?" These metaphors are designed to teach the cessation of all personal identity. The spirit received back again into the Divine Essence, from which it issued at the creation, is no longer subject to transmigration. It can never again possess a conscious and separated existence; in fact, it is *annihilated!* It is to thus laying down the burden of his being that the Hindu looks forward, after millions of centuries spent in change and suffering, as the only means of attaining the condition where the "wicked cease from troubling, and the weary are at rest."* How strikingly does this melancholy result of human philosophy contrast with the eternity of conscious union with our Heavenly Father, which the gospel opens to the believer, in that "rest which remaineth for the people of God"? †

The description given in the Shastras of the unseen world, are coloured with all the warmth of eastern poetry. The spirits of good men are conducted through delightful paths, under the shadow of fragrant trees, and among streams covered with the pleasant lotus. Sweet flowers are rained upon them as they

* Job iii. 17. † Heb. iv. 9.

pass, while the air resounds with the hymns of the blessed, and the still more melodious songs of celestial spirits. On the other hand, the wicked pass through dark and dismal roads, over burning sand, and stones that cut the feet at every step. Parched with thirst, and covered with mire and blood, they travel naked amid showers of hot ashes and fiery coals; they are terrified by frequent and horrible apparitions; the air is filled with shrieks and lamentable wailings. The several swargas and hells are depicted, in like manner, from all that is attractive or terrible to the senses.

These rewards and punishments, being often well apportioned to the moral merits and demerits of the deceased, might exercise a beneficial effect on the conduct of the living, if their influence were not largely counterbalanced by other characteristics of the Hindu religion. The doctrine of transmigration, while engendering a spurious tenderness for the lower animals (any one of which may contain the soul of an ancestor), is little calculated to promote the love of God or mankind. Though no remembrance is retained of the events of any former existence, it ascribes every human misfortune to the transgressions of a previous state. The calamities of others are equally regarded as the just reward of their deeds. "Men are born stupid (says Manu), dumb, blind, deaf, and deformed, *to be despised of the good*, according to the various actions they have performed; and penance must be performed to make expiation, or they will again spring to birth with disgraceful marks." Even crime and its punishment are attributed to a similar origin in some pre-existent state; the offender came into the world with his destiny already assigned him, and is only fulfilling it by a life of sin, and a shameful death. This gloomy fatalism quenches all compassion for the unfortunate, while it effectually stifles the motions of repentance in the sufferer; for where the offence is unknown it is impossible to repent. In like manner, every success in life being considered as the just reward of some previous (though equally unknown) merit, there is no room for gratitude to man, or thankfulness to God.

Another practical counterpoise to the moral influence of future judgment is the Brahmanical doctrine of *penance*. Hardly any crime, moral or ceremonial, may not admit of expiation, by means of certain prescribed ordinances, among which the giving money to the Brahmans always occupies a foremost place.

An anomaly still more singular is the power ascribed to sacrifices and religious austerities, irrespective of the moral condition of the worshippers. This notion is carried to such an extravagant pitch that the gods themselves are held subject to the claims acquired by the prescribed external acts of worship. An impious ascetic is able, by his curse, to punish the deity who judges him; and the most wicked of mortals may acquire so much merit by sacrifices, as to compel the gods to execute his criminal designs, and even to resign their heavens to his possession. Indra, hurled from his Swarga by the curse of a Brahman, was compelled to animate the body of a cat. Yama, the very judge of quick and dead, being cursed in the discharge of his office, underwent transmigration as a slave. The sacrifices of a wicked king threatened all the gods with destruction, and his power could only be arrested by an incarnation of deity for his overthrow. Another monarch, by this means, forced the gods to hide themselves under the shapes of different animals; a third compelled them to worship himself.

In later days, when the Brahmans and their sacrifices began to decline in repute, a new device took the place of this ritualistic devotion. The gods, it was said, all demand the respect and veneration of the worshipper: but their number is too great, and the services too burdensome, to be all known and attended to by the same individual. On this account a particular deity was selected from the pantheon to become the object of a more concentrated devotion; and an implicit *faith* in this divinity was held to be a sufficient substitute for the ever-growing ceremonies of the Brahmanical ritual. The worshipper was persuaded that to rely upon the god whom he had thus enshrined in his heart, under all circumstances, would dispense from every other religious obligation, while, without such an act of faith, neither sacrifice nor moral virtue was of the slightest avail.

3. Meantime the popular religion was moulded, not by the theories of philosophy, but by the traditions, customs, and prevailing opinion of the population. Its real Shastras were neither the Vedas nor the Institutes of Manu, but a compilation of quite another kind, called the *Puranas.* These are eighteen in number, with as many *Upas* or supplementary Puranas. They are filled with fragments of various systems of cosmogony and philosophy, and with innumerable legends of the gods and heroes, extending over a period of very uncertain antiquity. Their compilation is assigned by the Hindus to the same extravagant age with the Vedas, and is even popularly

supposed to be the work of the same arranger, Vyasa. Most of them, however, are obviously of a later date than the Institutes of Manu; and European critics assign the compilation to a date between the sixth and sixteenth centuries after Christ.

It is in the Puranas that the doctrine of *Avatars*, or incarnations of the deity, makes its appearance, in relating the exploits of the heroes, or in allegorizing the operations of spirit upon matter. Hence arose a new series of gods and demigods, which was not confined to the objects of Aryan veneration. The expedient by which the Brahmans reconciled their monotheistical philosophy with the polytheism of the Vedas readily admitted of a further application. God was to be adored under all his manifestations; but the Sudras or subjugated nations, who were excluded from the sacred rites of the Brahman, could hardly be denied the continuance of their former worship. Its objects, therefore, claimed to be ranked among the various manifestations of the Supreme. It was acknowledged that *all* the names and attributes of the Infinite were not enumerated in the Vedas. On admitting new nations into the system, their gods also challenged a place in the pantheon. Wherever a popular worship existed, the local rite was received into this elastic system, and its legend became enshrined in a new Purana.

Thus Hinduism multiplied its divinities as it enlarged its borders. The places of worship and pilgrimage, the ceremonies, and even the divine attributes, of other systems, were adopted as its own; and in the end some of the very demons, against whom the Vedas invoke the aid of Indra and Agni, became enthroned beside the gods of the

Aryans, in the heterogenous compound of Hindu idolatry.

To this process of incorporation the Hindu mythology seems to be indebted for the introduction of Siva, the god of destruction, and at the present day the great patron of the Brahmans. The Vedas and Manu are wholly ignorant of him. It is in the Puranas that he appears associated with Brahma, or rather elevated to the same ranks as a personal emanation of the Divinity, without regard to the claims of the former. Here also Vishnu, known to the Vedas only as a name for the sun, is represented as another equal and independent emanation. The attempt is made to harmonize these rival powers into a sacred triad, vested respectively with the powers of creation, preservation, and destruction. But no such distribution of functions is observable in their acts, or possible in theory, since these divine attributes intermingle of necessity in every operation. It is far more probable that Vishnu and Siva represent other and antagonist religions preserved in the Puranas, and the latter may be assigned, without difficulty, to the demonolatry of the aboriginal Dravidians.

In the same class with the Puranas may be ranked the two great epic poems, the *Ramayana* and the *Mahabharat.* The heroes of both were incarnations of Vishnu, and are at this day the most popular objects of worship throughout India. These poems are the *Iliad* and *Æneid* of Sanscrit literature. Both are popularly ascribed to Vyasa, the arranger of the Vedas; but there are two editions of the *Ramayana,* of which the more commonly known was the production of Valmiki, an author of uncertain date. The *Mahabharat* contains 400,000 lines, and after all professes to be but a fragment of the original poem as recited in the assembly of the gods. The *Ramayana* extends to 100,000 verses; while the *Iliad* contains but 24,000 lines, and the *Æneid* only half as many. Like the western epics these oriental writings are the chief authorities on the state of manners in the earliest ages;* they are also quoted as standards of religious belief, and are in that respect almost on a level with the Puranas.

This latter class of Shastras forms the real Scripture of the existing Hindu creed, which has no connexion with the Veda, and scarcely more with the speculative theology of Manu. Some specimens of the earlier writings having been given, it may be well to adduce an example, in this place, of the newer and popular style of divinity.

It is related in the Mahabharat, and in several of the Puranas, that Indra, the king of the gods, having happened to slay a Brahman, concealed himself in the waters to avoid the penalties of so great a sacrilege. The affairs of heaven and earth were in consequence thrown into confusion till a virtuous monarch, named Nahusha, at the entreaty of the gods, ascended the vacant throne. Becoming intoxicated with his elevation, the new king of heaven abandoned himself to dissipation. The gods remonstrating, were told he was no worse than his predecessor, whom they had never ventured to rebuke. At last, Indrani (the queen of the exiled Indra) was obliged to fly from the upstart's violence. She goes in search of her husband, whom she discovers hidden in the stem of a lotus at the bottom of a lake. She urges him to return

* The heroes, however, of the eastern epics claim to be at least as old as Moses, while those of Homer were coeval only with David.

and dispossess his unworthy rival, but the god, being afraid of the power acquired by Nahusha's austerities and devotion, sends her back to the Swarga with a device to overthrow his merit. The queen accordingly proposes to Nahusha that he should compel the Brahman *rishis* to bear his palanquin, an honour which not Vishnu, nor any other god, had ever aspired to. The king, immediately consenting, obliges 1,000 Brahmans to submit to this menial service. In order to be revenged, they demand if he considers the formulæ for the sacrifice of kine to be authentic; and, on his answering in the negative, a violent dispute ensues, in the course of which the king fills up the measure of his wickedness by touching the head of Agostya, one of the rishis (celebrated as the civilizer of the Deccan), with his foot. The enraged Brahman, conscious that this enormity had exhausted all the merits of the other, immediately commanded the sinner to sink from heaven to earth, exclaiming, "Fall, thou serpent;" and in the condition of a serpent he continued to crawl for ten thousand years. Meantime, Indra having offered a sacrifice to Vishnu, the guilt of Brahmanicide became "divided among trees, rivers, mountains, the earth, *women*, and living creatures, and was put away." After which, the king of gods reascended his throne.*

Such are the legends which have long taken the place of the Vedic hymns, and are recounted to the people in entire ignorance of the boasted monotheism of Brahmanical philosophy. The prominent feature of the worship they give rise to is *idolatry*, a practice foreign alike to the Vedas and to Manu. Temples, altars, and priesthoods have arisen to its service which

* *Muir's Sanscrit texts*, chap. iii., sect. 4.

had no place in the earlier systems. Local customs have acquired the force of revelation, and while the Brahman continues to repeat his barren assertion of one God, the heart of the people is crushed under a mountain of stupid and degrading idolatries. God is in fact *lost* to the Hindu; his religion is only a series of dark unavailing efforts "to feel after and find him."

In concluding this sketch of the leading elements of Hindu belief, the mind is struck by the similarity of its career to that of a truer religion in the other hemisphere. The world and the flesh exercise a uniform operation over the tendencies of a fallen nature. The Hindu system is seen to originate in a few sacred writings open to all, and the observance of which constituted the whole acknowledged religion. No sooner, however, had the Aryans obtained wealth and dominion in Hindustan, than the Brahmans began to desert their old ascetic life, and to assume the lead in commerce, war, and politics. At the same time they advanced pretensions to priestly functions before unknown. From conducting a domestic service, they raised themselves into mediators between the gods and their votaries. The sacrifices were multiplied in number and variety. Yet, too indolent to instruct their nominal proselytes from idolatry, the false priests contrived a distinction which excluded the masses at once from the scriptures and the communion of their conquerors. The Vedas, thus restricted to the upper classes, were next monopolized by the Brahmans, and then consigned to neglect. Voluminous glosses, comments, and expositions overlaid the sacred page. Practices were sanctioned among the neglected populace, which were in truth but continuations of the exploded idolatries. But schools of logic and philosophy arose to reconcile all with a belief in the One True God. The ritual was extended till the objects of veneration became too numerous for the worship, or even the memory, of the individual. Then came the selection of a patron divinity (like the patron saint of mediæval Christianity), an implicit faith in whose protection seemed to offer a refuge from the impossible round of ceremonial observances. This introduced a cloud of legends eagerly vouched for by contending champions. The Brahmans (like the secular clergy) were supplanted in the affections of the people by mendicants loudly extolling their several patrons, and, through an appearance of poverty and mortification, acquiring the reputation of superior sanctity. These, too, in their turn have become the objects of just contempt with the educated and reflecting Hindu; and attempts are now made to construct a purer religion on the text of the unadulterated Veda.

Here, however, the parallel fails: there can be no Reformation where there is no genuine Scripture to revert to. The more the Vedas are brought forth from the seclusion of centuries, the more clearly are they seen to be wholly inadequate to the necessities of a practical religion. To circulate them in the vernaculars of India, would, indeed, be to expose the falsehood of the assumptions on which millions are implicitly staking their belief. It would open many new and unsuspected truths, and give the death-blow to fables already tottering under the assaults of reason. But neither the Vedas, nor the whole circle of Brahmanical philosophy, can reveal to the natives of India the "unknown God whom they ignorantly worship."

One Book only is able to satisfy the long craving of a benighted nature, and make them "wise unto salvation." This Book is indeed primitive and divine; it is not a portion of the Creator's substance, but it is in very deed the "word that goeth out of his mouth, and which shall not return unto him void."

THE BIBLE is India's great want in the present state of the native mind, and the opportunity of giving the Bible is the highest distinction which the possession of India offers to the crown of Great Britain.

CHAPTER III.

IDOLATRY.

Brahmanical monotheism a philosophy, not a religion—The Supreme inaccessible to the creatures—Elementary worship of the Vedas—The sun—Demonolatry—Hindu triad—Antagonistic deities—Their consorts—Brahma—God of the philosophers—Vishnu—Avatars—Rama—Krishna—Names of Vishnu—Supposed resemblances to Christianity—Siva, only paralleled in Satan—Description—Relic of demonolatry—Wives of the gods—Sereswati, Lakshmi, Parvati, or Bhavani, Kali, etc.—Minor deities—Eleven principal—Ganesa—Surya—Others without temples—Stars, planets, rivers—Village gods—General effect—Idols—Temples—Pyramidal towers—Endowments—Connexion with government—Mode of worship—No common prayer nor preaching—Festivals—Cars—Procession—Hooli—Dusserah—Reflections on indecent rites—Brahmans—Gurus—Gosayens, Yogees, Byragees—Hindu sects—Marks on the forehead—The cow—Pilgrimage—Moral results—Incoherent and degrading particulars—Practical wickedness—Pantheism—Pope's lines—Illusion—Buddhism—Rejects Vedas and Puranas—Respect for animal life—No distinctions of caste—Relics—Priests—Monasteries—Buddhas—Jains—Comparison with classical philosophy—Need of the gospel.

It has been seen that the monotheism of the Brahmans was a philosophy, not a religion: it never offered the Supreme Being to the trust and worship of his creatures. It represented him as existing in a state of serene self-contemplation, careless and unconscious of all that goes on in the universe, the affairs of which were left to inferior divinities. The faith and worship of the people were naturally demanded for those who presided over their temporal and eternal destinies. These, and not the abstract conçeptions that lay behind them, constituted the real gods of the Hindus.

The primitive objects of adoration were the powers

of the elements invoked in the Vedas; and fire, water, earth, and air are still acknowledged as divinities, and daily worshipped by the Brahmans. This worship is naturally symbolized by the *sun*, who under the name of Vishnu monopolized a large proportion of the popular reverence, as the source of light and every natural blessing. His empire was divided by Siva, a conception borrowed from the earlier demonolatry, and representing the invisible powers of evil. These are still the two principal deities of the Hindu system. Brahma, with whom it has been sought to associate them in the Hindu triad, obviously belongs to another origin. He is the creation of philosophy, the personal emanation of the infinite, inaccessible Brahm, the active Creator of the universe. To constitute the triad, Vishnu and Siva are also recognized as emanations of Brahm, and a fictitious harmony is brought about by distributing the powers of the godhead amongst the three. Brahma is called the Creator, Vishnu the Preserver, and Siva the Destroyer; but this artificial distinction quickly disappears. The three deities are far from acting as consentient and co-operative emanations of one Essence. Each arrogates the functions of the other two, and the Puranas abound in grotesque legends of their conflicts.*

The three gods are each furnished with a consort, representing, it is said, the active energy of their respective powers; and from them are derived, either by birth or creation, the "gods many and lords many" of the existing Hindu system. These are in number far beyond arithmetical computation, of infinitely various degrees and characters, the subjects of innu-

* According to some, Brahma represents *truth*, Vishnu *the will*, and Siva *sensuality*.

merable legends, and the objects of the countless rites of a vast diversified idolatry.

Brahma is pictured of the colour of gold, having four faces and four hands. He is arrayed in shining garments, and rides on a bird resembling a swan. One hand holds the Vedas, another a vessel of water, the third is raised in the attitude of benediction, and the fourth is extended as bestowing a gift. They who would trace in such descriptions the material images of invisible things, may understand these as emblematical of the Great Being, "whose eyes are in every place, beholding the evil and the good," whose word is the law of the universe, who sends down "rain and fruitful seasons, filling our hearts with food and gladness," and who is the Giver of all good things. But such conceptions, if entertained by the first authors of the symbol, have long since disappeared under others of a very different description. The accounts of the creation are numerous, obscure, and contradictory. The common opinion is that Brahma created first the waters, then the earth, then a crowd of inferior deities, good and bad genii, etc., and finally mankind. The work of creation ended, Brahma offered an *aswamedha* in its honour, and returned to his heaven. From that moment it was consistent with the genius of Hinduism to dismiss the Creator from all further recognition and homage. A daily ceremony is performed in his honour by the Brahmans, his eldest and most favoured offspring; but Brahma has no place in the popular worship; his image is never made, and only one temple in India is known to be dedicated to his name.

The Puranas account for the neglect by pretending that he was solemnly cursed by the other gods for falsehood. Before this, he had five heads; but Siva, whom he had calumniated, was so enraged as to cut off one of them. This is an example of the manner in which the authors of those monstrous fables endeavoured to exalt the power of their favourite gods at the expense of the patrons of other sects. The true explanation probably is, that Brahma, the god of the philosophers, never attained to general reception. The populace was divided between the more tangible worship of Vishnu, or the sun, and the demonolatry represented in Siva.

Vishnu is depicted as a young man of a dark *azure* colour, in the dress of the ancient kings. He also has four arms and hands, holding respectively a war-club, a conch-shell, a water-lily, and a peculiar discus, or weapon termed *chuckra:* this appears to be a circle or wreath, darting out flame, and was originally, perhaps, an emblem of the sun's rays. He is represented as riding on a creature shaped like an eagle, with the face of a man.

This divinity is adored also under the forms of numerous *avatars* or incarnations, by which he is fabled to have interposed for the rescue of the universe, or the punishment of vice. In the first avatar, under the form of a fish, he recovered the Vedas, which had been swept away in a deluge by one of the demons; in the second, he appeared as a huge boar, to save the drowning world by lifting it out of the ocean on his tusks; in the third, he was a tortoise, supporting the mountain on which all things were sustained; in the fourth, a lion, destroying an infidel king, and vindicating the divine omnipresence. In the fifth, assuming the form of a Brahman dwarf, he outwitted and destroyed the king, who, by the merit of his austerities and sacrifices, had threatened to overthrow the gods. The sixth was Parasurama, a Brahman hero, who made war on the Kshettriyas, and extirpated their caste. The seventh was Rama, the great king of Oude, and conqueror of the Deccan, whose deeds are the subject of the epic poem, the *Ramayana:* the eighth, Bulla Rama, another hero, famous for the destruction of the giants: the ninth, Buddha the author of a religion which once rivalled the Brahmanical: and the tenth is yet to come, when the god is expected to appear on a white horse, with a scimitar blazing like a comet, to mow down the impenitent and incorrigible.

Of these *avatars* several appear to have been historical personages, whom their panegyrists sought to identify with the god. Such was clearly Rama, or Ramana, who is still worshipped in his natural form throughout Hindustan. Such, too, was Krishna, whom some accounts make to be the eighth avatar of Vishnu, instead of Bulla Rama. The more favourite notion, however, is, that Krishna was *more* than an *avatar*, being in fact Vishnu himself, the eternal, self-existing Creator. This distinction would seem to imply that the other ten forms were but *inspired* by the divinity, and that Krishna is the only *incarnation*, in the full meaning of the term.

Krishna was born of a royal family, on the banks of the Jumna, and his history abounds in legends which the Hindus are never tired of reciting. One large sect worships him in the form of a child, in which condition he stole milk and destroyed serpents. Females adore him as a handsome youth, playing on the lute, and captivating the affections alike of milk-maids and princesses. In his riper years he is renowned for exploits in the great war, which constitutes the theme of the other great epic, the Mahabharat.

Rama and Krishna are the most popular forms of Vishnu, and each is the exclusive object of adoration to a numerous sect. The former had a favourite general, Hanuman, who, being an aboriginal, was transformed by the Puranas into a monkey, and his image in that shape is common in the temples of the Deccan.* Rama is an object of universal reverence to the Hindus. His name is usually invoked in the hour of death, and a double repetition of it is the common form of salutation. His votaries appear to expect his return to earth, for the benefit of the Hindus; and in the mutiny of the Bengal troops, some of the revolted sepoys were heard shouting "Rama is come."

By far the greatest favourite, however, is Krishna, whose worship combines the opulent and luxurious classes, with almost all the women, and a very large proportion of all ranks of Indian society. In Bengal, more than half the Hindu population are his disciples. Yet this worship is full of practices more indecent and abominable than it is allowable to describe or imagine. Even the history of this popular deity cannot be repeated to European ears. The figures on a car, which Dr. Buchanan saw in Mysore, he declares to be the most indecent he had ever witnessed; and Dr. Allen pronounces of a long series of stone images which he saw in a celebrated temple, that if they were exhibited or offered for sale as statues, pictures, or engravings, or even described in any language of a civilized country, the offence would call for severe but merited punishment from the laws. Still these out-

* Ward represents this deity as a form of Siva, and analogous to *Pan*.

rages on modesty are publicly paraded in the ceremonials of Hindu worship, and a Christian government has not yet recognized the duty of protecting the general morals from so base a perversion of religious liberty.

Vishnu is often called the supreme God and Creator of the universe, quite regardless of the claims of Brahma. There are even pictures which represent the latter as proceeding from a lotus, which grows out of Vishnu sleeping on the waters of Chaos. He is also called the sacrificial male, priest and victim in one ; expressions perhaps not dissimilar in meaning from those applied to Agni in the earlier Vedas.

Some have wished to find in these expressions an allusion to the great truths of the Christian revelation ; an idea which was thought to receive countenance from other portions of the Hindu mythology,—such as its sacred triad, of which the persons are called three and yet one,—the derivation of the Creator from the inaccessible Deity, as it were "the brightness of his glory, and the express image of his person,"*—the incarnation of the second person for the benefit of mankind,—with several of the incidents attributed to Krishna, his birth of a royal line, his abduction when a child to escape the fury of the tyrant who sought his life, his retired education, his death by the piercing of an arrow or spear, and lastly the remarkable intensity in which the love and adoration of his worshippers have centred themselves on his person. A closer inspection, however, dispels the hopes once based upon these appearances. The most that can be conceded is, that some relics of primitive truth may be imbedded in the gloomy chaos of Hindu idolatry, as in

* Heb. i. 3.

the more familiar mines of classic mythology; but they lie too deep and scattered to be collected by human research.

The Hindu triad is so far from reflecting any idea of the Holy Trinity, that its three persons are not even of one mind and power. Their operations are not in harmony, but in continual conflict. Each receives from his own worshippers the ascription of supreme power; but it is an antagonistic not a co-ordinate claim. The glory of each is based on the depreciation of the other two; and all is so mixed with fables, monstrous and immoral, that the search after Christian analogies has been abandoned in despair.

The issue is equally disappointing when a comparison is instituted between the True Incarnation and the monstrous avatars of Vishnu. The name of Krishna, indeed, with some of the incidents assigned to him, dance for a moment before the eye, but they are quickly discovered to be wandering and deceitful lights, soon quenched in corruption. The heart recoils in horror from placing the life of the Holy Jesus on the same page with the ineffable abominations of Krishna.

The third emanation of Brahm, *Siva* the Destroyer, will assuredly find no parallel in the gospel scheme, unless it be with the evil one, "who was a murderer from the beginning." The Puranas describe him as delighting in blood, drunken and filthy in his habits, and only saved from universal contempt by the dread and horror of almighty power wielded by an ungovernable temper. One form depicts him with five faces, three eyes, and four hands; another exhibits but a single head, crowned with the crescent moon, with one pair of hands, which brandish an axe and a trident. His three eyes are inflamed with wine, and consume all who intrude upon him with their fire. He is mounted on a bull, naked or clothed in rags (occasionally exchanged for a tiger's skin), covered with the ashes of funeral pyres, girdled with snakes, having a necklace of human heads and a skull in his hands. In one of the Puranas he describes himself as wandering about like a madman, and dancing with demons in solitary places where corpses are burned. This frightful and ferocious deity has even more worshippers than Vishnu. His votaries style him *Maha Deva*, or the great god, claiming the same supremacy over Vishnu that others insist on for the latter. An emblem of Siva is the bull. His heaven is not with the other gods on Mount Sumeru, but lies in the eternal snows and glaciers of the remotest Himalayas. Disputes between his worshippers and those of Vishnu are of frequent occurrence, and occasionally require the intervention of government to restrain their violence.

Looking at the devil-worship still lingering in the south of India, it is impossible to avoid the conclusion that Siva is in fact the object of aboriginal terror adopted into the Hindu mythology, and elevated to a position commensurate with his importance in the older worship. At present he is the especial protector and patron of the Brahman caste.

The consort of Brahma, named *Sereswati*, is the goddess of learning and eloquence, and as such retains a larger share of notice than the long-neglected creator. *Lakshmi*, the wife of Vishnu, being the goddess of fortune and abundance, is everywhere most assiduously courted, though no temples are raised to her honour. She is described as resident with Vishnu, both shining like the sun, in a paradise of gold on Mount Sumeru, where the edifices are of jewels, and the flowers of surpassing beauty and fragrance. To this abode of delight their worshippers of every class hope to be admitted, and enjoy its pleasures till their stock of merit shall be exhausted, and they return to earth for another birth. Lakshmi is painted of a *yellow* colour, a hue with which Hindu women tinge their cheeks for ornament, and bearing a lotus in her hand. She is a favourite object of worship with females.

The consort of Siva is known by the various names of *Parvati*, *Devi*, *Bhavani*, *Durga*, and *Kali*. Under the first, the Puranas describe her as "an image of gold, a most beautiful damsel, the greatest beauty in the three worlds;" and lament over her sacrifice to so frightful a husband. The same attribute is preserved in the south, where she is worshipped as a beautiful woman, mounted on a tiger, and engaged in the destruction of the giants.

The destroying energy is symbolized in more repulsive forms under her other names. In Bengal she is represented under the name of Kali, with a hideous countenance of a *black* colour, streaming with blood; a very fury, and not a goddess. Her four hands are armed with symbols and instruments of death; a chain of human heads hangs from her neck, and new victims are prostrate under her feet. At Calcutta—for it is this fiend which has given name to the metropolis of British India*—the blood is never allowed to dry before her idol. A thousand goats are immolated monthly to renew the ensanguined dye.

* *Kali ghât*, *i.e.* Kali's stairs or landing-place.

Nor are these the costliest sacrifices required by the insatiate power. The Thugs, who associate for the purpose of murder and robbery, offer all their victims to Kali. She is the patron of their horrid fraternities. The noose which strangles the traveller unawares, and the pickaxe which digs his grave, have been first consecrated in her name. Her pleasure is consulted on every expedition; and when the omens have declared her will, the assassin proceeds to execute his bloody task, as an act of religious obedience. More than 1,500 Thugs have been arrested and brought to justice by the British government. Some of them had carried on their horrid trade for fifty or sixty years, and the number of their victims is beyond calculation: but no expression of remorse could be drawn from their lips. They expired on the gallows, believing that they had been true to their goddess. One of them, indeed, was scandalized at hearing of an act of mercy on the part of his brethren. "These are your north-country heresies," exclaimed the indignant devotee; "how can you expect the blessing of the goddess, if you rob her by exceptions of your own invention?" There can be little doubt that Hindu mythology has borrowed this demon, together with her frightful husband, from the aboriginal worship. This view is sustained by the midnight orgies included among the rites of the consort of Siva, and by the disregard of *caste* in admitting votaries to those infamous debaucheries.

The lower deities may be considered as without number, some authorities fixing them at 330 millions, while others pronounce the sum total to be infinite. There are, however, but *eleven*, in addition to the triad and their consorts, who are universally recognized as distinct deities entitled to a separate worship. The others are either the same gods, under different names, or the local divinities of particular districts, or, lastly, subordinate beings not entitled to the supreme honours of worship.

Of the principal gods two are hardly inferior in popular esteem to the sacred triad itself. *Ganesa*, or *Gunpatti*, the son of Siva, god of invention and remover of difficulties, has more temples in the Deccan than any other deity except his father. His idol is the figure of a corpulent man with an elephant's head, the united symbols of good living and good sense. Like Agni (and the Roman Janus) his name is invoked at the beginning of all sacrifices, to inaugurate the rite and render it acceptable to the other gods. The other is *Surya*, the sun-god, who is figured of a dark red colour, seated on a red lotus, in a chariot drawn by seven horses, and surrounded by rays of light. He has no idol like the other gods, but in its place the sun itself receives daily and universal adoration.

The foregoing are the only divinities to whom temples now exist in India. The other nine are supposed to have enjoyed that honour in former times; they are enumerated as follows:—

Indra, god of the air, called (like Jupiter) king of heaven and the gods. He is painted of a yellow colour, covered with eyes like Argus.

Varuna, god of water (Neptune).

Pavana, god of the winds (Œolus).

Agni, god of fire.

Yama, king of the infernal regions, and (like Pluto) judge of men. He is painted of a dark green colour.

Cuvera, god of wealth (Plutus).

Cartikeia, god of war (Mars).

Cama, god of love (Cupid).

Soma, the moon (Diana). The last is considered a malignant luminary, and but little worshipped.

Most of these retain an annual festival, at which their image is made and worshipped with a procession, and then thrown into the stream. Their actions, recorded in the Puranas, are at all times recited with a never-failing satisfaction to crowds of listeners.

The stars and planets also are objects of worship,* as well as a number of sacred rivers, especially the Ganges, personified in a female form.

Another numerous class of deities are the local gods, of which every village adores two or three as its especial guardians, or not unfrequently its most dreaded persecutors. This local worship is a form of the aboriginal creed, hardly recognized by the Brahmans. Its objects are either the ancient deities of the place, or the spirits of deceased persons who have wielded power in life, and continue to be dreaded after death. The latter are not unfrequently Brahmans who have killed themselves to resist or avenge an injury.

The general effect of the modern Hindu worship to the eye has been thus graphically described:—

"Every town has temples of all descriptions, from a shrine which barely holds the idol, to a pagoda with lofty towers and spacious courts and colonnades. To all these votaries are constantly repairing, to hang the image with garlands, and to present it with fruits and flowers. The banks of the river, or artificial

* The days of the week are named, as in Europe, from the celestial bodies. *Ruvee-varu*, Sun-day, *Soma-varu*, Moon-day, *Mungulu-varu*, Mars'-day, *Bhoodhu-varu*, Mercury's-day, *Vrihusputtee-varu*, Jupiter's-day, *Shookru-varu*, Venus'-day, *Shunee-varu*, Saturn's-day.

sheet of water (for there is no town that is not built on one or other), has often noble flights of steps leading down to the water, which are covered in the early part of the day with persons performing their ablutions, and going through their devotions as they stand in the stream. In the day, the attention is drawn by the song, or by the graceful figures and flowing drapery, of women as they bear their offerings to a temple.

"Parties of Brahmans and others pass on similar occasions; and frequently numerous processions move on, with drums and music, to perform the ceremony of some particular holiday. They carry with them images, borne aloft on stages, representations of temples, chariots, and other objects, which, though of cheap and flimsy materials, are made with skill and taste, and present a gay and glittering appearance.

"At a distance from towns, temples are always found in inhabited places, and frequently rise among the trees on the banks of rivers, in the heart of deep groves, or on the summits of hills. Even in the wildest forests, a stone, covered with vermilion, with a garland hung on a tree above it, or a small flag fastened among the branches, apprizes the traveller of the sanctity of the spot.

"Troops of pilgrims and religious mendicants are often met on the road; the latter distinguished by the dress of their order, and the pilgrims by bearing some symbol of the god to whose shrine they are going, and shouting out his name or watchword whenever they meet with other passengers. The numerous festivals throughout the year are celebrated by the native princes with great pomp and expense: they afford occasions of display to the rich, and lead to some little show and festivity even among the lower orders. But the frequent meetings on days sacred to particular gods are chiefly intended for the latter class, who crowd to them with delight even from distant quarters.

"Though the religion, presented in so many striking forms, does not enter in reality into all the scenes to which it gives rise, yet it still exercises a prodigious influence over the people, and has little, if at all, declined in that respect, since the first period of its institution."*

To the general description of the historian, some further particulars may be added. The idols are made of various materials—gold, silver, brass, copper, stone, wood, and clay. They are placed in temples, kept in the house, or made of mud for the occasion, and destroyed when the service is over. The idol is supposed to be the actual form of the deity, but its place is often supplied by a symbol or emblem. Idols are not worshipped in temples till they have been consecrated. This ceremony is performed by Brahmans, who bathe them in milk, burn incense before them, and invite the gods to take up their abode in them. They are then regarded as sacred, and those in the larger temples are not suffered to be touched or approached but by high-caste persons. The domestic idols are placed in a niche in the wall, not unlike the images of the saints in Russia, and in some Roman Catholic countries. Sometimes a Brahman is employed to perform the daily rites of bathing, burning incense, and offering flowers: in his absence they are performed by one of the family.

* Elphinstone.

The temples are very diversified in shape and size, being usually larger and handsomer in the south of India than in Bengal or Hindustan, where the Mohammedan persecution was more destructive. Their most striking peculiarity is, that they are not designed, like Christian churches, to accommodate a congregation, but simply as the residence of the idol. The primary feature is the sanctuary, where the image is placed. This is generally an oblong building without windows, having the door at one end, and the idol, with oil lamps burning before it, at the other. Thousands of such *swamee*-houses are scattered over the country, by the side of roads and lakes, only just large enough to admit the priest to walk round the idol, and wholly without ornament or architectural pretensions. In the pagodas the sanctuary stands in a court inclosed by a wall, with a tank and colonnade in the interior. Sometimes there are several courts, inclosed one within another, and enriched with sculpture. The temple of Seringham, situate on an island in the river, near Trichinopoly, is composed of seven such square inclosures, the walls of which are twenty feet high and four feet thick. The outer wall is nearly four miles in circumference; and some of the pillars which adorn the gateways are single stones, thirty-three feet high, and five feet in diameter.

In the south of India the gate of the outer court is usually surmounted by a tower, wrought in stages, in the form of a pyramid, and profusely ornamented with sculpture. A similar elevation often distinguishes the sanctuary containing the idol. These towers seem to be peculiar to the Peninsula; their origin is unknown, and they are not applied to any special use, like the steeples of Christian churches, and the minarets from which the muezzin summons the Mussulman to prayer.*

The temples are usually of stone or brick, and far more substantially built than ordinary dwelling-houses. They are often the work of individuals or families, who retain the appointment of the attendants, and the management of the rites. Others have been erected by the native governments. They are usually endowed with the land revenues (or a part of them) arising from one or more villages. These endowments, which are often very large, are applied to the repair of the fabric, the cost of the services, and the sustenance of the Brahmans and other attendants, amounting, with their families, to a very considerable number. The managers, or wardens, control the expenditure, and serve to secure a due performance of the ceremonies. This office is often the subject of appeals to the government. It is claimed by different parties; or complaint is made that the worship is neglected, and the funds appropriated by the Brahmans; or, again, the Brahmans allege that the villagers withhold their dues, and neglect the attendance on the festivals, required by their tenure of the temple lands. These disputes, with other abuses, have led, in some cases, to the assumption of the management by government officers; a proceeding not objected to by the natives, but which has resulted in implicating British authority in the appointment of priests and dancing-girls, the manufacture of idols, and the direction of a false worship.

* Mr. Caldwell observes a curious similarity in their shape and position to the rude devil-pyramids of Tinnevelly, and thinks it is possible that these stately pagodas are memorials of a kindred worship which has been superseded by Brahmanism. To the author, they always suggested the idea of altars to the sun.

Even personal attendance and participation in direct acts of idolatry have been thought necessary and justifiable by English gentlemen professing Christianity, and representing the British government. These degrading and sinful compliances were long defended, either as a politic concession to native prejudice, or as demanded by a just and equitable administration of the law. The latter plea, which is the only one that could deserve a moment's attention, arises out of the original fault of assuming into Christian hands the revenues allotted to idolatrous purposes. British administration thus lent a factitious aid to idolatries, which might otherwise have perished under their own inherent corruptions, and in their eagerness to prevent an abuse of trust, the public servants forgot the obligations of their own religion.

It was principally in the presidency of Madras, where the pagoda revenues have escaped Mussulman spoliation, that these exaggerated forms of British equity were exhibited. They have now been prohibited by repeated orders from home, directing that the natives shall be left to themselves in all that concerns their religion. Still the possession of landed endowments by the pagodas, with other legal or customary claims on persons and property, occasions questions which a Christian government may occasionally be unable either to decide or to escape from with entire satisfaction to itself.

The *poojah* or idol-worship is performed by perambulating the image, and bowing before it; or by prostrations on the ground, repeating the names of the deity, and making vows. Garlands of flowers are hung upon the idol, and offerings are presented of flowers, fruit, sweetmeats, jewels, money, or other articles, which are afterwards appropriated by the priests. One kind of worship consists in only standing before the idol, fixing the eyes upon it with joined hands, and bowing the head while repeating the name of the god. Short petitions, or *muntrums*, are usually added, expressing the desire of the worshipper for some advantage appropriate to the character of the deity invoked. With the single exception of Brahma, who is implored to bestow the knowledge of *truth*,* these petitions are all of a worldly and sensual nature.

The temple worship contains nothing analogous to the *common prayer* of Christianity. The pagodas, being regarded as the palaces of the idol, are to be entered only by the Brahmans and favoured attendants who minister to his state. The offerings of the people are received at the outer gates, where the votary attends, not at fixed hours or days, but whenever his private need or devotion may suggest. Neither reading nor preaching are included among the religious rites. The Brahmans often go about reciting the legends of the gods to auditories gathered for the occasion, when the utmost interest is exhibited; but it need hardly be observed, that these contain no lessons of morality or piety; nothing like a *sermon* is delivered at any time.

The only occasion on which a *congregation* can be said to assemble for religious purposes, is at the festivals which are periodically observed in honour of the several deities. These attract vast concourses of people at the larger temples. The idol is brought out from the pagoda,

* The object of this petition is to be made like the deity, in order to absorption.

and being mounted on a car, attended by his Brahmans and other ministers, is dragged on heavy wooden wheels by scores of natives harnessed with ropes. The roads being bad, the cars not unfrequently stick in the mud, and the god is then supposed to be displeased. Prodigious efforts are made, accompanied by loud cries, to extricate the car and continue the progress. The immense assemblage, the shouts and screams, the waving of flags, and clang of discordant instruments, with the discharge of guns and rockets as night advances, impart to these scenes an attraction often deepened into horror, as some poor frenzied fanatic casts himself before the wheels of the lumbering car, and is crushed to death as a voluntary immolation to the deity. These inhuman sacrifices, however, are now prevented by the British authorities; the Brahmans are also refused the aid of the civil power to compel the attendance of the peasants to draw the cars. The consequence is, that the gods are not unfrequently left in the lurch. Still these festivals exhibit in the strongest colours the power which Hinduism retains over the mass of the people. The vast concourse appears to glow with an intense excitement. The eyes of the Brahman, who at other times affects a calm and tolerant demeanour, gleam with all the ferocity and pride of his secret nature, while the surrounding multitude respond to his imperious voice and obscene gestures, with a cry of exultation which, to the Christian ear, sounds like the very triumph of Pandemonium.

The Hindu festivals are numerous, and of different esteem among different classes and localities. Some of them are prolonged over several days, during which a kind of fair is kept up in the streets and neighbourhood of the temple, surpassing any European concourse in license and debauchery. The two of most general observance are the *Hooli* and the *Dusserah;* the former kept about the time of the vernal, the latter at the autumnal, equinox.

The Hooli commences fifteen days before, and continues to, the full moon. It is held in honour of Krishna, and exhibits a saturnalia of the worst and most demoralizing description. It would be impossible to describe the depths of wickedness resorted to in celebration of the licentious intrigues of this popular god. No respectable woman ventures to appear in the streets, where the lowest and basest of mankind salute the passers with hideous jests, pelting each other with red powders, and revelling in the extreme of licentiousness. To the disgrace of Hindu civilization, the higher classes join in these excesses with as much zest as the lowest.

The Dusserah, called also the Durga-Poojah, is held for nine days, in honour of the victory gained by Durga, the wife of Siva, over the giant Mahisa. In Bengal, where this is the favourite deity, it forms a season of universal rejoicing. An image of the goddess, made of straw and clay, represents her as possessed of ten arms, each grasping a weapon, with one foot on a lion and the other on the prostrate giant. This terrific idol is worshipped for three days, and then cast into the river; after which mutual embraces and salutations are exchanged among the people. In other parts of India, this feast is connected with the exploits of Rama and the five sons of Pandu. It is everywhere considered an auspicious season for the commencement of new undertakings. The natives bring out their best clothes on its recurrence, and the several classes of society worship the implements of their respective employments; the soldier makes poojah to his arms, the husbandman to his plough, and the writer to his books and papers.*

This festival, like every other, is attended by indecencies which cannot be described. A prominent feature is the *nautch*, or dance performed by native girls, of whom a number are attached to most of the temples in the south, and whose wretched trade is but thinly disguised under the appellation of wives of the gods. Professor Wilson says that dancing-girls are not known in Hindustan, but are confined to Southern India. He adds, that "the cars with the indecencies upon them are restricted to Bengal and Orissa;† and the temples in Hindustan are free from the gross representations which disgrace some of those in the south." He further contends that such objects "have no warrant either in the Vedas or the Puranas, and are as foreign to genuine Hinduism as to every other religion."‡ These are statements which cannot be gainsaid, and it is a reproach to the British government that public decency should continue to be outraged by such exhibitions. The authority which felt bound to legislate against the destruction of human life, under pretence of religion, by suttee and female infanticide, should have no scruple in interposing the arm of the law for the protection of female purity, and the morals of society.

Of the Hindu system of religion the Brahmans are

* It has been often complained of, that at this festival the clerks in the offices of government are permitted to worship the official records in the building assigned to public uses, and belonging to a Christian government.

† He writes of the Bengal presidency only. These cars are numerous in Madras.

‡ Mill's History of India, vol. i., pp. 295-6—NOTE.

the authorized expounders and guardians. They compose the sacred tribe (answering to that of Levi among the Israelites), which supplies, at once, the priests, the judges, the teachers, and the philosophers of the nation. The sacrificial office, however, was not originally confined to them, and it is at this day less coveted than other more gainful occupations. A well-paid Brahman official under government loves to patronize and direct a temple, but does not condescend to minister in its rites. A Brahman sepoy will send for a priest to perform his religious ceremonies, and dismiss him with the wages of his office. There are even temples still where the oblations are made by priests of lower caste, though they are naturally regarded with contempt by the Brahmans. Ordinarily the officiating priests are members of this caste, appointed to the respective temples by the government or local managers. This privilege is often hereditary in particular families, who suffer no intrusion from other Brahmans in their villages or districts; and these rights are recognized and protected by law.

As religious guides, the Brahmans generally have greatly declined in influence. The authority of their colleges, however, is still deferred to in questions of caste and law; and particular individuals acquire great reputation and reverence as saints or philosophers. They possess little of the influence exercised in private life by the clergy of a Christian country: the people pay more regard to astrologers, fortune-tellers, and the various pretenders to sorcery, witchcraft, and augury. So far as Brahmans will undertake to cast horoscopes, and practise other branches of this imposture, they obtain a practical influence with their neighbours.

They are rivalled, in point of devotion, by men of other castes, who set up as *Gurus*, or teachers, and acquire considerable influenco with their followers. So estranged is the Hindu mind from any real knowledge of God, that many actually worship their teachers, saying, "They are to us instead of God." Their blessing is craved with enthusiasm; their curse dreaded as the worst of evils. These impostors are frequently followed by a tumultuous and fanatical mob, against whom the government is obliged to employ the military arm. Foremost among the Gurus are the *Gosayens*, or, as they have been termed, monastic orders. Many of these live in convents, maintaining large establishments, who are supported by grants of lands and the contributions of their disciples. They are usually devoted to some particular divinity, in whom they inculcate an exclusive faith. Other Gosayens wander at large, like the friars-mendicant, acquiring a character for sanctity by going without clothes, letting the beard, hair, and nails grow without clipping, or making vows to retain the head or limbs in some particular posture, till the muscles have lost the power of resuming any other. Some, who addict themselves to meditation, are termed *Yogees;* and another class of religious mendicants, called *Byragees*, vie with the Gosayens in enduring penances and voluntary tortures—casting themselves on spikes, thrusting swords into the flesh, swinging at a great height on hooks inserted into the muscles of the back, and sustaining extremes of heat and cold which it might be thought impossible to endure.

The Hindus are divided into many sects, devoted to the worship of particular deities. The principal are the *Saivas* (worshippers of Siva), the *Vaishnuvas* (of Vishnu), and the *Saktas*, who worship one of the *Saktis*, *i.e.*, the wives or female associates of the Hindu triad. Of the latter, Devi, the spouse of Siva, has by far the most numerous train of disciples. Surya and Ganesa, also, have their particular sects.

The Saivas and Vaishnuvas are distinguished by painted marks, carefully renewed, on the forehead, and not unfrequently upon the chest, when exposed to view. The followers of Siva wear three horizontal lines parallel with each other, while the Vaishnuvas have them in a perpendicular direction, but inclining together at the base, like a trident. These are usually called "caste marks," and Europeans often mistake them for badges of caste properly so called; they are, in fact, distinctions of *sect.* In Bengal three-fourths of the population are *Saktas*, and most of them worshippers of Devi.

Two familiar usages of Hinduism remain to be noticed;—the veneration of the cow and the practice of pilgrimage. It is a mistake to suppose that the cow is ever actually *worshipped.* It is universally considered as a sacred animal, and Hindus resent its being killed for food; but it is never made the object of *poojah*, nor, as a general rule, exempted from domestic and agricultural labour. The feeling is probably of great antiquity, descending from the times when the Aryans, like all other nations, offered sacrifices of kine. The bull is often carved in temples and other places, as the symbol of Siva, but this imports no peculiar honour to the living animal.

Pilgrimage is another ancient observance, of which

the Brahmanical system seems to afford no proper explanation. The confluence of rivers, termed *prayagas* or *prags*, are especial objects of Hindu reverence, as are also particular temples and the shrines of saints—a class in which even Mohammedan devotees are included. Vast numbers of natives constantly traverse the country on pilgrimage to these holy places. To add to the unavoidable hardships of the road by voluntary austerities, much increases the merit. Yogees may be seen measuring the whole way with their prostrate figures, or with the head inclosed in an iron cage, which prevents its being ever laid on a pillow. The cholera is a frequent attendant on the journeys and concourses of pilgrims, and vast numbers annually fall victims to famine, or other calamities, by the way.

The moral result of Hindu idolatry is to degrade and brutalize the whole mind and life. Not only is it altogether deficient in the Christian elements of faith, prayer, and thanksgiving;—altogether unenlightened by the reading of holy books, or by religious and moral instruction;—but the objects it presents to the senses and imagination are such as to vitiate, instead of to improve, the instincts of nature. The gods of the ancient classical idolatries were formed like men, and gifted with powers intended to express a higher condition of man's nature. Their majestic and beautiful shapes were adored in temples of exquisite architecture, with a worship which might, at least, exalt the imagination and improve the taste. But the Hindu idols, retaining the worst passions of humanity, are all monstrous, grotesque, and demoniacal. They are of all colours—red, yellow, and blue; some have twelve heads, and most have four arms; they indulge in impossible and degrading combinations of the human form with beasts and reptiles.

The character of the deities is as foul as their figures. Classic paganism personified the virtues, such as Justice, Fortitude, Mercy, and Chastity; the Hindu idolatry deifies vice, and worships it with a crime. Their divinities are often mad or drunk; always wild, capricious, and irrational. They are enraged without cause, and appeased without satisfaction. They are at once terrible and contemptible; mighty enough to destroy an enemy with a look, yet subject to accidents and chance, and impotent against their own creatures. Neither order nor harmony exists in their Olympus. Siva cuts off the head of Brahma; Indra, though called the king of gods, has no authority over the rest.

To all this confusion is to be added the unutterable wickedness in which the deities are made to revel, with an intensity proportioned to their gigantic dimensions. The licentiousness of Greek and Roman mythology is little when compared with the awful productions of oriental imagination in the Puranas. If it be true, as St. Chrysostom says, that men always endeavour to be like that which they worship, Hindu idolatry may explain—what nothing else can—the depths of Hindu immorality. It is scarcely possible for the European imagination to conceive a tenth part of the abominations which are practised in some kinds of worship. Mr. Ward informs us that, when reading their sacred books with a learned Brahman, his instructor often paused; and it was only, after repeated efforts, and with an overwhelming shame, that he brought himself to repeat to a Christian ear the directions of the holy Shastras for the worship of the gods.

Europeans who have been deluded into speaking of the Brahmanical system as a patriarchal religion, comparatively pure in faith and simple in worship, knew little of practical Hinduism. They were beguiled with the writings of philosophers and poets, having slight connexion with the actual rites and customs of the land. Those educated Hindus, also, who, to hide their own shame, pretend that the abominations, which they blush to see revealed in the light of Christianity, are corruptions engrafted by ignorance on the pure monotheism of their primitive religion, cannot be allowed so to ignore the traditions of centuries and the text of the Shastras. It is true that explanations have been attempted of ideas and practices, which seem to defy all system and arrangement; but they are little worthy of attention. None of them has ever approximated to a practical scheme of religion; and the philosophy, which could reconcile this prodigious mass of immoral and degrading rites with a belief in one holy and supreme Spirit, must ever remain as useless to mankind as it is offensive to God.

This philosophy, however, had yet another aspect, which still extensively affects the more educated Hindus. Encouraging the many to polytheism, the Brahmans beguile the more inquiring few with *pantheism.* The usual formula of this belief is, that God is in everything, or that God is the soul of the world; meaning, not that all is upheld by the indwelling of his creative and preserving power, but that his very person and godhead are contained in the works of his hands. One of the avatars of Vishnu is designed to illustrate this opinion. An unbelieving raja, being told by his son that God was in everything, demanded if he was in that pillar, kicking it at the same time to manifest his contempt. Vishnu immediately burst from the column, with the head and paws of a lion, and tore the blasphemer to pieces.

Pantheism was a favourite notion with some of the Greek philosophers, from whom it has passed, with too many other relics of classic paganism, into the language of our own poets. It is distinctly expressed in the lines of Pope:—

> "All are but parts of one stupendous whole,
> Whose body Nature is, and God the soul;
> That, changed through all, and yet in all the same,
> Great in the earth as in th' ethereal frame,
> Warms in the sun, refreshes in the breeze,
> Glows in the stars, and blossoms in the trees;
> Lives through all life, extends through all extent,
> Spreads undivided, operates unspent,
> Breathes in our soul, informs our mortal part,
> As full, as perfect, in a hair as heart;
> As full, as perfect, in vile man that mourns,
> As the rapt seraph that adores and burns:
> To Him, no high, no low, no great, no small;
> He fills, he bounds, connects, and equals all." *

Ward informs us that a learned Brahman, to whom these lines were read, started from his seat in admiration, and claimed their author as a genuine Hindu.

Another form of pantheism is very common in India, by which the existence of matter is altogether denied. It teaches that all we see and feel is a mere deception of the senses; in reality, nothing exists but God, who produces all the phenomena of the universe by the immediate and direct operation of his will. This doctrine of "illusion"—which the Brahmans exaggerate far beyond the hypothesis attributed to our

* Essay on Man. Ep. i. 267—280.

own bishop Berkeley—is carried to the extent of denying the existence of individual men. It is owing to the ignorance and darkness of the human mind, they affirm, that men think themselves distinct and individual beings, endowed with a power of voluntary action. In reality, they are only portions of the one supreme Spirit, and as soon as they acquire sufficient light and purity to disentangle themselves from present ignorance, they will be again absorbed into that Spirit, and lose their individual consciousness.*

These opinions, however, produce no practical difference in the worship or life of those who hold them. They join in the idolatrous ceremonies, and observe the laws of caste, like other Hindus. And the same may be said of those natives who, having received a European education, have discarded the Hindu religion without obtaining a better one in its place. The latter class, though sometimes pretending to a truer philosophy, founded on detached portions of the Shastras, and sometimes to an eclectic morality drawn from the Hindu, Mohammedan, and Christian Scriptures, are little better than deists in disguise, and seldom exceed the benighted idolater in practical holiness.

Side by side with Brahmanism, and descended from the same parentage, another religion has grown up, which claims to be noticed in this place. Buddhism,

* The Brahmans do not explain *how* these portions of the Great Spirit became involved in their present dark and erroneous ideas; nor what is the origin, nature, and operation of the entangling causes, where neither mind nor matter exists, save the Creator himself. Leaving them to settle these questions, the practical inquirer will not fail to notice that all moral responsibility must vanish with the loss of the separate existence. Where the distinctions, "I, thou, he, etc.," are pronounced to be "artificial, existing only for present purposes," it must be impossible to rely on the corresponding distinctions of *meum* and *tuum* between man and man.

once predominant in Hindustan, still retains ascendancy in Ceylon, Burmah, Nepal, Tartary, Thibet, and China, comprehending more worshippers than any other religion in the world. It is supposed by some to have formed the primitive faith of the Hindu race: in its present form, however, it is ascribed to a Kshettriya, name Sakya Muni, or Gotama, a native of the district of Gorruckpore, whose era is fixed by the best authorities about 550 B.C. This personage is considered the last of several human beings who have attained to the rank of Buddhas by transmigration, and is to continue the spiritual head of mankind for his allotted period of 5,000 years. According to his theology, the Supreme Intelligence, called Adi-Buddha, exists in a state of perpetual repose. From his essence were produced by his will five, or, as some say, seven, emanations, termed *Buddhas.* Each of these produced in like manner a *Buddhisatwa,* to each of whom was intrusted the creation of a world. The Buddhisatwa of our own universe is said by some to have produced the Hindu triad, on whom he devolved his functions of creating, preserving, and destroying. Many other celestial beings are acknowledged, some original, and some transferred with little alteration from the Hindu Pantheon.

The most ancient Buddhists denied the existence of God, considered matter to be eternal, and imagined the Buddhas to have raised themselves by their own actions and austerities, during a long series of transmigrations in various worlds, to that state of apathy and inactivity which they regard as the great object of desire.

The Buddhists reject both the Vedas and the Puranas; whence it may be inferred that neither was of unquestioned authority at the origin of the sect. Their own literature, however, abounds in fables not less extravagant and absurd. The sacred language is *Pali*, once current in Magadha, an ancient kingdom on the Ganges, where Buddhism was the prevailing religion for some centuries.

The Buddhists repudiate animal sacrifices of every description, carrying their respect for life to such an extent that their priests will not drink after dark, for fear of swallowing some minute insect. They carry a brush with them, also, to sweep the place where they sit, lest a living creature should be inadvertently crushed. Some even cover their mouths with a thin cloth, to avoid inhaling insects with their breath. The laity, however, partake freely of animal food; and the priests may do so also, provided that life be not taken expressly on their account.

The Buddhists differ from the Brahmanists in owning neither distinctions of caste, nor respect for fire. They also venerate the relics of saints—a feeling quite unknown to the Hindus. The cupolas or bell-shaped monuments which characterize this religion are erected over such relics—a few hairs, a bone, or a tooth. The priests, who are taken from all classes of the community, live in monasteries, shave the head and beard, and go barefoot, wearing a uniform yellow garb. They are bound to celibacy, eat in a common hall, and sleep sitting in a prescribed posture. In the services of their chapels, accompanied with processions, incense, and lights, a strong resemblance has been traced to the ceremonies of the church of Rome.

The Buddhas are represented by stone images standing, or seated cross-legged, in the attitude of profound meditation; with a placid countenance, and always with *curled hair*,—a feature of decidedly foreign origin. The chief object in worship is the attainment of quiescence, by means of abstract meditation. In morality and charity the Buddhists are favourably distinguished from the disciples of Brahma. They are now comparatively few in India, but many remains of magnificent temples attest their former importance. Several of the cave-temples at Ellora were constructed for this religion, and there is one between Poona and Bombay, with aisles and vaulted roof, recalling the idea of a Gothic cathedral.

An intermediate place between Buddhists and Brahmanists is held by the sect denominated *Jains*. They disclaim the divine authority of the Vedas, use no sacrifices, and show no respect for fire. On the other hand, they admit the whole of the Hindu gods, and have even augmented their number, and added to the absurdities of the system, by acknowledging sixty-four Indras and twenty-two Devis. Distinctions of caste are recognized, though not exactly the same with the four Hindu classes. Their priests, called *Jatis*, are admitted from all castes, and are dressed like the Brahmans. They never bathe, perhaps in opposition to the repeated ablutions of their rivals. The Jain temples are large and handsome; some resemble the pagodas in form; others are circular, surrounded by colossal statues of the Tirtankaras, or principal saints, who occupy in their system a position analogous to the Buddhas. The finest specimen of a Jain temple is found in remains of white marble on the mountain of Abu, in the north of Guzerat. There are also Jain caves at Ellora and in other parts. At Chinroypatam, in Mysore, a statue of one of the Tirtankaras is cut out in the living rock, nearly seventy feet in height. The Jains are still numerous in India, especially in Guzerat, the Rajpoot territories, and Canara. They mostly belong to the opulent and mercantile classes; many of them are bankers, and a large proportion of the commercial wealth of India is in their hands.

Whoever has studied the philosophy of ancient Greece, can hardly fail to be struck by the many traces of a common origin, which are exhibited in the religious views still prevalent in India. The Buddhists and Brahmanists of the modern East hold opinions in many points identical with those of the Epicureans and Stoics, with whom the apostle Paul disputed at Athens. As in Greece so in India, there is one teaching for the educated, and another for the common people. The former bewilder themselves with the efforts of the natural intellect to attain a philosophy, "falsely so called," which has communion neither with God nor man. It has no trust in Providence, and no sympathy with humanity. The latter are abandoned to foul and degrading rites, indicating the heart's sense of a moral ruin, together with some blind feeling after a propitiation. These are the two sources in which all religions take their rise. They called in vain upon Brahmanism for illumination or assistance; there was "neither voice, nor any to answer, nor any that regarded:" and the long craving of the fallen nature remained unsatisfied.

There is a wisdom, however, which understands and can respond to the appeal. India needs, at this day, the same gospel which encountered the philosophy, and overthrew the idolatries, of Greece and Rome. It is for the ambassadors of Jesus Christ to cry to her benighted children, "Whom ye ignorantly worship, him declare we unto you." * It is true, what their own teachers tell them, that sin has separated between God and man, and that we cannot by our own searching find out God. Let the heralds of his Son proclaim Him by whom alone the Father is approached—"the one Mediator between God and men, the man Christ Jesus."† It is true, as they believe, that in another existence we must all receive the things done in the body. Let them hear of "Jesus and the resurrection" ‡—the one true Judge of men, and the one resurrection which, rejecting the weary mazes of transmigration, shall reunite the justified spirit to its own body—the familiar home of its sorrow and its joy—and presenting both faultless before God, admit them to "a new heaven and a new earth, wherein dwelleth righteousness."§ It is true, also, that even in this life men can attain, by a second birth, to a participation of the Divine nature.‖ Let the Brahman be taught to find it, not in the introspection of his own polluted mind, but in the sanctifying communion of the Holy Ghost, when Christ shall dwell in his heart by faith.

* Acts xvii. 23. † 1 Tim. ii. 5. ‡ Acts xvii. 18.
§ 2 Pet. iii. 13. ‖ 1 Pet. i. 4.

CHAPTER IV.

CASTE.

Caste, suttee, and female infanticide, parts of one system—Name—Four classes—Immutable distinction—Acquired by birth—Nature of rules—Respect to another world—Unknown to aboriginal tribes—And to Buddhism—Authority of the Vedas—Five classes—Purusha Sukta—Allegorical meaning—Institutes of Manu—Brahmana—Inconsistencies—Puranas—Mahabharat—No uniform doctrine—Real origin—Changes—Extinction of caste—Brahmans the only pure caste—Subdivisions—Departure from original rules—Secular employments—Priesthood despised—Illegitimate castes—Trades—Mark of race and nation—Eating flesh—Prusad—Exceptions—Consequences of admitting the religious claim—Loss of caste—Act of 1850—Capricious distinctions—Early Christian missionaries—Roman Catholic—German—Swartz—Modern Protestants—Caste excluded from mission schools—Government encouragement—Bengal sepoys—Secular not religious—Analogous to slavery—Operates as a trades' union—Suggestions—Suppression of suttee and infanticide—Their connexion with caste—Concluding reflections.

The Hindu religion, however widely it diverged from the Veda, and the dogmas of Brahmanical philosophy, never ceased to be marked by the political and social necessities of the Aryan invasion. To this origin are to be referred the rules of caste, with the practice of suttee and female infanticide—all devised to perpetuate the superiority of the dominant race over the subjugated natives. The first endeavoured to establish an impassable barrier against a mixture of the races, and the other two sought to support it, by the destruction of those whose frailty might most easily endanger it. All three were numbered among the religious institutions of the Hindus, and caste is still thought entitled to the protection extended to creed, by men who have learned to punish its handmaids as crimes against natural justice.

Caste is a word of Portuguese origin, signifying *breed*, and so answers exactly to the native *zat* or *jat*. The Sanscrit *varna* (colour) indicates a similar etymology, since the Aryans prided themselves on the fairness of their complexions; and the Sudras are frequently denominated the *black* caste. It is now considered to be an article of the Hindu faith, that mankind was originally created in four distinct classes or species: the *Brahmans*, who sprang from the head of Brahma, the *Kshettriyas* from his arm, the *Vaisyas* from his loins, and the *Sudras* from his feet. Corresponding with this origin, to the first was assigned the office of teaching and guiding men; to the second, of ruling and bearing arms; to the third, the pursuits of commerce and agriculture; and to the last, the service of the other three.* The three higher castes are termed regenerate, or "twice-born;" they were all enjoined to read the Vedas, perform the sacrifices, and discharge the other rites of religion; but the fourth is expressly excluded from these duties. It is a sin to instruct a Sudra in the Vedas, or even to read them in his presence; to assist at his sacrifice condemns a Brahman to the lowest hell; while the Sudra who may acquire the forbidden knowledge is to be put to death.

These distinctions are declared to be fixed and immutable. No one can pass from one caste to another: it is a law of birth, not of creed; no profession of faith entitles to its privilege, and they are not forfeited by the neglect or refusal of religious

* The word Brahman is derived from *brahma*, signifying prayer, or sacred learning: in like manner the other castes have been referred to an etymology importing, respectively, *protection*, *agriculture*, and *service*.

rites. Finally, this law is wholly independent of *moral* requisites. Conviction for the highest crimes, or even capital execution, does not of itself entail the loss of caste. Acquired exclusively by birth, its preservation is dependent on certain technical rules, relating principally to marriage contracts, articles of food, and personal contact with particular objects. It has but a slight relation to any religious doctrine. The only effect of caste in the world to come seems to be that, according to the notion of transmigration, none but a Brahman can be directly absorbed into the Deity. The souls of other men must continue to pass through other births, till they reach the favoured caste which possesses the sole passport to annihilation. This prerogative is held to entitle every Brahman to a veneration almost amounting to worship. The exercise of the priestly function also is limited to this caste; but it is a privilege little coveted by those who have the means of pursuing a more lucrative employment.

Caste is wholly unknown to the aboriginal tribes, and is clearly therefore of Aryan origin. It is equally foreign to the genius and practice of Buddhism; raising the presumption that it was invented, or at least invested with the sanctions of religion, after the expulsion of the Buddhists by the Brahmans. It is disputed whether any authority can be found for its distinctions in the Vedas—the primary source of Hindu belief. Mankind is, indeed, spoken of in some of the Suktas as divided into "five classes," which the Brahmans expound to mean the four Hindu castes, with the addition of the barbarians, or aboriginal tribes, as a fifth. But for this interpretation they have no warrant in the text; and it is contradictory to a passage in Manu, which expressly asserts that *all* men are descended from the *four* castes.

A somewhat better authority is found in a hymn contained in the Tenth Book of the Rig Veda, which, being the only one of the kind, has been often referred to, and translated. The text is this:—"The Brahman was his mouth, the Rajanya was made his arms, that which was the Vaisya was his thighs, the Sudra sprang from his feet.* The deity alluded to is *Purusha*, apparently a name for Brahma; and the subject of the hymn is the sacrifice of his body, which is alleged to have been the origin of all religious rites. The whole composition is full of allegory. A native commentator conceives it to describe the sacrifice of the body of Purusha, as distinct from his spirit. If so, the meaning may not be unlike that of the apostle, when he terms the church the body of Christ, and Christians "members in particular," who are to offer themselves a living sacrifice, in union with the sacrifice of Christ.† In this sense the allegory would not relate to any creation of different orders of men, but simply to their place and function in the human family.

It is to be observed, that this text does not say that the Brahman was produced from the mouth of God, in the literal way now commonly believed, but that he *was* his mouth, *i. e.* his *mouthpiece* to men. So also the Rajanya was *made* his arms (not produced from his arms), and the Vaisyas his thighs. They discharged functions in society analogous to those of these members in the human body, and they might bear the name, in the same sense that Attila termed himself "the scourge of God." The Sudra, indeed, is expressly said to have *sprung from* his feet; but the next verse

* Muir's Sanscrit Texts, p. 7. † Compare 1 Cor. xii. 27, with Rom. xii. 1.

continues, "The moon was produced from his mind, the sun from his eye, Indra and Agni from his mouth, and Vayu from his breath." No one ever takes these expressions as describing a literal and material creation; and by the ordinary rules of interpretation, if one part of the passage be allegorical, the other must be so also.

This is the only passage in the true Vedas where the castes are, even apparently, enumerated. It is found in a late portion of the Sanhita, in connexion with much other very curious matter; and the most that can be safely inferred is, that it may have supplied the basis on which the existing superstructure of caste was afterwards erected. The *Brahmana* is far from being consistent on the point of creation. One text affirms that, "The Brahman is a caste derived from the gods, the Sudra is one derived from the Asuras."* Other passages seem to support the common tradition.

It is in the Institutes of Manu that we find the institution fully elaborated.† It is there distinctly stated, that in order "that the human race might be multiplied, he (Brahma) caused the Brahman, the Kshettriya, the Vaisya, and the Sudra, to proceed from his mouth, his arms, his thigh, and his foot."† The statement, however, is plainly inconsistent with the verses following, which say that mankind was created (in one species) by one of the ten great *rishis*, whom Brahma formed for the purpose. In a subsequent part of the code, also, the creatures are classified from their moral qualities, and this fourfold division is not observed.‡

Various other themes are found in different Puranas. One says that, "His creatures (Vishnu's) attained in

* Taittiriya Brahmana, i. 2, 6. Muir, 14. † Manu, i. 31. Muir, p. 14.
‡ Manu, xii. 43. Muir, 17.

the world the state of fourfold caste, being of one type but with different duties."* Another writer, in extolling the Satya *yug*, says, "There were no castes, orders, varieties of conditions, or mixtures of caste."† The Mahabharat, after describing the castes by their colour, (Brahmans, *white;* Kshettriyas, *red;* Vaisyas, *yellow;* and Sudras, *black*), adds, in express terms, that "there is no distinction of castes: this whole world is formed of Brahma, it became separated into castes in consequence of works," *i.e.*, as afterwards explained, by the pursuits to which men addicted themselves.‡ Cases are celebrated in the Vishnu Purana, where a member of one caste attained to a higher.§ Brahmans and Kshettriyas are said to be born of the same parents,‖ and the statement occurs that the system of four castes *originated* from Barghabhumi, the son of Bharga, one of the kings of the lunar dynasty.¶

These references suffice to show that no uniform theory on the subject of caste is to be found in the Shastras. In particular, its origin in a fourfold creation, and the consequent inalienability of the distinction,

* Harivansa, sect. 211. Muir, 35.

† Vayu Purana. Muir, 29.

‡ Muir, 38, 9.

§ The Mahabharata contains a long legend of the contests between *Vashistha*, the great Brahman rishi, and *Viswamrita* (or enemy of the gods), a Kshettriya monarch, who strove to rival the saint in the supernatural power obtained by devotion. The latter attempts to rob the other of his cow, affirming that force pertained to the caste of the Kshettriyas, and patience to that of the Brahmans. Being defeated in the attempt he abandons his kingdom, and devotes himself to the practice of austerities. By this means, having obtained perfection, he "*acquired Brahmanhood*, and at length drank soma with Indra." (Mahabharata Adi Parva, sect. 175; Muir, p. 98.) Viswamrita's son, Satyavrata, called for his sins Trisanku, was made an outcast or *Chandala*. Notwithstanding, his father (while still a Kshettriya) acted as priest at his sacrifices, compelled the attendance of the gods, and finally elevated his outcast son to heaven, in spite of their opposition. These legends, of which there are many, obviously show that Brahmans and Kshettriyas were of one stock, and their distinction was one of office and occupation.

‖ Vishnu Purana, sect. 21.

¶ Ibid. iv. 8. Muir, 52.

are not only not parts of their religious teaching, but are contradicted by several express statements.

There can be no doubt that these distinctions really originated in the higher classes assuming to themselves a monopoly of the most honourable employments, and condemning the lower to the most degrading. The three superior castes would appear to have belonged to the same or to kindred races, since they partook together of the religious rites. The fourth, being excluded from this privilege, was probably composed of the subjugated population, whom the invaders consigned to perpetual bondage, both in body and soul.

Immutable as the distinction is now pretended to be, no part of the Hindu system has, in fact, undergone greater changes. Of the four original castes the Brahmans affirm that none but their own remains in existence. The Kshettriyas were extirpated during a protracted contest with the Brahmans, and the Vaisya caste was suffered to expire through neglect. This account is disputed by the Rajpoots, who lay claim to the lineage and caste of the Kshettriyas, and also by some of the mercantile classes, who pretend to be genuine Vaisyas. The Brahmans, however, exclude both from the privilege of the Vedas and the sacrifices, and the others submit without a murmur to a decree which, if caste were indeed a religious distinction, must be resented as an intolerable privation.

It will surprise those Europeans, who have adopted the popular theory, to be told that there are nations in India who claim, as an honourable distinction, to belong to the *Sudra* caste. This is another testimony to the political character of these distinctions. That which in Hindustan was the servile, or "black caste,"

—the caste to which the Aryan invaders reduced the natives whom they subdued in war,—assumed a very different aspect in the Deccan, where the Brahmanical institutions were introduced by persuasion more than by conquest. The powerful tribes who accepted the new civilization could only be ranked in the Hindu system as Sudras, but their admission raised the caste to a position analogous to that of the Kshettriyas in the north. The Sudras of the south were, in fact, the martial classes, and next in place to their instructors the Brahmans. Such is still the position of the Nairs of Malabar, and of the whole Mahratta nation, who boast of a pure Sudra lineage, and look down upon Pariahs and Pullars—the outcasts and serfs of the south—as contemptuously as the Kshettriya disdained the Sudra of the north.

The lineage of the Brahmans is unquestioned throughout India: still their caste is no longer that which is described in the Shastras. Numerous sections have sprung into existence who refuse to eat with one another. Hindustan and the Deccan have their two grand divisions, each containing five sub-divisions, which may probably represent the ancient national distribution of the population. The Mahratta Brahmans acknowledge no less than *eight* internal distinctions, each exhibiting a perceptible difference of character and appearance.* Again, the Brahmans, in religious profession, are distributed into the two great sects of Vishnavas and Saivas, each of which admits a number of subdivisions holding no religious communion with the others.

In addition to all this unauthorized variety, the caste has almost universally departed from the rules and

* Grant's Mahrattas, i. 11.

practice of the original institution. The Shastras require every Brahman to pursue a fourfold routine of existence. In the first quarter he is to study the sacred books and rites under a competent tutor; in the second, to marry and keep house, teaching the Vedas, performing the sacrifices, and observing the other duties of religion. When he becomes a grandfather, he is to retire into the wilderness, and practise the severest austerities. Having thus attained to the heavenly light, he is released from all further observances, and is to spend the latter portion of his days in the house of his son, awaiting in intense meditation the hour of his reunion with the Deity. These injunctions are now generally disregarded. Individual Brahmans become students, ascetics, or devotees at their pleasure, and a sufficient number are always found to officiate as priests in the temples—a function clearly posterior to the times in which neither temples nor idols were in use. Some turn Gosayens, but though thus approaching more closely to the model of the Shastras, they are obliged to repudiate their caste on joining the fraternity. The bulk of the sacred caste is now entirely secularized. Brahmans engage without scruple in trades and professions of every kind, even those expressly forbidden in the Shastras.* In the north of India agriculture and arms supply their favourite occupations. In the south, they affect the civil service of government. "From the ministers of state down to the village accountant, the greater number of situations of this sort are in their hands, as is all interpretation of Hindu law, a large share of the ministry of religion, and many employ-

* Many deal in leather and hides, the most obnoxious articles to a genuine Hindu.

ments (such as farmers of the revenue, etc.), where a knowledge of writing and of business is required."* The duties of the priesthood are so little coveted, that the Brahmans who discharge them are looked down upon by their brethren. The secular members, on the other hand, rest their influence more on the force of numbers, wealth, and social rank, than on religious considerations; and it is certain that no appeal could be made in their favour to any of the Shastras, without at the same moment overturning all their existing usages and position in society.

The Brahman, however, is but one of the numerous classes into which the natives are distributed in the present day, and all of which assume the appellation of castes. For these there is, of course, no shadow of authority in the Shastras, their very existence being in direct violation of the most stringent obligations of the sacred books. All these so-called castes originated, according to Hindu theory, in the illegitimate mixture of the four original divisions; a statement which at once deprives them of a religious character, for such mixtures are strictly prohibited by the fundamental law of caste, and the offspring is declared to be for ever unclean.

It is impossible, however, to suppose for a moment, that the great bulk of the Hindu population is really descended from this scanty and polluted origin. The majority of the existing castes have nothing at all to do with the primitive four, or with the Shastras which describe them. In many cases they denote only the *trades* of their members, which, like political offices, usually become hereditary in India. There is a goldsmith's caste, a barber's caste, and an oilman's caste: the weaver, washerman, and sweeper, have

* Elphinstone, i. 104.

their castes: even the aboriginal Shanars of Tinnevelly assume the same appellation, and make a caste for the cultivation of the palmyra tree. In these instances the caste is clearly a sort of guild or craft, only constituted by birth, and admitting no apprenticeship from without. In other cases, especially in the Deccan, caste is the acknowledged distinction of *race* or *nation*. The natives call themselves of the Malabar caste, the Gentoo caste, and so on. There is even a caste for *thieves*, which probably represents some aboriginal race; and the Thugs, who worship Kali by assassination, call their fraternity a caste, though admitting Mohammedans into its number. In fact, the caste feeling is strongly shared by the Mussulman population throughout India, and (contrary to all religious theory) the Hindus assign to it a higher position in society than to some of their own inferior classes. All leads to the conclusion, that the distinctions established by the Aryan nobility, for the preservation of their own superiority, were imitated by other classes among themselves, and still with a social more than a religious object in view.

While the bulk of the existing castes are thus plainly without a shadow of religious origin, the rules in present operation are widely different from those contained in the sacred books. By the Vedas, the Brahman is not only at liberty, but on occasions of sacrifice he is *enjoined*, to eat flesh—even that of the cow. The restraints on marriage, and social intercourse generally, were less severe than those in modern practice. A ceremony still observed in the temples strongly testifies to the changes which have been introduced in the article of eating. Food which has been consecrated by dedication to the idol is termed *prusad*, and may still be freely handled and eaten by all classes without any violation of caste, proving that the latter was a social and secular distinction which gave way to religious duties. In a similar spirit the Institutes of Manu declare that the king, and those whom he employs in the public service, are never impure. So, again, the hand of the artist engaged in his trade is always clean; and the same immunity is extended to commodities exposed for sale in the public mart. Restrictions which admit of such frequent relaxation, for the convenience of society, seem to speak their own origin.

When it is insisted that caste is an essential element in the Hindu religion, it is important to consider what must be implied in that statement, to those who admit the Shastras as the proper standards of religious faith and practice. To give effect to the requisitions of these authorities it would be necessary to revolutionize at once native society and English jurisprudence. The Brahman would be the only caste remaining entitled to any distinction, and in order to enjoy it, its members must abandon their present modes of existence, and retire to the sacrifices and austerities prescribed in the Vedas. The Rajpoot and the Vaisya, who now assert the secondary and tertiary honours, must be informed that all social rank has been lost with the Vedas and the sacrifices, and they are in reality no better than Chandalas. The Mahratta, to sustain the title of Sudra, must renounce property, arms, and agriculture, and voluntarily serve the detested Brahmans. All other so-called castes must be relegated to the odious designation of *Shunkerjattee*, and submit to be accounted for ever unclean. Such are the sacrifices imperative on every Hindu who deems the institution of caste an essential part of his religious creed.

On the part of the British government, its courts of law must consent to accept the testimony of a Brahman before that of other men, and to acknowledge a distinction of persons in the punishments awarded to crime. It must rescind every enactment in favour of civil and religious liberty, in order to reinstate the condition of slavery. It must place the property, character, and in some instances the lives, of the natives at the mercy of the village pundits. In a word, it must recall every blessing granted to India, and consign its toiling millions, body and soul, to the grinding tyranny of a worthless few!

These considerations abundantly suffice to show that caste should be dealt with simply as an existing fact in Hindu society, not as an institution of Hindu religion. It was invariably so treated by the natives themselves, and has been modified from time to time accordingly. By the original institution loss of caste was equivalent to civil death. The outcast was denied admission to his father's house; the nearest relatives refused to eat or speak with him. He was excluded from religious ceremonies and social meetings. His very touch was pollution. His wife was released from the conjugal tie; his children belonged to him no more; his property was forfeited; and he was disabled from contracting or giving evidence in a court of justice. These formidable penalties, however, must have admitted of some easy remission, since in a long residence in India Mr. Elphinstone never met with an individual suffering under such disabilities.

The British government has swept them out of its path without scruple. Its courts of justice could never tolerate a distinction of persons in the eye of the law: their sentences are executed on the Brahman, as on the Pariah. Moreover, after sundry partial measures of relief, it was enacted by the famous *Lex loci* of lord Dalhousie in 1850 that "So much of any law or usage in force within the British territories, as inflicts on any person forfeiture of rights or property, or may be held in any way to impair or affect any right of inheritance, by reason of his or her renouncing, or having been excluded from, the communion of any religion, or being deprived of caste, shall cease to be enforced as law in the courts of the East India Company, and in the courts established by royal charter within the said territories."

To the high-caste men this righteous law was like the abolition of the Inquisition to the monks of St. Dominic; a violation of their dearest rights, an affront to the gods. Every effort was strained to procure its disallowance by the Crown, but the claims of caste were happily not allowed to be superior to the dictates of justice and freedom. They were left to assert themselves as a matter of private opinion and intercourse.

In that sphere they have continued to exercise a disastrous and extravagant authority. Loss of caste is still accounted the most grievous dishonour, and the inferior and spurious castes are equally sensitive on this point with the higher. The rules, too, which regulate the penalty are as capricious as they are irrational. A high-caste sepoy has been known to throw away his meal, because the space, which he had cleared for cooking it, was defiled by the shadow of his European officer accidentally passing by. On the other hand, thousands of Brahmans and Rajpoots in that army crossed the Indus in the Affghan expedition, at the bidding of the same officers, though in notorious breach of the laws of their caste. The Brahman officials in a collector's cutchery will refuse to sit in the same room with a low-caste, or Christian, native. Yet in the railway carriage the Brahman is seen side by side with the sweeper, enjoying the comfort and economy of the new mode of travelling without offence to his conscience. The Bengal sepoys consider themselves polluted by duties which are discharged, without a murmur, by their own brothers and relatives in the armies of Madras and Bombay, where the caste men are fewer in number and inferior in influence. In the Calcutta police, also, where caste is ignored, even the Brahman does not hesitate to assist in removing a corpse, the most unclean object he could possibly come in contact with. Numerous other inconsistencies might be pointed out, such as the wearing of leather shoes by all classes of natives, with a variety of conveniences borrowed from European habits. In view of these advantages, the requisitions of caste are silently dispensed with, and very extensive relaxations in its observance have been noted, in consequence, of late years.

Strange, however, to say, with all this voluntary innovation, it is considered that the highly prized distinction may be lost for ever by an *unconscious* defilement, or even by the act of another. Among the outrages committed by the robber chiefs of Oude on the peasants who fell into their power, the forcible privation of caste is accounted the most terrible. The victim's head was held back while a Mussulman *spat into his mouth;* or the bones of an animal were hung round his neck. This enforced pollution immediately destroys his caste. By no act or consent of his own, the offspring of Brahma's head falls in a moment lower than the dust under his feet. He might have murdered his greatest benefactor treacherously, and still have walked as a god amongst men.

The early Christian missionaries seem to have understood the distinction of caste as a civil rather than a religious institution. The Madura Jesuits even feigned themselves to be Brahmans, and, in order to keep up the deception, employed low caste agents to visit the common people, consenting only to carry the sacraments to the sick and dying, by dead of night, and with the strictest precautions of secrecy. Of these impostors it was not unjustly said, that instead of making the Hindus Christians, the fathers had themselves become Hindus. The remark may be extended to a large portion of the existing Roman Catholic congregations, which not only observe caste like the Hindus, but imitate their religious processions, and retain so many other heathen customs that an uninformed spectator would not readily distinguish them from the idolaters.*

Caste was tolerated also, though under very different arrangements, by the first Protestant missionaries. It appears not to have presented itself to their minds as a religious institution, or as necessarily connected with the idolatrous creed. They regarded it rather as a social prejudice, which might be borne with to a certain extent. Swartz allowed the higher castes to occupy one side of the church, and the lower the other. The former were permitted also to communicate before the others. It was hoped that by attempting no coercion the distinction would gradually

* It is remarkable that they apply the word *prusad* to the sacramental elements, in the same signification as it is used in the pagoda sacrifices, considering the consecration to render its common participation clear to all castes.

decline under the influence of Christian principles.* At the same time no opportunity was lost of exposing its inherent vanity. Swartz was visiting a heathen of the higher caste when a Pariah catechist came to speak with him. "Stop," cried the missionary, "I will come to you outside: these high-caste men have not yet learned humility: we must bear with the proud sinners." The rebuke was so effective that the catechist was instantly called in, and treated with kindness. By such methods it was sought to undermine rather than openly attack a distinction, which, though little consonant with Christian humility, might appear to the German missionaries not more sinful than the separation of the *noblesse* from the *canaille*, which was so strongly marked in their fatherland. The Lutheran missionaries in India still act upon similar views.

A more decided course has been taken by other Protestants. The British and American missionaries, having regard to the account of its origin contained in the Shastras, pronounce the distinction to be essentially idolatrous and sinful; caste is accordingly strictly forbidden in the bulk of the existing Protestant missions. Much resistance has been experienced in the enforcement of this prohibition in the south, where the first missions were founded on a different footing. The native Christians of Tanjore and Tranquebar, now under the care of the Church of England, complained long and loudly of the innovation. Bishop Heber inclined to agree with the views of the older missionaries; but the controversy was ultimately decided the other way, by the late metropolitan, Dr. Daniel Wilson. Enter-

* Perhaps the difference was once as strongly marked between Briton and Saxon, and Saxon and Norman, in England, though time and Christianity have now entirely obliterated them.

ing warmly into the feelings which demanded its abrogation as contradictory to the Bible and essentially idolatrous, that energetic prelate insisted on the entire renunciation of caste as an indispensable condition to church communion. A committee of inquiry subsequently appointed by the bishop of Madras arrived at the same conclusion; but the church missions are still agitated by the question, and many secessions have taken place. The remaining Protestant missionaries had, from the first, insisted on the renunciation of caste as indispensable to baptism.

Its pretensions have been resisted with equal zeal and firmness in the schools of all the Protestant missions. Offering an education which the higher natives have learned to prize, and steadily refusing the demand for separate classes, the missionaries found the caste-men, as usual, sacrifice their pretensions to their advantage. Brahman and Pariah now sit without scruple on the same form, and shoulder one another in the same class; and instead of losing popularity by the practice, it is ascertained that the mission schools, where caste is repudiated, are better attended than the Government educational institutions, in which its pretensions are still scrupulously respected.

By the British authorities generally, caste has been likewise identified with creed, but with the opposite result of entitling it to the protection extended to all religious observances. Its claims are ignored in the administration of the law; but in other departments of government they are guarded with an anxiety which seems both inconsistent and unnecessary. Natives have been rejected from civil employ, simply because clerks of a higher caste object to their society. In the army, concessions of this kind have been pushed to an extent actually subversive of justice and military discipline itself. When lord Hastings removed a sepoy from his regiment because he had become a Christian, he was actuated, it may be hoped, by a desire to protect the convert from persecution or discomfort. Still the act was received as an authoritative recognition of the claims of caste, and even as a censure on the conversion itself. In the Bengal army of later days, the high-caste men have been permitted to decline particular duties, and to object to other recruits, to an extent which no religious pretensions could justify.

Becoming aware of the evil, government sought to arrest its progress by directing that only a certain proportion of high-caste men should be enlisted in each battalion. But the regulation was extensively infringed upon. The men of Hindustan, where caste feelings are the strongest, are taller and more military in appearance and sentiment than other natives. Most of the Bengal regiments were recruited in Oude and the adjacent provinces. A kind of family party was formed in many corps, which commandants and adjutants were but too much disposed to defer to, in return for a soldierly appearance and general docility. The pampered sepoys were kept in good humour by increased concessions to the ever-advancing exactions of caste.

The fatal result was seen in the mutiny which dissolved that splendid army like a dream. The direst offence was taken just where the most anxious precautions had been used to avoid it. The suspicions of the sepoys augmented in proportion to the disclaimers of their superiors; and a government which, if it could have written its own epitaph, would have selected, with a clear conscience, the commendation that it had scrupulously respected the claims of the native creeds and castes, was suddenly and unanimously deserted by its own soldiers on the charge of fraudulently violating their most sacred convictions.

When it is remembered how much more jealous human nature is of its *honour* than of its *religion*,—how fiercely men fight for social esteem who care nothing at all for a creed,—and how tolerant the Hindu in particular professes himself to be of all theological opinions,—it must be concluded that caste is far more an affair of this world than of the next. Its connexion with Hindu creed is, at any rate, no deeper than that of our own orders of *knighthood* with the faith of the gospel; and its appeal to the Vedas may be fairly classed with that which is sometimes made to the Bible, in support of the "domestic institutions" of the Southern States of America.

Caste in fact originated, like slavery, in a war of races, and it breathes the true spirit of slavery still. A striking illustration of this is offered while we write. The recent proclamation of the Queen, directing that none of her Indian subjects shall be molested or interfered with on account of their religion, has been interpreted by the caste men in a way not altogether unforeseen.* In Tinnevelly, the corpse of a native Christian has been denied the use of the highway, because the deceased was by birth or descent of a low caste; and the heathen fanatics actually resisted the troops sent to enforce the public right. In Travancore, Christian women, who had acquired habits of decency, have been commanded to return to the old fashion of going half naked, the privilege

* The preface to a pamphlet entitled "The Company's Raj," in which the present author deprecated the then proposed abolition of the East India Company's administration, concluded with these words :—

of covering the bosom being the prerogative, forsooth, of the Sudra caste. In fact, the very essence of caste lies in the degradation of others; its only notion of liberty is to take away the liberty of all besides; and in such nefarious demands it claims to be *protected* by the proclamation of the Queen of Great Britain.

It is true that, during centuries of this slavery, the iron has so entered into the soul that the hereditary bondsman now hugs his fetters. Popular prejudice will, no doubt, long resist the light of truth on this, as on other subjects of education. The attempt to show the masses of India that the distinctions which they consider sacred have no sanction from the Vedas, or other Shastras, may be as little hopeful as to argue with the peasants of Italy, Spain, or Ireland, that their ceremonies are unauthorized by the Scriptures and the Fathers. Moreover, the existing condition of Hindu society renders caste as dear to the mechanic as to the Brahman. By confining each to his own hereditary occupation, it protects the labouring classes from the effects of competition, and so ensures a miserable subsistence to an unenterprising population.

These are no claims, however, on the respect of an enlightened government. There is no necessity to prohibit, or at all interfere with, any existing and lawful usage. We need not, as the Gosayens do, insist on a renunciation of caste as the condition of public employ; nor should the feelings of any servant

"Finally, the adoption of so great a change, at a moment when the native mind is widely and ruinously agitated by apprehensions of a government design upon *caste*, would in all probability be accompanied by declarations of non-interference, which might prove more injurious than the existing 'profession of neutrality;' for such declarations, put forth in the Queen's name, on the occasion of her Majesty's assumption of the empire, might be construed hereafter, both by governors and governed, as amounting to one of those '*treaties*' for the protection of the native religions, which have hitherto existed only in the imaginations of those who desired them."

of the government be wounded by unnecessary intrusion on prejudices which he holds to be sacred. This is quite a different thing from volunteering them a public sanction under the notion of a religious institution. The question is one of private opinion and feeling, on which every native may be left to his own judgment, provided that government extend no advantage to one which is unfair to another. The natives can observe what rules they choose among themselves; but the public service ought to be ordered exclusively on public considerations. In civil employ, it requires clerks and accountants, not Brahmans; in the army, soldiers, and not Rajpoots. Candidates have a right to encouragement according to official qualifications alone, without inquiring into their parentage, connexions, or habits at meals. The required duty should be everywhere insisted on: as in the Calcutta police, those who object to it may be permitted to resign the service; but no man should be held entitled to a dispensation from the duties of his situation on account of a distinction which is personal to himself.

These few simple and sensible principles, steadily acted upon, would soon alter the irrational state of opinion by which this so-called "institution" is sustained. Caste is a point of honour more than of religion; and the Crown is always the fountain of honour. The Queen's service would become itself a "caste," superior in general esteem to every other. The Brahman who should decline to enter it on the required conditions, would find himself surpassed in wealth and station by the inferior classes. He would immediately know how to reconcile his honour with his interest, and in a few years the distinctions of caste might be esteemed in Hindu society, about as much as a Norman pedigree and a coat of many quarterings are valued among ourselves.

Such expectations are justified by the results which have attended the discountenance of other practices, equally if not more closely connected with the Hindu religion. Self-immolation by fire is distinctly commended in the Vedas; and an example of it took place in the camp of Alexander the Great. Rama, one of the highest incarnations of Vishnu, was "reunited to the Deity" by means of suicide; and it is certain that the burning of widows on the funeral pyre of their husbands has been regarded by the Hindus, from very ancient times, as a religious duty or privilege. Thousands have been so sacrificed under our own rule; and the proposal to abolish *suttee* was denounced by the Brahmans, and their European patrons, as an outrage upon Hindu religion, and a dishonour to the sex. Nevertheless, lord W. Bentinck was not deterred from prohibiting its observance within the British territories, and branding its perpetration with the stigma of wilful murder. The inhuman practice not only ceased at once in British India, but the example was soon voluntarily followed in the native states.

Lord Wellesley had previously affixed the same penalty to the practice of *infanticide*, and a similar compliance with British example has been obtained from native princes and chiefs, who once thought it a point of honour to make away with their female offspring. The facility with which infants may be destroyed, no doubt, renders the entire extirpation of this piece of barbarism more difficult than that of suttee, and the numerical difference between the male and female population of some districts too plainly indicates that it still lingers among them. But the *principle* has received its just condemnation: the murder of infants is now perpetrated, like other crimes, in secret, and punished when discovered.

Both these abominations were intimately connected with caste, which, like polygamy, lays its heaviest burdens upon the weaker sex. While the man may freely take a wife from any of the lower castes, it devolves on the woman to maintain the purity of the lineage by marrying only in her own, or a higher, caste. The higher her birth, therefore, the more slender became her chances of a suitable alliance; and, to avoid the disgrace of an unequal match, or the scarcely inferior dishonour of no marriage at all, the unfortunate females were sentenced to immolation.

British equity has clearly seen that no ideas of religion or honour can be permitted to violate the rights of life, freedom, or property. It remains to give the full and legitimate effect to this principle, by protecting human nature at large against the injurious and irrational distinctions of caste. That God has made all men of one blood, is a physical fact as easy of demonstration as any truth in natural science. The government schools are not afraid of contradicting the Hindu schemes of astronomy, geography, medicine, and chronology, though all intimately connected with their religious belief, and distinctly taught in its sacred standards. Why should caste be entitled to greater tenderness or reverence, when, in addition to the physical falsehood, it is attended by so much injury to the moral and social improvement of the community? There are some hundreds of educated Hindus, who have learned to disregard the creed and worship of the Brahmans, but dare not encounter the reproach and trouble of renouncing caste. Some of these are "almost persuaded" to be Christians. The majority, for lack of a worthy substitute for the religion they have discarded, become sceptics and infidels. Clubs and associations exist among this class of persons for discussions and lectures, in which all religions are ridiculed and reviled. A large part of this increasing evil is to be laid to the account of caste, the laws of which, with all their free-thinking, these young reasoners are too timid, or too selfish, to oppose. On this account, as well as for its power in arresting inquiry and conviction generally, caste is considered by some missionaries a deadlier foe to the moral and religious progress of India than idolatry itself.

As for the danger of interfering, to the extent suggested, with native prejudices, many symptoms combine to show an extensive change of sentiment among the most intelligent Hindus. It is manifestly impossible that an educated mind should continue to believe in opposition to the demonstrations of science and the daily evidence of the senses, that mankind was really created in more than one species. One of the native papers of Bombay, alleged to be well acquainted with the state of native opinion, lately proposed the formation of a new *Shastra*, for the inculcation of a general and more suitable religion. It is observable, that this scheme proposed to abolish all distinctions of caste, as one of the worst portions of the Hindu system. Resting, as it does, wholly upon opinion, its simultaneous repudiation would be welcomed by thousands who have not the courage to effect a separate emancipation. It is surely the duty of a wise government to advance this desirable consummation, by at once steadily disowning all respect for a folly which it may still forbear to prohibit.

CHAPTER V.

MOHAMMEDANISM.

Fraction of the population—Various origin—Half Hindu—United only in religion—Islam—Salvation, or resignation—Moslem—Pious phraseology—Foundations of Islam—Koran—Its compilation—Not the work of Mohammed—Magian contributions—Sergius—Jews—Respect for Holy Scripture—Kebla—Subsequent change—Mecca—Ignorance of Old and New Testament—Apocryphal writings—Talmud—Mistake as to the Holy Trinity—Paraclete—Mohammed the last of the prophets—Doctrine of abrogation—Pretended eternity of the Koran—The night Alkader—Style—Tokens of veneration—Gibbon's admission—Comparison with Job—Indebted to older religions—Mohammed's friends in search of a religion—His disordered imagination—Former revelations debased and corrupted—Inferiority of views of God—His names—Rosary—Predestination—Angels—Jins—Resurrection—Monkir and Nadir—Day of Judgment—Hell—Paradise—Omission of women—Tradition—Sonnites and Shiyahs—Different collections—Corruptions in India—Four practical duties—Prayer—Accompanied by ablutions—Five times daily—Repetitions—Congregational prayer or Khotbeh—Sermon—Recited by sovereigns—Definition of a king—Inconsiderate indulgence to king of Delhi—Alms—Fasting—Ramadhan—Mohurrum—Origin—Imitation of Hindu feast—Tazzias—Lamentations—Peculiarities in India—Procession—Saturnalia—Faquirs—Characters represented—Taboots—Plain of Kurbulla—The Barawagat—Prophet's footstep—Booraq—Remarks on. processions—Pilgrimage to Mecca—Relic of heathenism—Arab tradition of the Caaba—Ishmael—Mohammed's inconsistency—Sacrifice unmeaning—Heathen ceremonies—Omar's remonstrance—Obligatory on true believers—Description—Sacred spots—Difficulties of the pilgrimage—Extravagant enthusiasm—Animal sacrifices—Buckra-eed—Medina—Shiyahs—Pigrilmage in India—Attachment to the prophet—Summary—No redemption, atonement, nor regeneration—No grace—Morality inferior to other systems—Sensuality—Position of the female sex—Mussulman polygamy worse than Hindu—Obstacles to conversion—Self-righteousness.

THE Mohammedans, though numerically but a small fraction of the population, are entitled by former power and present influence to particular consideration among the natives of India. They are not a homogeneous people, nor inhabitants of any particular district, but descended from various nations, and scattered throughout India. About half their number are of Hindu extraction, differing only in religion from the other natives of their respective localities. The moiety of foreign descent spring from several ancestries, widely differing in blood and policy, and only united by the institutions of Mohammed. These, however, are to all Mussulmans not only the guide of religious belief, but the source of civil law, and the standard of social esteem.

Notwithstanding its pretensions to simplicity and immutability, the Mohammedan religion has in fact admitted many modifications in India, which will be best explained by a reference to its original standards. Its proper name is *Islam*, from an Arabic root, signifying "peace." The same verb is also the parent of the common salutation *Salaam*, and signifying in some of its conjugations *saved*, "Islam" is frequently translated "*salvation*." The Mohammedan writers prefer to render it "*resignation*," professing that submission to God's will is the beginning and end of all true religion. *Moslem* (*i.e.* a believer in Islam) signifies, therefore, a man resigned to God; in this meaning, Abraham is called a Moslem in the Koran.

This fundamental characteristic of Islam is strongly impressed on all Mussulman conversation and literature. On the occurrence of any calamity the Mohammedan exclaims, "It is God's pleasure." When talking of the future, his invariable proviso is, "If God please." Every undertaking is commenced with the expression, "In the name of God, the Merciful, the Compassionate;" and its completion is regularly hailed by the corresponding ejaculation, "Praise be to God." Phrases to this effect abound in common conversation, and are freely scattered over all poetical and historical writings. Educated Moslems stuff their letters and ordinary speech with verses of this sort, quoted from some favourite poet; and these expressions, being always uttered with an air of devotion, impart an aspect of piety to the whole Mussulman existence. The charm is broken when it appears that they are forms of speech required by the usages of society, and often uttered, like other established phraseology, by persons whose conduct and avowed intentions can by no exercise of charity be reconciled with truth or justice.*

Islam is said to be based on four foundations; 1. The *Koran*, which, with the Arabic article prefixed, is written "*Alcoran*;" 2. The *Sonnah*, or tradition; 3. The *Ijmaa*, or consensus of orthodox theologians; and 4, in default of the rest, on *Kias*, or reasoning. The latter two are resorted to only in explanation of the former.

* Two respectably dressed Mohammedans once called upon the author at his house, and after an amount of ceremony which recalled the preludes employed by Esther to introduce her petition to king Ahasuerus, requested his intercession with the commissioner of the country for the restoration of the younger to a military command, from which he had been, of course unjustly, dismissed. Both being entire strangers to the desired intercessor, he could not but marvel at the effrontery with which natives in general prefer such applications. The elder of the visitors, the father of the discharged *rissaldar*, was an old man of venerable aspect, clothed in spotless white, with a silver beard descending to his breast. Addressing him, the author said that his business in the country was to teach religion, and offer prayers: he had no right to interfere in disposing of troops of horse. The old man stroked his beard with a sanctified air as he repeated the words *Khooda-ki-kam* (literally, "God's business"). "A good business," he ejaculated, "a holy business," and took his departure with many a lowly reverence. It turned out that both were men of very indifferent honesty.

By far the first authority is the Koran, containing the revelations which Mohammed professed to receive, from time to time, during the twenty-three years of his ministry. The prophet being, according to general opinion, unable to write,* repeated his visions verbally to his friends, by some of whom they were taken down on skins, palm leaves, or pieces of bone. These rude records, after being circulated among his immediate followers, were thrown into a chest belonging to one of Mohammed's wives, whence they were collected, two years after his death, by Abubeker his successor, and formed into a volume, along with others which had been preserved by oral tradition. Othman, the third caliph, finding no little diversity in the copies in circulation, caused an authorized text to be made, and then destroyed the manuscripts. How far the received version is indebted to either of its royal editors, or to their respective assistants, it is now of course impossible to say, but while the perplexity of various readings has been avoided, it is clear that the existing Koran is so far from being the actual production of Mohammed, that it does not even appear that he ever intended such a work to be compiled.

It has been questioned whether the revelations so recorded were the unassisted productions of Mohammed. He was suspected, even in his lifetime, of being aided in the forgery by various persons whose names are mentioned by Mohammedan writers; and it is pretty plain that his descriptions of heaven and hell, with the narrow bridge over the abyss, were borrowed,

* Mohammed styled himself "the prophet of the illiterate," but some suppose this to mean only "prophet of the Arabs," who were called illiterate, as possessing neither Scriptures nor prophets, as the Jews and Christians did.

through a Persian friend, from the Zend-Avesta. Other passages, also, have been traced to a Magian origin. The early Christian writers affirm that one of his assistants was Sergius, a Nestorian monk: and the Jews have a tradition that the Koran was compiled by twelve of their doctors. Certainly some portions of it manifest a desire to conciliate the believers in the earlier revelations. Both Jewish and Christian Scriptures are declared entitled to equal respect with the Koran. It is even said that the followers of Moses, of Jesus, and of Mohammed, will be all judged by their respective laws. In a similar spirit Jerusalem was at first made the *Kebla*, or quarter to turn to in prayer,* though this was afterwards changed to Mecca, the birthplace of the prophet, and the metropolis of the old Arabian religions.

In spite, however, of these friendly indications, the Koran exhibits but little acquaintance with the Scriptures either of the Old or New Testament. It supposes a hundred sacred books, delivered to Adam, Seth, Enoch, and Abraham, to be now lost. The four still extant are described as the Pentateuch delivered to Moses, the Psalter to David, the Gospel to Jesus, and the Koran to Mohammed. The writer of these statements could not have seen either the Jewish or the Christian Scriptures. The Arabians were possessed, it seems, of a corrupt copy of the Psalms of David, and of one of the apocryphal writings of the heretics of the Eastern Church, called the "Gospel of St. Barnabas." These, together with the fables of the Talmud current among the Jews, who had been settled in Arabia for some centuries before Mohammed, appear to have furnished all that he

* Compare 1 Kings viii. 44 with Daniel vi. 10 and Ps. v. 7.

knew of the older revelations. Of Christianity he was so ignorant as to imagine the Three Persons of the Holy Trinity to be God, the virgin Mary, and her Son. The Koran is accordingly very severe on those who give God a wife and a child. Another blunder equally ridiculous was his mistaking the Greek word *Paraclete*, signifying Comforter, for *Periclyte*, which means "*Illustrious*." The latter being equivalent to his own name Mohammed, this blunder supplied the exposition that he was the successor spoken of by Christ, and the last of the prophets.*

Finding little encouragement among those who could so easily refute his pretensions, the impostor changed his tone, charged the Jews and Christians with corrupting their Scriptures, and in several new revelations incited his followers to destroy them with the sword. These contradictory passages in the Koran are now accounted for by the doctrine of *abrogation*, which pretends that a later Scripture abrogates a former one. So low was Mohammed's own idea of

* The Gospel of Barnabas, rejected as apocryphal by pope Gelasius, A.D. 494, is thought to have been an interpolated corrupted copy of St. Matthew, compiled at the close of the fifth century. In the library of prince Eugene was an Italian manuscript, entitled "The true Gospel of Jesus called Christ, a new prophet sent of God to the world, according to the relation of Barnabas the Apostle." In this work Mohammed is expressly named as the Paraclete promised in John xiv. 16, 26, and xvi. 7. Jesus is called by no higher name than a prophet, and it is related that as the Jews were about to seize him in the garden of Olives, he was carried up to the third heaven by the four angels, Gabriel, Michael, Raphael, and Uriel, *and Judas was taken and crucified in his place*. So great a resemblance was miraculously effected between them that the Virgin and the apostles were deceived, but afterwards Jesus obtained permission to reappear and comfort them with the assurance that he should not die till the end of the world. Jesus is further made to say that the shame of the cross was imputed to him because men called him God and the Son of God, and that this reproach should endure till the coming of Mohammed, who would deliver all who believe from this error. Mr. Jones pronounces this MS. to be a late Mohammedan forgery; still, it shows the source from which their ideas of Christianity were derived. —*See Jones's Canon of N. T.*, i. 147.

the Divine counsels, that on one occasion he declared a revelation to be abrogated on the same night that it was delivered. On this pretence, many verses actually published and circulated in Mohammed's lifetime are omitted from the Koran: moreover, its chapters not being arranged chronologically, but in the order of length, it occasionally happens that the abrogating verse *precedes* that which it repeals.

Notwithstanding these proofs of alteration and confusion, the Koran is believed to have existed entire and uncreated in the heavens, being inscribed by God himself, with a pen of light, on the table of his everlasting decrees. From this table it is affirmed to have been brought down to the lowest heaven, and thence communicated, as required, by Gabriel to the prophet. For this assertion an express passage is quoted from the 44th chapter:—"By the perspicuous book of the Koran, verily, we have sent down the same in a blessed night, wherein is distinctly sent down the decree of every determined thing as our command; the night Alkader, the night which is better than a thousand months, it is peace until the rising of the morning."

This doctrine was accused, after the prophet's death, of making two eternals, the Deity and the Koran. After much controversy it was agreed to acquiesce in the explanation, "that the Koran is pronounced with the tongue, written in books, and kept in memory, and yet is eternal, subsisting in the divine essence, and not separate from it." The doctors of Islam were ignorant that there is, indeed, a "Word which was in the beginning with God,"* and who has manifested himself in the gospel of Jesus Christ.

The Koran, though written in prose, terminates its

* John i. 2.

sentences with a long-continued rhyme, which greatly enraptures the Mussulman ear. It is considered not only the purest standard of Arabic style, but beyond the power of man to equal. Mohammed more than once refers to its composition as his best answer to the charge of forgery, being a greater miracle than the raising of the dead. Pretending to report the very words of God himself, the Koran is regarded by all Moslems with the deepest veneration. They wash their hands before they touch it, swear by it, and decide disputes by dipping at random into the sacred text—ceremonies, by the way, which were all practised by the later Jews with their own more authentic Scriptures.

Notwithstanding these pretensions, Gibbon, a critic by no means unfriendly to any opponent of Christianity, and who pronounces the Koran "a glorious testimony to the unity of God," is constrained to admit "its endless, incoherent rhapsody of fable, and precept, and declamation, which seldom excites a sentiment or an idea, which sometimes crawls in the dust, and is sometimes lost in the clouds." He adds, what no one who compares the two can doubt for a moment, "that its loftiest strains must yield to the sublime simplicity of the book of Job, composed in a remote age in the same language."* If Mohammedans could be persuaded to extend this comparison to the whole Bible, they would discover that the best portions of their boasted book are borrowed from the older Scriptures, and that the Koran is, in fact, very deficient in imagination, no less than in true philosophy.

Its origin can be easily traced: both Jews and Christians had been some time settled in Mecca and Medina; the colonies of the former, in disputing with

* Decline and Fall, chap. l.

their pagan neighbours, were often heard to exclaim, "Oh! if the time of the Messiah were come we would go to him."* There is evidence that some of Mohammed's family had heard of these aspirations, and it is recorded among the motives of his earliest adherents, that they wished to anticipate the Jews in the recognition of the long-expected prophet. Before Mohammed opened his pretensions, the more reflecting of his countrymen were already beginning to tire of a dark and barbarous idolatry. "Our tribe," exclaimed one of them, "is corrupting the religion of Abraham, and are worshipping and walking round a stone, though it can do them neither harm nor good."† Four men renounced the idol, and set out in quest of a better faith; three of them eventually became Christians, and the fourth remained a sceptic. These were men of Mohammed's own tribe, and one of them was related to his first wife and benefactress, Kadijah. It was this person who, after embracing the gospel, and then relapsing into Judaism, was the first to hail in the young camel driver of Mecca the prophet whom Moses had foretold.

It is matter of doubt whether Mohammed himself were more impostor or dupe. He thought himself at one time the sport of *jins*, or genii, at another, possessed by Satan. The convulsions and other derangements attending his supposed revelations are strongly symptomatic of epilepsy, and certainly much of the Koran is no better than the ravings of a disordered imagination. In spite of the extravagant panegyrics of its adherents, no impartial reader can wade through its puerile and wearisome iterations without impatience and disgust. It has borrowed from the earlier

* See Psalm liii. 7.

† Macbride's "Mohammedan Religion Explained." 1857.

and authentic Scriptures the great doctrines of the unity and personality of God, the immortality of the soul, and the identity of the human species, together with the resurrection of the body, the day of judgment, and an endless state of bliss or perdition hereafter. These constituted the strength of Islam in its early struggles with the superstitions of the barbarous Arabs; and these, accompanied by great physical superiority, gave its disciples an easy ascendancy over the idolatrous Hindus. Every one of these ennobling truths, however, is debased and weakened by the treatment received in the Koran, where Magianism and Heathenism have also their representative elements.

The mystery of a Trinity in the Divine Unity was unknown to Mohammed, and it is allowed by the best Moslem commentators that he entirely mistook the Christian faith on this article. His assertions of the Unity itself are disfigured by much poverty of conception in regard to the Divine personality. The Deity of the Koran is an idea in some respects inferior even to that of Brahmanical philosophy, and infinitely below the holy and spiritual majesty revealed in the Bible. He is seated on a material throne, writes with a pen of prodigious dimensions, and swears by his own creatures; as if to show (in opposition to the apostle)* the *mutability* of his councils. He abrogates his own scriptures and decrees. Instead of hating all unrighteousness and sin, while pitying and loving the sinner, his affection for his messenger is allowed to authorize in Mohammed sensual practices forbidden to other men. He is *called* almighty, just, and beneficent, but these attributes are but magnified from the good qualities of an earthly monarch. He is not the

* Heb. vi. 13—17.

"Lord, high and holy, whose thoughts are not as our thoughts, nor his ways our ways." He pardons, when entreated and propitiated, like a generous man, but he is far from being "the God of consolation and Father of all mercies" revealed to the Christian, or even to the Jew. The hard, flinty unity of this notional God may please the self-righteous rationalist, but it was the gross and sensuous clothing with which the Koran invests him, that proved the attraction to the Arab armies, and still encourages its disciples to rapine and lust.

The great truth of the Incarnation being unknown, the Mussulman is, of course, an entire stranger to the exquisite sympathies of the God-Man, seeking, searching, regenerating, and finally glorifying human nature in himself. In place of this only Way to the invisible Father, the Koran presents its disciples with a hundred *names* of God, which it is thought highly meritorious to repeat, by the aid of a rosary.* Some of their own writers doubt whether these epithets do not imply a real polytheistical distinction injurious to the very foundation of Moslem theology.

The Koran asserts the Divine predestination in language so crude, that the Turkish confessions of faith openly ascribe all unbelief and wickedness to the *will* of God, though not to his *satisfaction*. Mohammed himself discouraged speculation on a mystery which he felt his incapacity to deal with; nevertheless, it has become the distinguishing feature of Mussulman divinity. In India the belief amounts to a fatalism as dark as the Brahman's, who imagines all events to be the results of a previous existence, and every man to bear his destiny within him, inscribed on the bones of his forehead.

* The first invention of this implement of devotion seems to belong to the *Buddhists*, from whom it was copied by the Mussulmans; the Saracens lent the toy to the Crusaders, by whom it was brought into Europe.

Under the confession of God the Koran includes "a belief in his angels, scriptures, and messengers." Two of the former are assigned to every man, and changed daily, in order to record his actions for good and evil. The names of Gabriel and Michael, revealed in the genuine Scripture, are augmented by those of Azrael, the angel of death (borrowed from the Magians), and Israil, who is to blow the trumpet of the resurrection. The leader of the fallen angels is named Iblis; their expulsion from heaven is attributed to their disobedience in refusing to worship Adam. To these invisible beings are added in the Moslem creed the *jins*, or genii, a race of beings supposed to have inhabited the earth under a line of kings, who were all called Solomon, before the creation of mankind. Though still living and unseen, they are not of the nature of spirits, but have bodies of fire, and are mortal. Mohammed declared himself to be a preacher to jins and men.

Not less strangely disfigured is the doctrine of judgment after death. The spirits of prophets are supposed to be wafted immediately to paradise; those of martyrs are lodged in the *crops of the green birds who feed on the fruits at its entrance.* All others hover near their graves till the day of judgment, when they will be called to attempt the passage over the narrow bridge which spans the gulf of hell. In this perilous attempt they are to be assisted by the animals whom they may have offered in sacrifice while alive. The resurrection of the flesh is gravely explained as effected by means of a particular bone, which is preserved in the dust of death, to be the seed of the future body. A fable scarcely less puerile, received from the Jews, forms an article of most implicit faith with all Mussulmans. Soon after the body is laid in the grave, it is visited by two tremendous angels or demons, named *Monkir* and *Nakir;* by these it is set upright in the grave, and the soul is recalled to undergo the question, Who is thy Lord, and who is thy prophet, and what is thy religion? They who can answer in the orthodox formula, "There is no God but God, and Mohammed is his prophet," are dismissed with honour, and their rest is visited with sweet airs from paradise. The unbelievers are beaten with iron maces, and gnawed by dragons, till they fill the cemeteries with howlings, which are audible alike to angels and jins, but mercifully withheld from men, whose nerves might be less equal to the sound, or their hearts more moved to compassion.

The day of judgment itself is described with many of the particulars revealed in the Bible. The beast, the sealing of the elect, the rise and overthrow of Antichrist, are explained as in the revelation of St. John. We are further told, that the false Messiah shall be slain by Jesus, who is to descend on the mosque of Damascus, and enjoy a glorious reign, having the last of the Imams for his vizier. The books and the scales used in the Divine judgment are dwelt upon in a similar literal and grovelling spirit.

The portion of the wicked is set forth in language which has been traced to the Zend-Avesta of the Magians. Across the depths of perdition is stretched a bridge of steel, finer than a hair and sharper than a sword, on which only the feet of true believers are preserved to pass into paradise. All others drop into the abyss, which is divided into seven compartments. The first is a purgatory for unworthy Moslems, it being declared that "no one shall remain for ever in hell who has but as much faith in his heart as the weight of an atom;"* the second is assigned to the Jews; the third to Christians; the fourth to the Sabians; the fifth to the Magians; the sixth to idolaters; and the last and lowest to all hypocrites professing a religion without believing it: these alone, it would appear, are to abide in everlasting torments.

In depicting the heritage of the faithful, the imagination of the Arabian prophet was unable to ascend above a gross and sensual paradise. Fruit-gardens, luxurious couches, silk clothing and pearls, wine (an indulgence forbidden in this life), and *houris*, created out of musk for endless enjoyment, are the delights to which Moslems are taught to aspire, as the ultimate rewards of their religion. They are fiercely and passionately realized in their carnal minds, infusing an ardour which conquers all apprehensions of death. In the battle-field, where all who fall under a Mussulman leader are reckoned as martyrs, and entitled to pass straight to their reward, the power of this superstition has been often attested. Some attempts have at other times been made to *spiritualize* the language from which the orthodox Mussulman draws his inspiration, but the explanations are generally condemned as heretical and dangerous to the honour of Islam.

It is singular that in its descriptions both of heaven and hell, the Koran should have made no mention whatever of *women:* the *houris* of Paradise being creatures of quite another species. The omission has led to the common notion that women have no souls. This error is repudiated by the more intelligent Moslems, but no authoritative or satisfactory belief seems to exist on the real condition, in another world,

* Algazalis Creed. Macbride, 133.

of the companions so indispensable to men in that which now is.

These serious defects are observable in the Koran itself, and in the very points which form the strength of its claim to attention and submission. No religion rises higher than its source, and the doctors of Islam, instead of improving on the crude notions of the Koran, have proved unable to preserve its better parts from the common corruptions of time and place.

Second, and to the orthodox sect hardly inferior in authority to the Koran, is the *Sonnah*, or Tradition. The Koran pretends to record the actual and literal words of God, as repeated by the archangel to the prophet: the Sonnah contains the sayings of Mohammed himself, as a commentary of co-ordinate authority. These sayings were the subject of frequent conversation during his lifetime. On one occasion he is said to have encouraged their being recorded, saying, "Write, for by God nothing but truth comes from my mouth." At another time, however, he said, "Do not write anything from me except the Koran." The contradiction is thus resolved, in a tradition which appears in the Sonnah itself, "I have left you two things in which it is impossible for you to err—the word of God and my Sonnah." In spite of the impossibility, however, this infallible exposition of an infallible revelation has met the fate which usually befalls the traditions of men. The Koran is universally received among Mussulmans; but the Sonnah divides them into two irreconcilable sects. The largest, called Sonnites, receive the six canonical collections of orthodox traditions compiled in the reigns of the caliphs, Abubeker, Omar, and Othman. These are rejected by a large minority of the Mussulman world, who consider the prophet's son-in-law Ali to have been his rightful successor, and anathematize the three intervening caliphs as usurpers. The disciples of Ali assume the designation of *Adaliyah*, or followers of justice, but are better known by the name of *Shiyahs* (separatists), given them by their adversaries. The Arabs, Turks, and Affghans, with most of the educated Mussulmans of India, are Sonnites. The Persians are chiefly Shiyahs, and from that quarter the royal family of Oude (originating in a trooper of the Mogul army), with many of the lower orders in India, have received the same persuasion.

The most approved collection of the Sonnah, is that of Abu Abdallah, called, from the place of his birth, Bokhari; it contains 7,275 traditions selected out of 600,000; which, however, are reduced by deducting repetitions to 2,000. The Shiyahs also have four collections of traditions, but regard them as of inferior authority to the Koran. Still their opponents are considered the better Mussulmans, the Shiyite creed being largely adulterated with mysticism.

Neither sect has preserved the faith of the Koran, or their own acknowledged traditions, free from admixture. In India, especially, the proximity of idolatry exercises considerable influence over the Mussulman population, more than half of whom are of Hindu extraction. The former fierce hostility between the two religions has yielded to a less rancorous feeling, under the pressure of time and common subjection to another rule. Both ascribe much to the power of astrology and witchcraft; both tremble at local demons; and the latter being in many places the objects of Hindu worship, the Mussulman owns a dread of the idol akin to that which not unfrequently urges the Brahman to offer a second homage to the aboriginal devil. Custom, too, always so powerful in India, has not only reduced the Mussulman colonies to a toleration of idolatry, which their ancestors accounted dishonourable; but effected no little assimilation in their popular rites. In some districts the Mussulman population is so largely Hinduised, as to incur the contempt and indignation of the more faithful, and reformers not unfrequently arise, who create much disturbance by their endeavours to resuscitate a purer zeal for Islam.

The practical duties of the Mussulman religion are four: *Prayer*, *Alms*, *Fasting*, and *Pilgrimage*. The first must be accompanied with certain minutely specified ablutions, according to the prophet's saying, "Ablution is the half of prayer." The hands, mouth, nostrils, face, arms, head, ears, neck, and feet, are to be separately washed, and most of them three times (a specified petition being offered with each), for the morning prayer of a devout Moslem; with the generality, however, all is performed in about two minutes. Five hours in the day are enjoined for prayer,—daybreak, noon, afternoon, evening, and the first watch of the night. The prayers are mostly but ejaculations or recitations from the Koran, which the worshipper utters in the prescribed postures,—standing, sitting, kneeling, and lying prostrate,—concluding with some short petition for himself or his friends. In these devotions, such phrases as *Allah Akbar* (God is most great) are to be repeated thirty-three times by the help of the rosary. Still it seems that in practice five or ten minutes suffice for the whole exercise.

The Koran recognises no priesthood, and all who

can read the sacred text are at liberty to expound and teach it. Public prayer, however, was declared by the prophet to be more efficacious than private, and he assigned Friday for its weekly observance, as being the day on which Adam was created. On this day the men assemble in the mosque (the women being allowed to enter no further than the porches), and a prayer called Khotbeh is recited. The first part of this contains a commemoration of the prophet, his wives, the five caliphs, and the imams Hussan and Hossein. After this some verses from the Koran are recited, the muezzins chanting the *Amen*. The second part of the Khotbeh prays for Mohammed and all his posterity, the caliphs, the reigning sovereign, the orthodox armies, the pilgrims, and the whole Moslem people. This prayer is often followed by a sermon; both are delivered from a pulpit looking towards a niche in the wall which marks the Kebla, or position of Mecca. The remaining furniture of the mosques consists of carpets or mats on the floor, with lamps and ostrich eggs suspended from the ceiling.

Mohammed was accustomed himself to officiate at this service, and his appointment of Abubeker to act during his last illness, was taken as a designation of that officer to the succession. The Khotbeh was accordingly recited by the succeeding sovereigns in person, and Mohammed II. signalized his capture of Constantinople by performing this act in the church of St. Sophia, thenceforth converted to a mosque.* The Mussulman definition of a king is "he whose coin is current in the

* Decline and Fall, cap. lxviii. The statement that Mohammed "performed the *namaz* of prayer and thanksgiving *on the great altar* where the Christian mysteries had so lately been celebrated before the last of the Cæsars," is perhaps more epigrammatical than exact.

realm, and in whose name the prayers are offered after the Khotbeh."* The two parts of this definition have been strangely separated in British India, where the coin has long borne the impress of the royal effigies, with the name of the East India Company; yet the Khotbeh has been permitted to retain the name and style of the puppet king of Delhi. The *imam* who reads the prayers, and the *khuteeb* who preaches the sermon, with the *muezzin* who calls to prayer, and the other servants of the mosque, are appointed and paid by the British government: they might surely have been required to acknowledge the real, and not the pretended, sovereign of India. It is owing to such inconsiderate concessions that the power of the native religions is often found wielded against the authority, which their own principles would require them to uphold.

The Koran follows the Bible in connecting alms and fasting very closely with prayer; but while the latter receives the pre-eminence in Christ's Sermon on the Mount, the Moslem teachers quote with approval a saying of Omar, that "Prayer will bring a man half way to God, and Fasting to the door of his palace, but it is to Alms he will owe his admission." The disposal of his alms is remitted to the private conscience of the Mussulman, save that their bestowal is expected to accompany marriages, funerals, and some other ceremonies. It is a duty which few are known to neglect; indeed it is often discharged with a liberality worthy of a purer religion. For *Fasting*, besides private and particular occasions of sorrow, two special seasons are assigned by public appointment, the *Ramadhan*, expressly enjoined in the

* Qanoon-e-Islam, p. 263.

Koran, and the *Mohurrum*, which is observed in commemoration of the death of Hussan and Hossein, the sons of Ali and last of the imams.

The Ramadhan endures for a whole month, which, in consequence of the lunar computation used by the Mohammedans, falls in different seasons of the year, and must at times severely task the resignation of the devout. A total abstinence from drink, as well as food, is prescribed from sunrise to sunset, and the regulation, though said to be violated by the richer classes in private, is to all appearance very strictly and generally observed. At sunset the shops are opened and entertainments freely given, but many spend a large portion of the night in the mosques, praying and giving alms. The conclusion of this rigorous fast is celebrated with great rejoicings as an *Eed*, or festival.

The *Mohurrum* is observed with far less rigour, resembling in most parts of India a festival more than a fast. The tradition runs that the ancient prophets observed a feast on the 10th of the month Mohurrum, which Mohammed continued with some additional ceremonies. The day is now chiefly remembered on account of the death or martyrdom of the *Hossein*, *i.e.*, of the two sons of Ali and the prophet's daughter Fatima. They perished in the forty-sixth year of the Hegira: the first by poison, and the other by the sword, under circumstances which, though variously related, still affect the Mussulman mind with the liveliest emotions. Since this event the ancient rejoicings have been exchanged for lamentations; and the observance is, in India, extended to the first ten days of the month, in imitation of the Hindu festival of Durga. For the whole of this period (which in the Deccan is often prolonged to thirteen days) the entire Mussulman population abstains from every description of work, from strong liquors, and from nuptial festivities. Some deny themselves the use of a bed, of meat, fish, and even the darling *betel* leaf. *Tazzias*, or models made of ivory, ebony, sandal-wood, and other materials, from the precious metals to bamboo or paper, and supposed to represent the funeral chapel of Hossein, are exhibited in the streets, carried in procession, and finally deposited with funeral rites in the cemetery. Assemblies are held daily, at which poems are recited in honour of the martyred imams. The streets resound with shouts of "*Ya Ali!*" "*Shah Hussan!*" "*Shah Hossein!*" "*Doolha! Doolha!*" (bridegroom) "*Haee Dost!*" (alas! my friend) and "*Ruhero, ruhero!*" (stay, stay!)—repeated, again and again, at the top of the voice. Among the Shiyahs, who are devoted to Ali, these exclamations are accompanied by exhibitions of despair, which the Sonnites hold to be inconsistent with "Islam." The women beat their breasts, with loud shrieks and lamentations, and even the men appear affected with the most passionate grief.

An observance peculiar to India is the erection, in the streets, of sheds or booths, called *astroorkana* (ten-day house) and *tazziakana* (house of mourning). In front of these booths bonfires are kept burning, round which the idle people dance and leap during a large part of the night. The buildings themselves are decked with lamps, flowers, and fishes made of paper or tinsel. They contain the *ullums*, or representations of Hossein's standard, with the *neesa*, or spear, on which his head was borne by his enemies, and the *nal*, or shoe of his horse. These articles are paraded in the streets, amid loud cries and mimic representations of the incidents of the martyrdom. Sometimes a figure, or a man representing a corpse, is carried in the procession, pierced with knives and daggers, and covered with an imitation of blood. These more tragical parts of the show are diversified with buffooneries rivalling the saturnalia of the heathen. They are performed not only by the ordinary faquirs or dervishes, who attend in force, but by numbers of Hindus, who assume the garb of faquirs in order to participate in the license of the Mohurrum. These men parade about in dresses representing a variety of characters, male and female. *Mujnoon* and *Leila*, the Abelard and Heloise of the East, are enacted in one place; in another a group of African negroes run wildly, shaking cocoa-nut shells filled with gravel. Others imitate a *hukeem*, or quack-doctor, vending his nostrums; or a Mogul chief, with his attendant; or a couple of drivelling *hadgis*, or pilgrims. An old man and old woman (*Boodha*, *Boodhee*) are exhibited in ridiculous postures on a scaffold. Others dress up as tigers, crows, paddy birds, etc. All are provided with stories, jests, and practical jokes, by which the buffoons amuse a large concourse of followers in their progress to the several astroorkanas, not forgetting to levy contributions of rice or money from the bystanders.

The *taboots* (also peculiar to India) are a larger kind of *tazzias*, built of bamboo, illuminated with lamps and sparkling with plates of mica. The glitter of these playthings, when variously coloured by Bengal lights, attracts and charms the multitude; but all these imitations of Hindu observances are disapproved by the more educated and religious Mussulmans.

The Mohurrum closes with a grand night procession to what is called the plain of Kurbulla (the scene of Hossein's fall); after this the taboots are stripped of their finery and thrown into the water, in obvious imitation of the Hindu practice with the Durga idol. The Mohurrum is the occasion of many disputes between the rival Mohammedan sects. When it happens to coincide with the Hindu *Dusserah*, the collision of the two religions creates no little alarm. Violent conflicts sometimes occur in the street, and the attendance of the troops is necessary to preserve or restore the public peace.

Similar processions are practised in India on the two days of the *Bara Wagat*, a fast observed in commemoration of the death of Mohammed. On this occasion, notwithstanding the Moslem abhorrence of idols, images are exhibited of the prophet's footstep impressed upon stones, which are kept in caskets with great reverence. A figure of the *Booraq*, or flying steed on which Mohammed made his journey to heaven, is drawn about in procession: both these idols are not unfrequently exhibited also amid the fooleries of the Mohurrum.

These religious processions, both of Hindus and Mohammedans, are offensive to one another, and odious to the rest of the community. They are always dangerous to the public peace, and no respectable person of either creed undertakes to defend the obscene abominations by which they are usually attended. It is surely time, therefore, for the impartial hand of government to prevent such violations of public order and decency, by prohibiting processions altogether, and restraining the rites of all religions to the temples or enclosures appropriated to their observance.

The last and most anomalous requisite of Mohammedanism is the Pilgrimage, sanctioned in the Koran and by the personal example and positive precept of the prophet, yet obviously a relic of heathenism, inconsistent with any worthy idea of God. The main object of the pilgrimage is the *Caaba*, a temple in Mecca, which the Arabs believe was originally raised by Adam, and re-edified by Abraham out of the ruins occasioned by the deluge. It was here (they say) that the Father of the faithful displayed his resignation and constancy in the sacrifice of his son, the intended victim being, as they maintain, not Isaac, but their own ancestor Ishmael. He was snatched away at the critical moment by the angel Gabriel, and a broad-tailed sheep substituted in his place. The worship then founded became, in course of time, corrupted with divers innovations. When the city fell into Mohammed's possession, he purified the Caaba from hundreds of idols—the accumulated store of several successive systems, and restored the worship of the God of Abraham.

In violation, however, of all consistency, many of the heathen observances were continued and sanctioned by the prophet. He himself, at his first visit, shaved and sacrificed the hair of his head, along with sixty-three victims, according to the years of his age, and thirty-seven for his son-in-law Ali. The doctrine of atonement being explicitly rejected from his scheme, these sacrifices could have had no *moral* signification, typical or commemorative. The notion that the victims may lend aid in the passage over the bridge of steel is a puerility obviously borrowed from some *heathen* tradition. This blind and dumb rite Mohammed accompanied by other ceremonies not less irrational and unworthy, such as circuiting several times round the Caaba, running seven times up and down a street, pelting the devil with pebbles, and, above all, kissing and adoring a black and a white stone in the walls of the Caaba. This last undisguised act of idolatry sat heavy on the conscience of the caliph Omar. "I know," he exclaimed, in paying the accustomed homage, "that thou canst neither help nor hurt me, and if I had not seen the prophet do the same I should never have kissed thee." The famous stone is in all probability an aerolite, which the idolatrous Arabs adored in their ignorance, just as the Ephesians worshipped a similar object as "the image which fell down from Jupiter."* It has been built into the wall of the Caaba, where it continues to receive from the deluded Mussulman the adoration paid by his heathen ancestors. Some of the other ceremonies are now traditionally connected with incidents in sacred history, but it seems probable that all really originated in the days of heathenism.

The Koran makes it obligatory on every Mussulman, who possesses means to defray the journey and maintain his family during his absence, to make the pilgrimage to Mecca once in his life. Mohammed himself declared "that a Mussulman who should neglect the pilgrimage, when in his power to observe it, might as well die a Christian or a Jew." So great is the merit attached to its performance, that the corpses of those who die on the way are carried on by their companions to acquire the sacred title of *Hadgi;* and though the poor are dispensed from the obligation, it is not uncommon to see them begging their way, in whole families, from Bengal and Chittagong to the western

* Acts xix. 35.

coast of India, where the wealthier Mussulmans keep vessels, called God's grace, or bounty, ships, to transport them free to the shores of Arabia.

The pilgrimage has been made by three Christians, in spite of the jealous precautions of the Arabs, who would have immolated the intruders had they been detected. One was carried thither as a slave by a Mohammedan master; the second was the German traveller Burckhardt; and still more recently Lieut. Burton has verified his description. The two last assuming the garb and character of Mohammedans, obtained admission to all the rites; but surely it was purchasing the information at too high a price, when disciples of the Lord Christ consented to share in the observances, and professedly avow the creed, of a false, deceitful, and debasing religion.

The Mohammedans, it seems, are not content with making their favourite temple the scene of the devotions of Adam and Abraham; they crowd into its precincts divers notable events, without regard to sense or probability. Here is shown the well *Zemzem*, gravely affirmed to be the same which gushed out in the desert for the relief of Ishmael. Here, too, the pilgrim adores the spot where Adam and Eve, long wandering apart after their expulsion from Eden, were at last happily reunited. With all this want of reason and imagination, one cannot but marvel at the fanaticism which induces so many thousands to undertake the pilgrimage, and manifest such unintelligible raptures at its accomplishment. Independently of the miseries of a sea voyage, which to a native of India are uniformly odious, the city itself lies in a narrow sandy valley, wholly destitute of shade or refreshment. The wayworn pilgrim approaches it on every side through a weary desert. Many perish from disease, exposure, and starvation. Burckhardt saw corpses daily brought into the enclosure; and others who just survived to crawl within sight of the house of God, deemed themselves happy to be sprinkled with water from the sacred well, and so expire in the arms of the prophet and the guardian angels.

The impressions generally appear to be vivid and extravagant. In some places the spectator might suppose himself at an American camp meeting. An African burst into tears, exclaiming, "O God, now take my soul, for this is paradise." With all his usual gravity and reserve, the Mussulman never seeks to conceal his religious emotions: and Pitt, the first English visitor at Mecca, expresses himself greatly moved by the sight of "so many thousands in their garment of humility and mortification, with naked heads, and cheeks watered with tears, begging earnestly, with grievous sighs and sobs, for the remission of their sins, promising newness of life, and using a form of penitential expressions for four or five hours." All enthusiasm is respectable, but it is difficult to comprehend or sympathize with such extravagant emotions, in men whose avowed religion contains nothing to justify them. If the Moslem wished indeed to "worship the Father in spirit and in truth," he should know that he is to be approached neither on this mountain nor on that, but wherever the sacrifice of a broken spirit is offered him through the mediation of his Son.

The number of sheep and goats sacrificed at one of these annual pilgrimages is reckoned at several thousands. The season is celebrated in India by an annual festival called the Eed, or Buckra-eed, in which many goats, sheep, and even camels, are sacrificed.

Mecca was the birth-place of Mohammed, but Medina, which received him on his flight from Mecca,* and was the first to acknowledge his mission, is the city honoured with the custody of his remains. It lies about 250 miles distant from Mecca, and though not a commanded place of pilgrimage, usually receives the compliment of a voluntary visit. The Shiyahs, who might scarcely find it safe to avow their tenets at the more orthodox places of pilgrimage, have others of their own at Meshed Ali and Kurbulla, where the attractions of the Caaba are rivalled by the tombs of Ali and Hossein. The practice has extended itself in a lower degree to the burial places of many other Mussulman worthies. Dervishes and devout people of both sexes visit these tombs, and say their prayers over the dust which they contain, with all the fervour of an Italian Christian at the shrine of a confessor, or a Hindu at the altar of his divinity.

The rite of circumcision universally obtains throughout the Mohammedan world, and is doubtless regarded as a religious institution. Yet it is not commanded or alluded to in the Koran, and is the sign of a covenant which pertains exclusively to another religion. The sons of Ishmael received it by tradition from their father, but the promise was restrained to Isaac and his seed. Its perpetuation among nations of another race can only be attributed to a blind following of the Arabian prophet.

The most interesting feature in the aspect of this

* It is from this flight that the Moslem æra, called *Hegira*, is dated. It corresponds with A.D. 612.

religion, is the extraordinary attachment exhibited by every true Mussulman to Mohammed himself. Hard and straitened in its idea of the Divine Being, Islam has succeeded in investing its prophet with the concentrated and passionate affection of his followers. A good Mussulman looks to Mohammed as more than a father or a brother; "their love to him is wonderful, passing the love of women."* The highest title claimed by himself was that of the Friend and Messenger of God. So far from deeming his life an example to mankind, he has introduced into the Koran special exemptions, granted to himself, for sensual indulgences forbidden to every other man. Still his followers are never weary of extolling the personal merits and dignity of Mohammed. His name is thought to bring good fortune upon all who have the happiness to bear it. It is associated with the Divine Being, and invoked on every occasion. He is called *Mustapha*, the chosen one. The Sonnah prefers him above all preceding prophets, and the angels of heaven; declaring that he alone was found worthy to undertake the office of *Intercessor* with God, which had been declined by Adam, and Noah, and Abraham, *and Jesus*, as transcending their abilities. So audacious a transfer, from the true Mediator between God and men, of an office which Mohammed never laid claim to, and which the Psalmist tells us "no man can discharge for his brother," suggests the suspicion that the authors of these traditions were actuated by a determination not to allow their prophet's inferiority to the Christian Saviour in *anything*.

This regard for the person of Mohammed has defied the power of time, and communicated itself to various

* 2 Sam. i. 26.

races. Persia and India own it at this day, in a degree hardly inferior to his immediate companions and followers. Poems are still composed and recited in his honour: in one of these, entitled "Twinkling Stars in praise of the Best of the creation," the author declares that "he never had recourse to the prophet without finding him an invincible patron and protector, nor desired of him any good, temporal or spiritual, without some grant from his liberality."* Whatever else may be vague and notional in Islam, it is certain that the prophet is no abstraction. He is the object of a real and personal love, which forms the mainspring of the whole system, and is doubtless the secret of its long hold upon mankind. It were well if the followers of a Greater than Mohammed—One who is, indeed, the Intercessor on high—the Friend and the Son of God—"the chiefest among ten thousand, and altogether lovely"—the Saviour of sinners—the Example and the Judge of men—were ever looking unto him with that trustful love which the deluded Moslem throws away on a sinful man like himself.

In other respects, Islam has been correctly described as "a faith without mysteries and a morality without love." The affection centred on Mohammed is not extended to mankind, with whom the Mussulman acknowledges none of the relations originating in the gospel of Christ. Redemption has no place in his scheme: the fall of Adam is related as an historical fact; but original sin is only dimly alluded to, in a tradition that the angel Gabriel extracted the black 'drop' from the liver of Mohammed. Though all men are pronounced sinful, the Koran is ignorant both of *atonement* and *regeneration*. With no con-

* Macbride.

ception of *grace*, or the implanting of new affections by the Spirit of God, its aim to awaken the conscience, and restrain the passions, is of a confessedly imperfect nature. Its morality is, in fact, inferior to that of some heathen systems. Temperance is enforced by the clumsy expedient of total abstinence in one particular, accompanied by unlimited indulgence in another. The conceptions of a future life are sullied with the impurities of the present; its felicity resides neither in being, nor in doing, *good;* its paradise is simply a boundless harem; and the errors which vitiate the standard of religion are but too faithfully reproduced in the lives of its disciples.

In India the morality of the Koran has been further lowered by association with the impure revellings of the heathen. It may be questioned, indeed, whether in one great article the Hindu has not attained to a superiority over the Mussulman. The female sex certainly enjoyed a higher place in the older, than in the later, civilization. The ancient Hindu drama exhibits a delicacy and refinement not to be found in the sensuous pages of the Koran. A far higher sense of female honour appears in Hindu history, and the institutions of native society have clearly suffered in this respect from contact with those of Mohammed. His polygamy is coarser and more degrading than the old Hindu practice. The *harem* is a Mussulman usage, partially adopted by Hindus to preserve their families from the outrages of the foreigners. The freedom with which women of the Brahman caste still mix in male society, attests the former liberty of the sex; and though it has now become a point of honour, with other Hindu females, to seclude themselves from the eyes of men, they enjoy a degree of domestic and social liberty unknown to the Mussulmans, and their character is proportionably higher, both in intellect and morals.

It has been thought that the light which the Korân has borrowed, though by very distorted mediums, from the Scriptures of truth, together with its intense abhorrence of idolatry, would render the Mohammedan more easy than the Hindu of conversion to the gospel of Christ. The reverse, however, is well known to be the fact, and the reason may be found in the greater *self-righteousness* which is nourished in the disciples of Islam. The publicans and the harlots go into the kingdom of God before the scribes and Pharisees. True conversion is in every instance the work of the Holy Spirit, through faith in Christ Jesus; and the soul most prepared for the reception of this grace is not that which has attained to the finest intellectual ideas of the Creator, or the most rational conceptions of his service, but that which is the most burdened with its own sin and most anxious for a Redeemer. "Come unto me (exclaims the true Messenger of God), all ye that labour and are heavy laden, and I will give you rest." The Hindu, like the publican of old, sometimes wearies of the burden of his idolatrous rites, and sighs for a more spiritual object of reverence. The Moslem is sustained by an arrogant, undoubting satisfaction in his prophet and in himself.

The impediments to Moslem conversion would doubtless yield before a serious comparison of the Koran with the Bible, and of the history and character of Mohammed with the human life of Jesus Christ. If Mussulmans could be induced to such a comparison, it would be seen how ignorant was the author of their much-vaunted "book" of the older and wiser Scriptures which he so rashly condemned, and how inferior in nature, office, and holiness, to the Son of man. The immaculate character of Jesus Christ is confessed in the Koran itself. He is even acknowledged as the future Judge of men. A further acquaintance with his mission and work of righteousness would leave no room for any subsequent prophet; and the exposure of Mohammed's error with respect to the promised Comforter, together with his admitted misapprehension of the doctrine of the Holy Trinity, might go far to remove the prejudice which now operates in the Mussulman mind. It might then appear that all, and more than all, which they so fondly assign to the son of Abdallah, had already been accomplished for the restoration of the true faith, and the salvation of mankind, by another and a higher Messenger. It might even be thought that had he been acquainted with the true gospel, instead of an apocryphal forgery, the teacher of Mecca might himself have been persuaded to become a Christian.

It is deeply to be deplored that Christianity should have been presented to the mind of Mohammed, and of so many of his disciples, in connexion with rites and traditions hardly to be distinguished from idolatry, and which accordingly provoked the contempt and indignation of those ardent monotheists. Could the Bible, in its simple integrity, be submitted to a dispassionate perusal, an intelligent Mussulman could hardly fail to discern its superiority to the Koran, considered as a "*book*" or that authentic record of Revelation which he justly requires as the basis and standard of faith. Nor could he avoid the conviction that the great doctrines, which it is the merit of Islam to have rescued from the corruptions of tradition, are far more clearly and powerfully enforced in the gospel. The unity and spirituality of God are taught with equal energy and a loftier purity; the vanity of idols, and all merely external rites, is exposed with a zeal which leaves nothing wanting; while faith and prayer, and resignation and love, are insisted upon in terms which no Mussulman can surpass or equal, as the reasonable service of a rational and immortal creature.

Over all, too, the gospel sheds a light which Islam has not attained to, in the revelation of sin, and its sufficient remedy, the atoning blood of the Redeemer, followed by the gift of the Holy Spirit for the regeneration of the heart. These great evangelical truths of justification and sanctification soar far above all the teaching of Mohammed. Without yielding to the Mussulman in the assertion of the Divine sovereignty, they proclaim, what he is ignorant of, that "God is LOVE." They would subdue the world by persuasion, not by force. Armed with no carnal weapon, but with the sword of the Spirit, the Gospel Herald addresses all nations with a nobler and more victorious truth than the battle cry of the Moslem—"There is one God, and one Mediator between God and men, the man Christ Jesus."

CHAPTER VI.

POLITICAL GOVERNMENT.

Influence of government—Former despotisms—Constant war—Ignorance of representative institutions—Arbitrary power—Injury to native character —No political virtues or qualifications—British government—Public employ—Native army—Pay—Native officers—Advantages of the service —Military character — Mutiny —Disloyalty of caste—Native aristocracy —Tenure of land — Villages — Cultivation of lands — Tanks — Jungle — Municipal system— Crown rights — Property of the soil — Permanent assessment—Ryotwar—Village system—Regulations—General indigence —Police — Madras collections — Elastic system in the North-Western provinces—Questions of title—Popular preferences—Administration of justice—Native system—Dewannee—Nizamut—Supreme court of Judicature—Company's courts—Litigiousness of natives—Judicial integrity— Perjury—Punchayets—Indifference to the law—Connexion with religion —Patronage of idolatry—Home reprobation—Despatch of Mr. C. Grant —Cessation of the system—Difficulties of government—Spirit of the public servants.

NEXT to the traditions of religion and the pride of race, the character of a people is determined by the form of government under which they live. In this respect the Oriental mind has seldom risen above the savage simplicity of pure despotism. No other form evokes the sympathies, or has apparently entered into the imagination, of the natives of India, whether Hindu or Mohammedan. Their history presents nothing but a ceaseless succession of absolute monarchies, ranging from petty states to great empires, but all uniformly *absolute*. Local customs, and the influence of religion, served to protect particular interests from violence, but the subject neither enjoyed nor aspired to the smallest share in the political government. This indisputable truth compels us to receive with distrust the panegyrics both of Hindu and Mussulman writers on the empires of former days. It is certain that India never possessed a government which was administered with any reference to the wishes of the people; nor, till the rise of the British power, was any considerable portion of it united under a ruler strong enough to protect the subject against foreign outrage and internal discord. The earliest period exhibits a vast number of petty rajas continually at war with each other. The larger empires of later times were the results of military conquest, submitted to with reluctance, and continually disturbed by insurrection. Such circumstances are not only incompatible with the existence of public liberties; they do not admit of security to private property, honour, or life itself.

Of course a people so governed can have no political institutions. Physical force supplies their only foundation of law; and morality, public and private, is reduced to the lowest ebb. The civilization attainable under such disadvantages must, of necessity, be partial and deceptive. Still there is reason to think that both Hindus and Mohammedans were once possessed of qualities which have disappeared in their ill-assorted political association. The virtues which won the admiration of Alexander the Great, and those which shed lustre round the throne of Akbar, would now be sought for in vain among any of the peoples or princes of India.

The deterioration is largely to be ascribed to the absence of political institutions; a defect which still operates to defeat the wishes of more benevolent rulers. The one idea of government common to Hindu and Mussulman is power, and that of the elemental kind described in the poet's "good old rule"—

> "The simple plan,
> That they should take who have the power,
> And they should keep who can."

Of anything like *representative* assemblies, or constitutional law, no idea exists beyond the village communities and caste meetings, to which the direction of social life seems to be confided. No tribunal ever had power to try the title of a landed proprietor who rode with a score of spears at his back. The king himself governed only by force of arms; his law was respected in proportion to the power at hand to uphold it. The restraints of custom and religion were themselves dependent on the conscience of the strong hand. In the Puranas, the Kshettriya raja continually alleges his "right divine to govern wrong;" and the foundations of Islam lay a sacred obligation on the Mussulman prince to pillage and enslave the unbeliever. A very different estimate of right and wrong exists among communities where the public voice is heard in the exercise of government, and every individual asserts an interest in the execution of the law.

This universal prevalence of despotic power, combined with frequent subjugation to foreign conquest, could not but exercise a disastrous influence on the native character. The Hindus were admired by the Greeks for their veracity, and the Moslem of other lands is too proud to stoop to a lie; but, in India, deceit and perjury have long been the familiar *opprobria* of both. These are the vices of men who have lost at once confidence and self-respect: they have been generated in one class by the long struggle against an odious and intolerant usurpation, and in the other by a contempt and hatred of the idolater, akin to the doctrine that no faith is to be kept with heretics.

As for public morality, it may be fairly said to be unknown in India. To the native the state is simply a master exacting all that can be obtained, the community a slave pledged to never-ceasing resistance or evasion. It matters little what the impost is demanded for: the tax-payer contributes nothing that he can withhold; and when compelled to pay, cares nothing for the application of the spoil. The possession of office is so avowedly sought as a source of private emolument, that its tenure is thought a property rather than a trust, and is made the subject of contract and inheritance, like any other estate. Public works may be admired as proofs of power and wealth, or commended as generous additions to popular convenience; but the people neither consult for their erection, nor willingly contribute the smallest coin to their cost. Good laws are preferred to bad ones; but the natives, instead of aiming to bring the law into accordance with the public good by seeking a share in the legislation, prefer to fall back on a private resistance to all ordinances whatsoever.

A condition of society so absolutely destitute of political qualities and aspirations is almost unintelligible in England, where the desire is unceasingly cherished to impart her own franchises to her subject millions in the East. The apathy which refuses to appreciate such a gift seems to her as revolting as the ingratitude which attends every endeavour to bestow it. But public liberties can only rise on historical foundations, and history cannot be created at pleasure. In lacking the tradition of political rights, the natives lack the first qualification for their exercise. Divided among races, languages, and classes, owning little or no common intercourse, India is so far from demanding national liberties that she has not yet realized a national unity. A powerful government she both understands and needs; but the power must be wielded, not in deference to a public opinion which has no existence among the natives, but under the sanction of the ruler's own conscience and moral responsibilities. The Indian administration must be content to discharge its trust to the crown and parliament of the empire: it will long be in vain to expect the co-operation of the natives, or even a general appreciation of the advantages they enjoy from British dominion.

To this entire absence of political institutions must be ascribed the facility with which India has ever been made the prey of foreign conquerors. The Hindu population is broken up into a number of local communities, satisfied to preserve their social and family relations, and bowing without difficulty to any sceptre that, from time to time, may be extended over them. Their relations to the crown are like those of tributary states to an emperor, more than of a nation to its sovereign.

It would be a mistake, however, to infer that the constitution and action of government are matters of indifference to the natives: on the contrary, they are more deeply interested in their rulers than any people of Europe. The want of political institutions throws the administration of public affairs wholly on the government officers; and the nature of Indian society further subjects an enormous amount of the population to their immediate orders. A large number are in the *service* of government, civil or military; the *land-tenure* places almost all the agricultural classes in the condition of crown tenants; all are directly and peculiarly affected by the administration of *law and justice;* while the most extensive interests are connected with the state patronage of *religion*, and with its system of *education*. The last kind of action is peculiar to the British government, and will be considered in a subsequent chapter devoted to the state of knowledge and education in India. The others have been inherited from the native administrations, and are universally regarded in the East as constituting the natural and necessary relations of the ruler with the ruled; they will accordingly be noticed in this place, and in the order above stated.

1. The Oriental mind regards the state as preeminently the fountain of honour; and its service is the most coveted, as well as the most lucrative, profession. The ambition to enter it has always in India outweighed every objection of race, rank, and religion itself. The Hindu rajas freely employed Mussulman officers to command and discipline their troops; and the most intolerant of the Mohammedan usurpers have never refused the services of Hindu financiers to regulate their exchequer. The same indiscriminate mixture is still found in the service of the Native States, where, as of old, a mechanic may aspire to be elevated to the head of the administration, or a trooper win his way to the topmost step of the throne. Under the British government the adventurer can no longer dream of so brilliant a career.

The principal offices—all in which power might be abused to private ends—are intrusted to European holders: still in British India the passion for public employ continues unabated and insatiable. Large numbers find occupation in the lower grades of the civil establishments: of late years natives have been admitted to offices of trust, with greatly augmented salaries, in the judicial and revenue departments: the introduction of railways and the electric telegraph has provided places for many more. The determination had been long announced to open the avenues to still higher distinctions, as candidates should be found qualified by education, when the late disastrous mutiny shook the foundations of European confidence, and proportionally impaired the prospects of native employment.

It was in the military department, that the British government had reposed the largest and most generous confidence in the faith and good feeling of its native subjects. At the outbreak of the Bengal insurrection, as many as 200,000 natives were serving in the East India Company's army. The service was entered by enlistment as private soldiers or *sepoys* (from the Persian *sipahee*), and promotion was offered by seniority and merit to the ranks of non-commissioned and commissioned officers. The pay of a sepoy varies from fourteen to eighteen shillings a month in the infantry, and is somewhat higher in the artillery and cavalry. The highest native officer, bearing the designation of *subadar major*, receives from ten to twelve pounds a month in pay and allowances. The lower grades, enjoying proportionate allowances, are *subadars* and *jemadars* (who rank with captains and subalterns), and *havildars* and *naiks*, equivalent to sergeants and corporals.*

The native commissioned officers enjoy relative rank with the European in private intercourse, and sit with equal authority on native courts-martial; but on parade and in the field the youngest ensign is entitled to command them. The rank was instituted to be a link between the sepoys and their European commanders; but the native officers having all risen from the ranks, where their relations are still serving, are naturally found to sympathize exclusively with the men. Their relations with the European officers are artificial and constrained. If some professional ambition is kindled by promotion, it is again damped and fretted by their unavoidable subjection to the dominant race. Little advantage, therefore, has been experienced from their good offices

* The rates of pay are as follows:—

	Pay per Month. Rupees.	Half Batta. Rs.	Full Batta. Rs.
Cavalry.			
Subadar Major	85	20	40
Subadar	60	20	40
Jemadar	24	8	16
Havildar	15	5	10
Naik	12	4	8
Trooper according to service	9½, 8½, 7½	1½	3
Infantry.			
Subadar Major	77	15	30
Subadar	52	15	30
Jemadar	17	7½	15
Havildar	9	5	10
Naik	7	5	10
Sepoy...	7½, 6½, 5½	1½	3

Full batta is drawn, in addition to the pay, when serving at stations more than two hundred miles distant from the presidency town. Half batta at all other stations.

in reconciling differences, or revealing conspiracy. In great emergencies they have usually failed altogether. During the recent disturbances, the native officers were almost invariably in the councils of the sepoys, and the instances were but few in which they apprised their European superiors, in time even to escape with their lives.

The rates of pay before mentioned may appear small in England, where the cost of living, and the remuneration of labour, are about six times as high as in India; but the lowest which a sepoy receives is double the usual wages of a day-labourer; and his position, as compared with the rest of the population, is in every respect far superior to that of a private soldier in any country of Europe. The profession is honourable, the pay more than equal to their wants, the treatment indulgent; and what is more valued than all, pensions on a liberal scale are enjoyed by all grades after serving their periods with fidelity.

The estimation in which the service is held is proved by the natives themselves. Recruits are never wanting; the old sepoys, on the contrary, procured their own sons to be enlisted to an extent which, in many corps, had created a kind of family party sometimes difficult to manage. Discharge is so severe a penalty that it has been deemed safe to abolish corporal punishment altogether, and the sepoy has long been exempt from a degradation still inflicted on the British soldier.

The employment of a native soldiery is as old as the British dominion in India. Clive, Lawrence, Munro, and Coote, won their victories mainly by their co-operation, and all the subsequent triumphs of British arms in the East were largely indebted to the same assistance. Their exploits in the field are second only in renown to the foremost that adorn our military annals, while in garrison their general steadiness and tractability have earned them a confidence, which must now be adjudged to have been too generous and unsuspecting. These military good qualities were ever mixed with a disposition to mutiny, imperilling from time to time the very existence of government. The history of native states is one continuous chronicle of military insubordination and outrage. Ill-clothed and unpaid, the army was a source of constant terror both to the prince and the subject; at one moment threatening the overthrow of the throne, at another seeking to recover their arrears of pay by plundering a village. A soldier was a common marauder; the peasantry hid themselves at his approach, or, cautiously combining, shot him down from their ambush like a beast of prey.

Excesses of this sort quickly vanished under British discipline, aided by its punctuality in payments and general good faith. But the tendency to mutiny is not easily eradicated in troops so absolutely mercenary as those of India. Our earliest successes in Hindustan were interrupted by it in the field itself, and at a later period the mutiny at Vellore shook the government to its foundations. Symptoms of the same spirit had long been notorious in the army of Bengal, and though from time to time overlooked or indulged, it could not be appeased till it had kindled the flames of civil war over Upper India, and alarmed the world for the civilization of the East.

This disposition is perhaps inseparable from the existence of *military castes*,—men who place their honour and existence in fighting, and acknowledge neither conscience nor patriotism in choosing their side. These hereditary and professional soldiers are numerous in India; they comprise most of the Rajpoots, a considerable number of Brahman and Mahratta families, and all the more adventurous portion of the Mussulman population. Like other mercenaries, these men acknowledge the professional law of honour, so far as to fight faithfully for the master that pays liberally; in Oriental language, they boast themselves "*true to their salt.*" But this fidelity disappears in questions of caste and religion. Neither Hindu nor Mussulman allegiance is proof against the suspicion of interference with the faith: consequently, this is always the cry which a conspirator endeavours to excite.

The British government had become so aware of the danger impending from this quarter, that regulations were made to limit the recruiting from the higher castes, to a manageable proportion in every regiment; but these precautions were too much disregarded, from indulgence towards the family predilections of the older sepoys. Such, too, was the confidence still reposed in these troops, that single regiments were scattered about in isolated stations, where the lives of the officers lay absolutely at the mercy of the men. The artillery, also, formerly composed exclusively of Europeans, was largely intrusted to native gunners, while the proportion of European troops was at the same time suffered to decrease.

These palpable errors will doubtless be guarded against in future. The British government will not again allow itself to be surprised in the unreadiness of a weak and misplaced confidence. But every precaution will prove in vain, if the system of caste be allowed to taint the recruiting, and undermine the discipline, of the native regiments. A service so justly popular stands in no need of the patronage of Brahmans or Rajpoots. Millions of the lower castes, men such as won all the great victories in the south, are ready to crowd into its ranks, though the Brahmans should retire to their temples and solitary meditations, and the Rajpoot go to nurture his hereditary turbulence in the service of some native prince, who may be willing to pay a gentleman for neglecting, instead of performing, the duties of a soldier. The British army would lose nothing from the exchange, save the anxiety of watching and controlling a disaffected soldiery. The truth, however, is, that there would be no secession. No affront need be offered to the pretensions we decline to encourage: all castes may be equally and impartially admitted, and the best soldiers will always receive the preference. What is needed is to place the test of superiority in the better discharge of military duties, not in the curiosities of a pedigree, or the ceremonial of cooking.

An important feature in the regular native army, is that it is wholly drawn from the lower classes of society,* natives of rank and wealth being excluded by the necessity of enlisting as private sepoys. In former times this was otherwise; the native gentleman obtained his commission at once as a subadar, and brought his recruits with him, marshalled under his own banner. The commandant and adjutant of the corps only were European officers; the rest fought under their direction, and won promotion from their approval. The chiefs and warlike spirits of

* *Caste* is, of course, not to be confounded with *class:* a peasant may enjoy distinctions on the former score, which chiefs and princes will readily acknowledge as superior to their own.

the land had then an interest in British ascendancy, from which they have been too much excluded by the subsequent progress of military organization. The "Irregular Corps" are still officered on the former plan, and the higher natives gladly take service in them as of old. But, no doubt, the greatest defect in the military, as in the civil establishments of the British, is that so few openings are left for the native aristocracy.

It is true that this term bears a very different meaning in India and in Europe. The dissimilar structure of society, and the confusion resulting from repeated conquest and revolution, leave no classes there resembling the landed proprietors, or professional gentry, of our own country. The titles, even of reigning princes, would hardly bear judicial investigation, while hundreds of displaced and discontented chieftains have simply lost by the strong hand, what nothing but the strong hand acquired. Neither does native society exhibit those wide distinctions of education, breeding, and social habits, which render the descent to a lower class so painful in Europe.

Still the country abounds with those who consider themselves, and are considered by others, as entitled to lead in their respective spheres. Descendants from fallen princes and chiefs, — representatives of old families,—(even old *intruders* acquire a title to Hindu respect)—children of high government officials,—with hundreds more, to whom various accidents contribute to give importance, feel themselves precluded from entering the army as sepoys, or the civil service as clerks. Neither do they often possess the education which would stand them in stead at a competitive examination. These classes find their only field of action in the dominion of the native princes; they are discontented and declining under British rule. The latter is felt to be everywhere unfavourable to this portion of society, and the point is worthy of being weighed, notwithstanding the benefits undoubtedly conferred on the labouring and commercial classes, who form the bulk of the population. The evil may be alleviated by judicious regulations, but it is perhaps without a cure in the total absence of political institutions.

2. The next particular in which the government sustains peculiar and extensive relations towards the people, is connected with the tenure of the land, and the collection of the revenue arising from it. Of personal property there is but little, and that in the simple forms of jewels, bullion, and coin. The large funded investments arising, in European nations, from manufacturing and commercial wealth have only begun to exist under British rule, and are limited to a few moneyed individuals. The mass of the people, including all the gentry and upper orders of society, are sustained from the land; the ownership of which gives rise to what in India approximates the nearest to a political institution.

The soil is owned and occupied on quite a different system from any now known in Europe; and the lifference shows itself on the face of the landscape. No manor residences, farm-houses, or rustic cottages, impart variety to the scene. The whole rural population is lodged in villages, often enclosed by walls strong enough to resist the predatory horse which scoured the country under the native governments. Every village is surrounded by its belt of cultivated land, the amount of which is regulated principally by the supply of water. On the banks of rivers, the villages are numerous and near together; further off, they are seated on natural lakes, or on artificial reservoirs termed *tanks*, made by enclosing the valleys with a mound or *bund*, which causes the waters to accumulate in its rear. These bunds are fitted with sluices for the irrigation of the lands below. The construction of such tanks, with one or two main roads, composed the chief public works of former princes, and the government is still charged with their repair. In some parts there are chains of tanks at intervals of eight or ten miles, which successively receive the water from the irrigated lands above, and re-distribute it on the lower levels.

Land without a permanent supply of water is necessarily unproductive, the rains being confined to particular seasons. Such land the natives term *jungle*, a term applied not only to forests, but to the open uncultivated waste. Millions of acres lie thus barren and unreclaimed, which by irrigation and labour might be converted into fruitful fields.

The cultivated lands are not divided into separate estates or farms. A portion is assigned to the village officials, and the remainder belong to a common proprietary. Every inhabitant of the village is not of necessity a member of the proprietary body, which is confined to the original settlers, or their representatives, called *meerasdars*. Other families have been associated in the village, sometimes as tenants of particular portions, sometimes as hired labourers; and, according to the genius of all Hindu proceedings, both these classes acquire rights of continuance and descent, so long as they perform their respective duties. The rights of all parties are registered by the village accountant (or *curnum*), and the crops being secured distribution is made to each according to his share.

The village is presided over by a headman (or *potail*) with a kind of magisterial authority. Separate freeholds, with some advantage in the general partition, are assigned to him and to the other village officers, in order to secure the continuance of at least one family pursuing the vocations requisite to the little society. These are usually the *headman*, *accountant*, *Brahman priest and schoolmaster*, *astrologer*, *silversmith and money-changer*, *barber and surgeon*, *smith*, *carpenter*, *potter*, *washerman*, *tailor*, and especially the *watchman*, who is often (as before observed) of aboriginal descent. Some villages include a *minstrel* or genealogist, and some a functionary to regulate the distribution of water for irrigation. The little community, thus complete in itself, forms a sort of republican municipality, transacting its affairs with the state government through the headman and accountant, and levying in the village senate the necessary rates for the pagoda, the sacrifices, walls, feasts, and charities. The property is all strictly entailed: no individual can alienate his share, even with the general consent, and wills are unknown.

By native theory, land not settled belongs to the crown, but, once reduced into a township, the right of the sovereign merges into a claim on the produce, which, combining the characters of a *tax* and a *rent*, has been spoken of under both appellations. The proportion to be taken by the crown is placed in the Institutes of Manu as low as an eighth, a sixth, or a twelfth, to be determined (say the commentators) by the difference in the soil and the labour required for its cultivation. It is added, however, that a military king, in time of war or other necessity, commits no sin in requiring a *fourth*. A sixth would appear to have become the ordinary proportion under the Hindu princes. The Mussulman government exacted a half, or even more, in fact assuming the *property* along with the *sovereignty* of the land, and dividing the produce with the actual cultivator.

The rights of the sovereign were often leased to a farmer-general, or granted, in particular districts, either in perpetuity or for a term, in reward of distinguished services. This kind of grant is called *enam*, and the person who holds it an *enamdar*. All such assignments of the government revenue were legally without prejudice to the rights of the villagers. They simply paid to the lessee or grantee of the crown what before they were bound to pay to the crown. The contracts and grants were often varied or resumed: still the villagers insisted upon their rights, though too often unable to realize them against the strong hand of the superior.

Upon this theory, which is supposed to have been once of universal application, the *fee* of the land must be held to rest in the *meerasdars*, or village proprietary, subject on the one hand to the demand of the lord, and on the other to the wages of the cultivator. The Moslem, however, finding himself limited by no definite law or usage of sufficient strength, often augmented his demand so as to sweep off all that remained after paying the expenses of cultivation. By means, too, of under-leases granted to rapacious middlemen, the share of the *ryot* was often reduced to a sixth, and seldom exceeded a fifth, of the produce. Often the labourer himself was left destitute, and the whole population took to the jungle, leaving the fields uncultivated.

From the operation of these abuses, the proprietary body, as distinguished from the labourer, had in many parts disappeared, and the produce was shared between the actual cultivator and the government, or those who represented it, including the various personages designated *zemindars*, *talookdars*, *enamdars*, etc. Some of these were ancient Hindu rajas or chiefs, whom the Mohammedans left in possession of the revenues, imposing on them a certain tribute to the emperor. Others were simply farmers of the revenue at a specified sum, whose contracts, like everything else in India, became hereditary. Others, again, held assignments of the revenue arising from particular districts, and others had possessed themselves of some of these claims by purchase, or more often by forcible entry, in place of the original holders. These are the classes which in India correspond to the nobility and gentry of Europe, and are popularly styled land-owners. They have no legal title to the *occupation* of the soil, which belongs to the village. On the other hand, they have *power* to augment the assessment, so as to drive out the cultivators in despair, and substitute others in their place. Still the natives seldom lose sight of their rights, and after long evictions they return in better times to claim their restoration.

Such was the general state of the land when the British came into the sovereignty of the provinces of Bengal, Behar, and Orissa. The contending claims of the government, the zemindar, and the *ryot* (or cultivator), were warmly disputed in oblivion of the true owners, the village proprietary. It was determined by lord Cornwallis to establish a permanent assessment on behalf of the government, and, subject to this payment, to recognise the *zemindar* as the proprietor of the district over which his agency extended. In further accordance with European ideas, powers of sale and ejectment were granted to the new landlords, by which the whole agricultural population was reduced to the position of tenants and labourers. The force of custom has imposed many restraints on these powers: still the Permanent Assessment unconsciously effected a greater change of property than any conquest or change of sovereignty that ever passed over these provinces.

At a later period the inquiry was taken up by sir Thomas Munro in the south, where Mohammedan usurpation had been less effectual in obliterating the ancient Hindu institutions. It was then perceived that rights existed in the ryots, which had been overlooked in Bengal; and the conclusion was arrived at that the government officers should deal with these, on the footing of tenants holding immediately of the crown, which was still conceived to be possessed of the fee.

More recently still, the village system has been revived in its integrity in the North-Western provinces, and the ownership of settled lands is there generally acknowledged to reside in the representatives of the ancient proprietary.

The question thus diversely determined would be of comparatively little practical import, and the land revenue might be indifferently termed a tax or a rent, if the government share could be accurately defined, and the villagers protected in the enjoyment of their own. But the division being always uncertain, the rights of all parties depend on the title to the *fee*. If the sovereign be also the proprietor, the produce is only liable to the wages of the labourer and the charges of collection: all the surplus belongs to the public exchequer. If the zemindar is to be held as landlord, the surplus is his, subject to the payment of the taxes. If the villagers, or any class of them, are the true freeholders, then the zemindar can only represent the government, and the claims of both ought to be included in an equitable tax.

These were questions very difficult to settle, and which have been actually settled differently in different parts. On their settlement, however, depended the proportion to be levied as land revenue by the British government. A committee of the House of Commons in 1810 assumed *three-fifths* as the proper share of the produce, and that, moreover, in money payments; whereas the old Hindu rajas took it in *kind*. This assumption was justified only by the fact that a much larger proportion had been often exacted by the zemindars or their lessees, while money payments had become the common usage under Mohammedan rule. But these excesses of power had not then been sufficiently compared with previous rights and customs.

The permanent settlement of Bengal, made upon these faulty principles, is now generally admitted to have effected much injustice. The attempt to create a landed order out of the revenue agency has signally failed. The zemindars have become ruinously entangled and insolvent, while the cultivators are represented as oppressed and impoverished. The loss of revenue to the state, too, is considerable; but *that* was deliberately incurred in view of the other advantages anticipated from the settlement.

Such is the general testimony of writers acquainted with the present condition of those provinces. On the other hand, the principle of lord Cornwallis' arrangement is not without its defenders, and it may reasonably be questioned whether *all* the evils now complained of are fairly to be laid at its door. The difficulties of the zemindars seem to have arisen more from the complicated system of law and jurisprudence introduced at the same time, than from the revenue settlement itself. The latter may have been placed too high: but it was undoubtedly a remission of the burdens sustained under former governments; and it is hard to reconcile the manifestly increased production of these provinces with a state of fiscal oppression and ruin. Other causes, too, can be assigned for the prevailing indigence. The natural increase of an Asiatic population, when not arrested by war or famine, is enormous; the openings for new kinds of employment are few, and no relief is afforded by emigration. In such circumstances a state approximating to general pauperism would seem almost inevitable. It is promoted by the very excellence of the government, which preserves in tranquillity a population whose religion and habits stimulate its growth, while they close up the avenues of enterprise and improvement.

Another share of the evils charged on the revenue settlement are plainly due to the defectiveness of the *police*. Under the native system every village had its watchmen, whose fidelity and practical habits rendered them a very tolerable rural constabulary. These are now often overborne by the retainers of the zemindar —ruffians armed with bludgeons called *latties*, who not unfrequently perpetrate the grossest outrages on the defenceless peasantry. This state of things has long been a reproach to the British government; it is now about to be rectified by the formation of a military police for service in the lower provinces. Ten corps of infantry, commanded by military officers, and amounting to upwards of 10,000 men, have already been sanctioned, and it is further proposed to attach 100 *sowars* (or native horsemen) to each police battalion. The condition of society may be imagined when in our oldest provinces such a force is found necessary to "resist armed aggression and afford protection to the peaceably disposed against outrage and violence." *

It can hardly be expected, however, that any reforms in the police or the revenue can preserve a vast population from sinking to the lowest level of subsistence, so long as it is chained to the paternal soil, and debarred from all internal improvement by the restrictions of Hindu religion and caste. Similar complaints are heard in the presidency of Madras, where the revenue settlement was conducted on the exactly opposite principle. There the collector treats with the cultivator direct, on the principle of allowing him the fair costs and wages of cultivation, and carrying the surplus rent to the government exchequer. Annual journeys are taken for the inspection of the lands, and the receipt of the revenue. Advances are made for the purchase of seed, and remissions liberally granted on the score of droughts or unexpected calamities.

Still the rent audit (called *jummabundy*) is invariably a kind of civil war between the government officer and the ryots. The former takes the field attended by an army of *peons*, whose business it is to meet and expose the false accounts anticipated

* Despatch of lord Stanley, March 9th, 1859.

from the tenants. The latter, on their part, are inexhaustible in mendacity. The rains have been too heavy or too light; the tanks have burst or dried up; the ground has gone mysteriously wrong; the god has been displeased; the crops are an utter failure; the village was never so poor. Sometimes the government survey is affirmed to be imaginary; there are no such lands in existence; or they are smaller and poorer than is laid down. These allegations are supported by "witnesses" in abundance, and no form of adjuration is too sacred to be had recourse to.

This testimony is met by the collector's peons with equal boldness of asseveration. The seasons were excellent, the waters abundant, the crops above the average, the fields larger and better than was supposed, and the *jumma* ridiculously light: the "collector sahib" ought to *increase it* on the spot. When the excitement of the game rises to a boiling heat, some too zealous peon extemporizes a little torture, after the native fashion. The village delegate is placed in the sun with a weight on his head, or ingeniously pinched between slips of bamboo, to bring him to reason. The point of honour on his part is to stand out to the last; and after a conflict, of which the European officer seldom knows more than the duel of words which is fought in his presence, a sum is decided upon, which usually leaves the ryots more or less victorious. Still there can be no doubt that the agricultural population of Madras, as at Bengal, is everywhere in a state of extreme poverty, and the revenue exacted cannot but be considered excessive when contrasted with the miserable condition of those who pay it. A new survey and re-assessment were ordered by the Court of Directors in 1856, and the work is expected to be completed in *fourteen years*.

The North-Western provinces are thought to exhibit more hopeful results, and it is obvious that an arrangement, which leaves a surplus in the hands of a local proprietary, presents a better prospect of social improvement than either the *zemindary* or the *ryotwar* settlements. The more recent arrangements have the further merit of not attempting too much. The pedantry of system has been avoided: existing usage is accepted as the basis of the settlement in each locality, and the temptations of theory are postponed to the facts of the case. A similar system—or a similar happy want of system—is observed in the territories placed under commissioners; as the Punjab, Berar, Mysore, Tennasserim, and the later acquisitions of Pegu and Oude. This form of administration being confessedly provisional, it is committed either to civil or military officers, according to personal qualities more than official claims. It thus combines the two elements of popular usage and administrative energy; and being unfettered with rules (too often adopted on crude and insufficient reasoning), it is at liberty to develop the local resources to the greatest advantage. The elasticity of this loose and ready administration adapts it to the condition of our rule and the tastes of the people; and it might have been better for the whole empire, if parts of it had been longer retained under some such transitional and tentative arrangements.

The chief error committed under this system seems to have arisen (like so many of our administrative faults) from the English propensity to be "righteous over much." The discovery of rights long unjustly suppressed, gives birth to a zeal for investigating *titles*, in the spirit of European rather than of Oriental justice. Inquiries have been instituted into assignments of revenue held or claimed in *enam*, and have resulted in their resumption by government, to an extent which has roused the apprehensions of the whole class to which the deprived parties belong. The alarm and indignation generated in the minds of the talookdars of Oude by the indiscriminate proposal to restore the *meerasdars*, were doubtless the chief causes of the opposition lately experienced in that province.

Those persons were well aware how little any of their claims could abide the test of a legal investigation; but what is more surprising is, that these robber chiefs actually retain the support of the very classes whom the reform was intended to benefit. The peasantry desire the residence of "great men" among them, with all the oppression and spoliation incident to their unbridled tyranny, in preference to the dead level and monotonous indigence which follow the British rule. When sir W. Sleeman made a tour through Oude, under the government of the late king, scenes of robbery and torture were disclosed, which seemed to cry not only for the transfer of the sovereignty, but for the extermination of the local chiefs, who were spreading terror through their respective districts. Nevertheless, the cultivators, who had fled into the nearest British district, were found returning after awhile to their homes, determined to take their chance with the local oppressor, rather than bear the yoke of an uniform law, foreign to their habits, and administered by courts whose procedure was a mystery and a dread. Bad as the "regulations" are admitted to be, it is reasonable to suppose that other considerations entered into this resolve; and none is more probable than that, with all the suffering under native misrule, the chances of individual improvement, and the natural desire for a resident aristocracy, outweigh the more civilized, but less appreciated, advantages of order and law.

A sufficient remedy for the evils pointed out would hardly be found in a general remission or reduction of the revenue. Higher assessments were borne with less reluctance under the native and Mohammedan governments, and, with the exception of a property tax on all classes, no substitute could be easily suggested for any extensive reduction of the land revenue. Possibly, the soundest reform might be some scheme for its redemption, on the principle observed with the land-tax in England. A combination of this principle with that of the Encumbered Estates Act in Ireland might possibly result in the establishment of a real and efficient landed proprietary, capable at once of sustaining the government and protecting the population.

3. A third department, in which the political government acts with a peculiar effect on the natives of India, is in the administration of justice and law. The native system recognised a two-fold jurisdiction, corresponding to a frequent partition in the general administration of government. The management of the revenue was entrusted to a high officer, called the *dewan*, while the other functions of government were administered by another, termed *nazim* or *nizam*. Each of these viceroys exercised judicial as well as executive authority in his department: the

dewan had his courts of revenue jurisdiction, and the nazim his tribunal of criminal justice.*

This distinction was transferred to the British judicature, whose authority first arose from the grant of the *dewannee* in the provinces of Bengal, Bahar, and Orissa. That authority necessitated the establishment of courts, in the name of the East India Company, for the exercise of revenue jurisdiction. The nawab, or subadar, remaining as *nazim* at the head of criminal justice, should have held his own Court of *Nizamut* accordingly; but his authority quickly became so purely nominal, that Warren Hastings established criminal courts without consulting him, and placed them, like those of the dewannee, under the administration of Company's servants.

Soon after, to correct the evils of these imperfect tribunals, the British Parliament established by their side a Supreme Court of Judicature at each of the presidency towns, armed with the usual powers of the superior courts of law and equity at Westminster, but invested with no powers of appeal from the Company's courts. A double system of jurisdiction was thus called into existence—"the Queen's and the Company's;" and the anomaly has not disappeared with the extinction of the Company's authority. The original design of the Supreme Court was the protection of European residents, and it was constituted to administer British law under the national institution of a jury. The natives it seems to have been intended to leave to the courts of the country. The royal tribunals, however, would naturally extend their protection to all the subjects of the crown of England; and, after some

* Somewhat of the same distinction may perhaps be recognised in the titles of our own Courts of Exchequer and Queen's Bench.

collision with the Company's governments, their authority was established in all civil and criminal cases arising within the towns of Calcutta, Madras, and Bombay, as well as over Europeans generally throughout the *mofussil*, or inland parts. They were precluded, however, from interfering in revenue causes, as well as in other proceedings in the Company's courts; and it is presumed that the same restrictions continue since the abolition of the Company's authority. The judges of the Supreme Courts are appointed by the home government, from the English or Irish bar, and were wholly independent of the Company's governors: some change in their relations will probably ensue from the recent elevation of the latter into representatives of the crown.

For the present, the courts of the old Company continue in the peculiar position derived from their origin. They consist of a chief court of original jurisdiction and appeal at each presidency, with a number of inferior tribunals in the mofussil. The superior court is called the *Sudder Dewannee* and *Nizamut* (or *Foujdarree*) *Adawlut;* immediately below it are the "civil and session judges" in their respective circuits; and under these the "Zillah" (or district) Courts. The judges of the Sudder and Sessions Courts are members of the Indian civil service, appointed by the local governments; but the Zillah and inferior courts are commonly intrusted to native judges, styled *sudder ameens*, or *moonsiffs*. The exchequer jurisdiction being now conjoined with the civil and criminal, collectors of revenue exercise no higher functions in administering the law than those of magistrates. European police magistrates are appointed, in addition, at the presidencies and some other chief towns. The mofussil police is intrusted to native officials, under the orders of the sessions judge.

The Company's courts were erected on the principle of administering "native law," that is to say, the law of the parties in civil controversies, and the law of the government in criminal proceedings. So long as the fiction of the Mogul empire was acknowledged, the Koran was the principal authority for the latter; but its barbarous and unequal procedure was mitigated by a code of "Rules and Regulations" issued by lord Cornwallis, and augmented from time to time by orders of the different governments, till the year 1835, when a Legislative Council was established by Act of Parliament at Calcutta. This council, which possesses authority to legislate for British India with the force of an Act of Parliament, has continued to enlarge, without simplifying, the Anglo-Indian statute-book. Various attempts at codification have failed; and the result is, that the courts under the *aeen* and *kanoon* (rules and regulations) administer a confused medley of native, British, and government law, of which the best that can be said is, that it *aims* at dispensing Hindu law to the Hindu, and Mussulman to the Mussulman, correcting both by the milder and freer dictates of English jurisprudence.

Unfortunately, the execution has proved unequal to the design. The Rules and Regulations, intended to secure a simple and equitable procedure, have been found to labour under both the antagonist vices of bad legislation; they are at once too loose and too technical; at one time leaving justice open to audacious frauds, at another hampering her action by rules unfitted to native character and opinion. Swarms of *vakeels*, scribes, and lawyers, fill the courts, and not unfrequently possess themselves of the property in litigation. The English ideas of title, with the power of sale granted to a successful creditor, effect changes in landed property wholly irreconcilable with native feeling. When a zemindar sues his ryots, his first application is usually to his banker, or vakeel, to supply funds for the costs. Indolent and bewildered, the unhappy suitor at last sees his estate put up to sale, and the agent who had transacted his affairs, or accommodated him with a loan, declared its proprietor. Again, the Hindu law of equal succession, admitting no testamentary disposal, leads to extensive sub-divisions of land, or to joint-tenancy, on a scale which frequently reduces families, once accounted wealthy, to a state of impoverishment. Unwilling to forego their ancestral position, they resort to the native banker; a suit ensues, with sale and execution as a matter of course.

None of the parties thus ejected admit the justice of the process. The ousted proprietor almost invariably remains on the estate, a tenant in law, but in native opinion a robbed and injured man. The invader of an hereditary property, more especially the stranger who comes into co-parcenary with a family, never conciliates the native respect. A feeling of resentment and disloyalty is cherished against the government, by whose orders the injustice was perpetrated, and on the first political disturbance the attempt is made to restore the ancient rights by force. The extent to which these feelings prevailed during the recent disturbances has obliged the government to consider whether any remedy can be found in buying up the claims of the auction purchasers, and imposing some restraint on the sale of landed estates for the future.

With all this aversion to the operation of English law, the natives are not deterred from crowding the courts in vast numbers. Their character is astonishingly litigious: the rights of property are complex; and a cause is seldom abandoned till it has been carried through every stage of appeal, or the subject in dispute has disappeared in the costs. One great attraction is the incorruptibility of the judge. From the time of Solomon the reproach has attached to all Oriental tribunals of "taking a gift to pervert the ways of judgment."* In India a superior is never approached without a present "to make his face white." Kings must be mollified with *nuzzurs*, and the ordinary forms of salutation uniformly require a present. The practice was extended to the seat of judgment, even when occupied by the monarch in person. The European traveller admires the simplicity of eastern manners, where the monarch sits at the gate of his palace, and his subjects seek justice from the royal lips, with no impediment from technical pleadings or hired advocates. The Oriental knows there is another side to the picture. It is easy for a plaintiff to take the defendant by the girdle, crying, "Justice, mighty raja;"—easy for each to detail his story in the unadorned accents of native sincerity; but with the first word a courtier whispers into the royal ear the amount of the "present" received from one of the parties, and the judgment is determined at once. The defeated party, however, enjoys the privilege of repeating "the simple process" on the next audience day, when a larger bribe may reverse the judgment, and perhaps inflict chastisement on the adversary who dared to deceive his prince at

* Prov. xvii. 23.

the former hearing. It is only in the British judge that the natives discover the prodigy of an arbitrator who cannot be bribed. They dislike our institutions, stand aghast at our law, and despair over its intricate and defective procedure; but they estimate to the full the advantage of a just tribunal. Probably it is the judicial integrity, in conjunction with the pecuniary good faith of the British government, which form the strongest bulwarks of its power in India.

It must be acknowledged, however, that the example is admired more than followed among the various classes of natives connected with the administration of justice. Venality, the most unblushing, prevails alike among suitors, advocates, and witnesses. All the terrors of the Vedas and the Koran cannot impose an oath too sacred to be violated for a trifling gain. Lying is so little thought of, that the most opprobrious reproach to a European calls up no shame in the countenance of Mussulman or Hindu; and where men can smile at being detected in a lie, perjury is sure to be no uncommon or shameful offence.

The difference between native and European ideas of justice is strikingly illustrated in the procedure observed by the *punchayet*, an institution of the nature of a jury, which is often used with good effect in the determination of civil causes. It consists of five persons; but instead of being drawn like a jury by lot, and liable to be challenged on suspicion of partiality, two are named by the plaintiff, two by the defendant, and the fifth by the judge. This tribunal seldom fails to arrive at a satisfactory verdict; but it is often reached by discarding the evidence sworn to in court, and relying on some private, hearsay information picked up from other quarters.

With all his litigiousness in questions of civil and personal right, the native is utterly indifferent to the vindication of public law. Criminal prosecutions are resorted to, like civil actions, from personal and vindictive motives. But even a murder excites no thirst for pursuit and conviction, when the victim is of another family or caste. One of the difficulties experienced by the authorities in detecting and suppressing the atrocities of Thuggee, was the indisposition of the natives to give evidence. Notorious Thugs were allowed to reside unmolested in a village, on condition of carrying on their horrible trade at a distance, and even the corpses of murdered men, found in the fields, were privately got out of sight, in order to avoid the burden of a journey to the Sessions Court in support of a prosecution. The English practice of compelling persons to attend as witnesses, in a cause which does not concern their private interest, is considered an insupportable infliction by the natives. The want of political cohesion leaves them without public spirit or true patriotism, and the effect of caste is to dry up their sympathies with humanity. Hence the law is respected only as far as it can be wielded for self-interest; no government must expect native support any longer than it makes itself feared for its power, or valued for a present and tangible gain.

4. The patronage and direction of religion forms, according to native ideas, one of the most important functions of government. Hindu tradition makes it the glory of a prince to protect the Brahmans, and augment the splendour of the ceremonies. The Mussulman considers the church identical with the state, and invests the sultan with the entire control and responsibility of its religious duties. The ideas of

toleration and neutrality are not to be found in either the Vedas or the Koran, and the disciples of both never hesitated in the day of their power to impose their religious rites on the vanquished.

The British government has been so far from imitating the example of proclaiming its own religion, that it has been weakly and wrongfully induced to accept the functions of native governments in patronising and sustaining the heathen worship. A course so injurious to the interests both of the gospel and of civilization, could never have been entered upon with any deliberate foresight of the consequences: it has long been condemned by the unanimous voice of the Christian public, and is now so universally repudiated, that there is a difficulty in comprehending on what grounds it could ever have been justified or palliated.

It will be seen, however, from the account already given of the peculiar endowments bestowed on pagodas and mosques, that they almost necessarily entailed an intercourse with the political government unknown to the practice of Europe. The most common form of endowment was the assignment by government, or by those who held of it and represented it, of the whole, or a portion, of the land-revenue arising on a particular village or district. In the one case the district might be made over to the temple as to a zemindar or enamdar; in the other, the revenue was collected by the government officers, and the temple received its share from them. Another form of endowment was an annual grant of money, made by the government, for some charitable or religious purpose: these obligations were conceived to be inherited by the British along with the exchequer on which they were charged. Again, the *patronage*, or right of appointing the Brahmans and other ministers of the temple, naturally followed the endowment, and was either in the government itself, or the government was appealed to, to decide between rival claimants for the privilege. Other disputes, too, were of frequent occurrence. The Brahmans were charged with neglecting the duties for which the endowment was granted; or the peasantry withheld the customary services on which, it was alleged, their lands were held of the temple. All was brought to the English magistrate for redress, and, as in analogous abuses in the administration of native states, the attempt at reform often terminated in assumption and annexation. The European officer found it easier to administer the temple himself than to enforce their respective duties on the native officials. The Hindus, always leaning to government protection, were pleased rather than offended at the intrusion. It magnified the official character of their establishments, added to the dignity of the Brahmans, and afforded the worshippers a tribunal of appeal.

In this way the appointment of the priests and dancing-girls, the decoration of the temples, the performance of the sacrifices, the adorning of the idols, and even the manufacture of new ones, came to be conducted under the immediate orders of the Christian magistrate. The offerings at the idolatrous shrines were sold by his direction to the credit of the account. The collector attended, and made oblations in person for the benefit of the concern. All was conducted with the method and regularity of English business; and such was its superiority over native inefficiency and corruption, that a handsome surplus was realized from the estates, while the natives acknowledged that the ceremonies were never so gorgeously celebrated.

The native religions being thus taken under the patronage of the state, the collector was called on to supply all that was requisite for its observances. If the harvest was threatened with drought, his authority was issued for prayers and ceremonies to be made to the gods for rain. His own office was permitted to be the scene of idolatrous rites. His peons were active in procuring attendance at the festivals; and so gratifying was the position to the minds of some of these authorities, that they began to regard the Hindu rites with a tenderness approaching to veneration, and censured the zeal of the Christian missionary as an unjustifiable interference with the "national religion."

Foremost among those who enjoy the unenviable distinction of inaugurating this policy, was Mr. Lionel Place, the collector of the "Company's jaghire" at Madras. He found the great temple of Conjeveram under a management so corrupt and inefficient, that the ceremonies were neglected, and the buildings out of repair, while the funds were embezzled by the native officials. There seemed to be a danger that "the temple should be despised, and its magnificence be destroyed, which (in orthodox Hindu opinion) all Asia and the world worshippeth."* Mr. Place hastened to the succour of what he was pleased to denominate "the Established Church." He represented to government the inefficiency of the native "churchwardens," and the alarming condition of the "church funds." His report acknowledges that this pagoda had been hitherto independent of the government, but he considered their "interference and control"

* Acts xix. 27.

indispensable to the morals and happiness of their native subjects. His request being complied with, he assumed the management in 1796, and saluted the great idol with an offering of jewels, still exhibited at the temple, and said to be worth one thousand pounds. This Brahmanized collector was in the habit of personally attending the festivals, which he caused to be celebrated with extraordinary pomp, distributing presents to the Brahmans and dancing-girls with his own hand.

While the civil servants of government were thus openly abetting and partaking in the idolatries of the Hindus, the native army was thought to require concessions almost as dishonouring to British Christianity. As our dominion extended in Hindustan, and large numbers of Brahmans and Rajpoots were admitted into the ranks, a respect began to be shown for their usages, almost exceeding the demands of the natives themselves. Every "custom" was assumed to be religious, and entitled to protection; rights of conscience were invented for the Hindu before he claimed them himself; at last it was deemed essential to his religious liberty to compliment it with the sacrifice of Christian duty. Military officers stooped to gratify their sepoys by subscribing to, and attending, their idolatrous ceremonies. The government fired salutes, and sent their troops to do honour to the festivals of the idols, and the remonstrances of more consistent Christians brought down ridicule or displeasure from their superiors. In some instances actual persecution was inflicted.

It was long before the voice of Christian principle could make itself heard with sufficient force to procure the disallowance of this connexion with idolatrous usages on the part of men professing the gospel of Christ. The Indian governments and the Court of Directors justified it as the necessary and traditional policy of the East India Company. By the larger Court of Proprietors, and by the public in general, it was seen in a truer aspect. At last, lord Glenelg, when at the Board of Control, in 1824, despatched orders for its entire abandonment. Many of the practices complained of continued, however, to a later date, and, in 1837, the author was himself interrupted, during the celebration of the Holy Communion in the garrison church of Fort St. George, by the roar of the guns saluting an idolatrous festival.

These undue compliances have now happily ceased. Orders have been issued to prohibit the attendance of troops, and the intervention of civil officers, at religious festivals; the temples are made over to native trustees, and the doctrine is proclaimed that, in all which concerns their religious observances, the natives are to be left to themselves. The British government will not impede, but neither will it encourage, their belief or worship; it will no longer "touch the unclean thing." Still the public faith requires the continuance of the endowments guaranteed to the temples, and this necessitates, it may be feared, a closer connexion than is desirable. It would be neither just nor safe, for instance, to allow the Brahmans to collect the land-revenue; this is still managed by the government officers, by whom the proportions are paid over to the native managers; but this pecuniary connexion is obviously open to considerable risk of misapprehension, and requires to be jealously watched.

Acceptable as the recent changes must be to the enlightened mind, it may be doubted how far they are relished by the bigoted Hindus. The Brahmans would, probably, prefer the European supremacy to that of a native trust. If they have been relieved from a powerful check on their rapacity, they have lost a protector who brought authority to their side, and often compelled an attendance which would not be voluntarily rendered. Altogether there can be little doubt that, to a system so thoroughly corrupt and corrupting, independence must prove a destructive boon. Deprived of the illegitimate countenance of British authority, it will stand defenceless against the assaults of the gospel and the progress of civilization.

Much has been learned by the British public from the continually recurring conflict of European and native opinion. It no longer cheats itself with the idea that Hindus and Mussulmans *prefer* Anglo-Saxon institutions to their own ; it has found out that liberty and knowledge are plants of a tardy and uncertain growth ; but it is still far from being sufficiently impressed with the difficulty of a free nation undertaking to govern a people so little desirous, or qualified to govern themselves. It might be comparatively easy to rule India (as some express it) by the sword ; that is, as a conquered and tributary country, with exclusive regard to an imperial policy : and such a government, administered by a civilized power, would, beyond all question, insure to the natives more of happiness and contentment than was known under either Hindu or Mohammedan ascendancy. Great Britain, however, has proposed to herself the infinitely higher and harder task of ruling India *for the natives ;* in this she must lay her account to meet with protracted disappointment and delay. The difficulty of conducting the necessary struggle with the indolence, the timidity, the want of public spirit, and general incapacity of the native races, is enormous: and justice has, at times, been hardly done to the motives and exertions of the civil and military officers engaged in this arduous undertaking. Taken from the bosom of our Christian families at home, educated in our schools and colleges, glowing with every English sentiment, they carry out to India at an early age, a spirit which draws its after inspirations from the great mother who nurtured them, and in whose lap they hope to die. Why should such men be thought less impressed with the grandeur of England's mission, or less sensitive to India's need, than those who form their opinions at a distance, and pronounce judgments which they leave it to others to execute? The failures of the public officers in India have at no time been more conspicuous than those of other men in circumstances of far less difficulty: their successes have surprised the world, and shed an imperishable lustre on their country's annals. Happily, many of these servants of the British crown have learned to conjoin with a knowledge of native customs unrivalled in Europe, and an industry and vigour of mind which the lassitude of the East cannot vanquish, an earnest love of God their Saviour, and, for his sake, of the creatures that were made after his image and redeemed by his blood. India, which has absolutely nothing to expect from the efforts or aspirations of her own benighted children, may hope for every liberty that can elevate mankind, from those who administer their charge under a sense of the highest responsibility, with a zeal that never flags, and a purpose that embraces the undying interests of their fellow-creatures.

CHAPTER VII.

PRIVATE LIFE.

Strength of family ties—Early marriages—Widowhood—Astrology—Hindu marriage rites — Procession — Expenditure — Mussulman rites — Legal requisites—Polygamy, Hindu and Mohammedan—Kuleen Brahmans—Tippoo Sultan—General practice—Divorce—Condition of female sex—Seclusion introduced by Moslems — Children — Preference of sons — Inheritance—Birth ceremonies—Names—Hindu—Mussulman—Religious initiations — Hindu funeral rites — Banks of Ganges — Firing the pile — *Shradh* — Mussulman obsequies—Death and burial — Funeral procession —Zeearut in imitation of the Shradh—Repetition of the Koran—Sorcery —Exorcism—Possession—Medical science — Astronomy—Physiognomy—Clothing and ornaments — Houses — Furniture — Daily habits — Shops — Money lenders—Streets—Conveyances—Mode of travelling—Palanquins —Food—Tobacco—Pawn—Bang—Strong liquors—Amusements.

THE absence of political institutions seems to draw closer among the Hindus the ties of family life. No people, perhaps, are more deeply sensible to the force of domestic relations. Marriage is universal, and celibacy a reproach in either sex; the parental and filial feelings are strong, and the obligations of kindred are owned, to an extent seldom found where the claims of country and humanity are better understood. To support a relative out of employment, even though himself in indigent circumstances, is so common to the Hindu, that the claim is advanced without scruple, and conceded almost as a matter of course.

Marriage, the foundation of domestic society, is contracted at an early age, and as an obligation of religion. A Brahman youth marries immediately after assuming the sacred string (which takes place at about eight years of age), and boys of other castes as early as the parents may choose. A girl is almost always wedded before ten years of age, and to a husband older than herself. The parents consider it as much a part of their duty to provide suitable marriages for their children, as to feed and clothe them. If a Brahman allow a daughter to remain single till eleven years of age, he is visited with suspension from his caste. The law, however, strictly forbids the sale of a daughter, or the receiving of any pecuniary consideration for giving her in marriage; but this law is often disregarded where the girl is eligible enough to command a price.

The first consideration in forming an alliance is the caste of the parties. A Brahman or other high-caste man may marry a female of inferior descent; but the female must always be mated in her own, or in a superior, caste. This artificial restraint, coupled with other conditions of Hindu life, makes the marriage of girls by their parents almost necessary to their future comfort and respectability, and the practice could hardly be abandoned with safety in the present state of education and manners. Neither are the results so unfavourable to the weaker sex as might be supposed. A marriage dictated by prudence is at least preferable to one which is the offspring only of passion. Transferred from the care of her father to that of a husband, before any other attachment can have been formed, the Hindu wife experiences little subsequent temptation. Her affections naturally centre on the father of her children, and if her life be monotonous, it is free from many sorrows which often follow a wider liberty of choice. The principal evil attending the custom is the danger of being left a widow while yet in the opening of life. A female of the Brahman caste, once betrothed, is not allowed to contract another union, even if her husband should die before she has quitted her maiden home. She is thenceforth doomed to inexorable widowhood, denied the privilege of wearing her hair and other ornaments, excluded from all festive meetings, and humiliated in social life. These restrictions properly apply only to the Brahmans; widows of any other caste are permitted to marry again. But the example of the higher Hindus creates a strong prejudice against such reunions, and they are very uncommon. No doubt the prospect of so desolate an existence went a long way to reconcile so many poor creatures to sacrificing themselves on the funeral pyres of their deceased husbands.

The prejudice against the re-marriage of widows extends to Mussulmans also, notwithstanding that their prophet's first and most honoured wife was a widow, and the Koran expressly authorizes a second union, in four months and ten days after the death of the first husband. The marriage of a widow, however, is solemnized without the *shadhas*, or rejoicings, which distinguish the nuptials of a virgin.

In commencing the marriage ceremonies, the astrologer plays an important part, both among Hindus and Mussulmans. The horoscopes of both parties are cast, and great attention is bestowed in determining the "lucky day." The Hindus further consult their idols, sometimes by sticking flowers, which have been first wetted, against the cheeks or breasts of the image, accompanied by a prayer, that if the union is to be auspicious the right hand flowers may fall first.

When the indications are favourable, a time is appointed for the marriage rites. These are numerous, tedious, and in many parts far from delicate. All, however, being expressed in Sanscrit, and recited by the officiating Brahman with the utmost rapidity, no one understands what is said. The principal rites among the Brahmans are walking three times round a fire, and tying the garments of the parties together. The bride has also to make *seven steps*, at the last of which the marriage is complete.

The marriage is usually solemnized in the house of the bride's father, where she continues to reside till of age to join her husband. The latter then proceeds to her father's house, attended by his friends, and conducts her home in a grand procession, usually by night, with torches and great rejoicings. On both occasions considerable expenditure is incurred in feasting the friends and relatives, and in providing ornaments, music, processions, and illuminations. The wealthy spend freely on these objects; and the poorer classes often incur debts which burden them for many years. The costs incurred by the fathers, on both sides, in celebrating a marriage, form a heavy item of Hindu expenditure; and one of the motives to female infanticide is doubtless laid in the desire to avoid this charge.

Among Mussulmans the marriage contract is solemnized, after the customary interchange of presents, by reading the first chapter of the Koran, called the *Fateeha*. This may be done by a cazee, moulvie, moollah, or any other respectable person. At the marriage itself (called *nikah*) the bridegroom repeats certain other chapters of the Koran, with the five creeds, the articles of belief, and the prayer of praise; after which he joins hands with the vakeel, or proxy for the bride (whose presence in person is contrary to Mussulman notions of delicacy), and their mutual faith is plighted in a prescribed formula. Prayers are then offered by the cazee, who concludes by sending some sugar-candy to the bride, with a message that she is married to such a person.

To a *nikah* three conditions are required:—1, Consent of the man and woman: 2, evidence of two witnesses at the least: 3, the settling a dowry on the wife. If either of these be wanting, the marriage is unlawful.* The portion, when not paid at the time, becomes a sacred debt on the husband; but it is forfeited if the wife should leave him of her own accord. If divorced by him, he must pay her the dowry; and if she dies it becomes due to her parents. The bride is conducted home in a palanquin, the bridegroom usually riding on horseback; and on arriving at the door he carries her into the house in his arms.

Polygamy obtains among all classes of the native population, Hindu, Moslem, Jew, and Parsee. Among the Hindus, however, a second wife was originally permitted only in some default of the first. The Institutes of Manu allow "a barren wife to be superseded by another, in the eighth year; one whose children are dead, in the tenth; one who brings forth only daughters, in the eleventh; and one who speaks unkindly, without any delay." These exceptions seem to indicate that monogamy was the original rule: and the first wife still retains the chief place in the household.

There is a class of Brahmans in Bengal, termed *Kuleen*, which was erected by an ancient raja (Bullalsen) as a distinction for the more learned and pious members of the caste. Becoming hereditary

* Qanoon-e-Islam, 135.

like all other Hindu honours, it is now a sort of nobility, everywhere receiving pre-eminence, and much sought after in marriage connexions. The inferior Brahmans give large sums for the honour of such an alliance; and the sons of Kuleens are consequently easily contracted. The daughters, however, as with other castes, are not allowed to marry below their rank. Hence every Kuleen ordinarily takes, at least, two wives; one from his own caste, as a duty to the order, and another from some other family with a valuable portion. The latter consideration induces many to multiply their wives still further. There are even some who gain an infamous subsistence by the practice, marrying from twenty to a hundred women, with each of whom they receive a fortune. Their wives are left with their parents, and the lordly polygamist visits them at his pleasure, being sustained and clothed by his numerous fathers-in-law in turn.

Mussulmans are allowed by the Koran four wives, but restricted from the same degrees of relationship as are prohibited in the Levitical law. Additional wives or concubines are added, by wealthy persons, apparently without limit or law. Tippoo Sultan married no less than nine hundred women, and the palaces of some of the royal family of Oude contained apartments for more than eighty. The domestic habits of the natives make it difficult to say how far polygamy is generally practised in India. It appears, however, to be scarcely more common among Mussulmans than Hindus, and with the lower orders the expense must always operate as a powerful restraint. Perhaps not more than a fifth, and in some districts not more than a tenth, of the community have more than one wife.

Polygamy is naturally accompanied by great facilities

of divorce. The Hindu law permits a husband to repudiate his wife for a variety of causes, among which it is remarkable that the one only sufficient reason, allowed by the gospel, is *not* enumerated. Adultery was, in fact, punished with death. The crime was presumed from the slightest evidences of familiarity, and the offence of a Sudra with a woman of the Brahman caste was accounted the most aggravated depravity that human nature could be guilty of. The Hindu law seems to allow no right of divorce to the wife, except the husband forfeit his caste, which is equivalent to civil death. In cases of aggravated misconduct upon his part her relations occasionally interfere, and even take her back to her father's roof.

The Mussulman husband exercises an equally absolute power of divorce, limited, however, by the necessity of repaying the dowry to a wife repudiated without sin. The wife may induce him to divorce her at her own instigation by consenting to forego her dowry.

It is difficult to ascertain the amount of married happiness enjoyed in the privacy of native life. The female sex is certainly in a much lower social position than the other. The wife is not allowed to eat with her husband, or to appear as his equal: if seen with him in public she walks behind, and is more like a servant than a companion. In the lower orders women assist in agricultural labours, and are not unfrequently seen staggering under heavy burdens, while the men walk at their ease. It is common also, in this class of society, for the men to beat their wives; and in all ranks great coarseness and want of delicacy characterize so much of their intercourse as reaches the European eye. On the other hand, much deference and personal attention are shown to mothers and elderly female relations. The Hindu annals record the deeds of noble ladies worthy of all admiration; and their drama often attests a high conception of female character.

It seems probable that the educated Hindu was in this respect (as in many others) more civilized than his Moslem oppressor, and that the female sex has suffered a considerable depression in the social scale, by the introduction of Mussulman rule. Their rigid seclusion from society is certainly a custom of Mohammedan origin; doubtless copied in the first instance as a refuge from the license of the spoiler, and afterwards, like some other marks of inferiority, turned into a point of honour through the example of the ruling powers. The Brahman women still exercise the ancient liberty, appearing before men without scruple; but other Hindu females, especially of rank, live like the Mussulman ladies secluded in their own apartments, and would deem it an insupportable dishonour to be even seen by a man, save a husband or son.* The etiquette is so strict that a native gentleman will only speak of his wife or daughters in conversation, under the term of his *family*, and by the same indefinite appellation it is customary for others to make inquiries after their health.

* The raja of Mysore was in great tribulation for one of the widows of his father, whom he loved as his mother. She was afflicted with a cancer in the breast, for which the raja entreated the aid of the resident surgeon. He himself accompanied this gentleman to the ranee's apartment, and bowing with much veneration before the *purdah*, or screen, behind which the lady was concealed, entreated her to admit the surgeon to her presence. But all that could be obtained from her was permission to feel her pulse, for which purpose a hand was put out from behind the screen. In vain the surgeon represented the impossibility of affording aid without inspection, and in vain the raja renewed his entreaties. The princess was inflexible, and her life actually fell a sacrifice to this unreasonable etiquette, which, "after all (observed the raja), is no custom of ours, but purely a Mussulman usage."

On the whole, it seems probable that as much conjugal harmony exists in India as in many parts of Christian Europe. The standard of female education is low; their range of information is therefore limited, and their amusements frivolous and unprofitable. But to the extent of their capacity, native wives are perhaps as happy as European ones. It is Christianity alone that could alter their condition for the better; and in no respect is the gospel attended with so great a social revolution as in its consequences to the weaker sex. Independently of the abrogation of polygamy, the immediate alteration effected in female habits and ideas by embracing Christianity is enormous. The simple fact of attending public worship, in common with the men, is sufficient to indicate what a gulf is crossed in passing from heathenism into the kingdom of God's dear Son. The equality of the sexes, however, is so utterly repugnant to native ideas, that their women are sedulously instructed to recoil from it as immodest, hugging the chains of their own degradation. There is no doubt that these mistaken feelings of delicacy constitute a great obstacle to the spread of the gospel. The females of a family are seldom accessible to the missionary, and they are often earnest opponents of the truth, when their husbands or sons show a disposition to believe.

Natives of all ranks and classes exhibit much fondness for their children, though greatly more for sons than daughters. The latter, partly in consequence of the difficulties in the way of marriage, are regarded as a very doubtful blessing, and in the higher castes, it may be feared, are still at times ruthlessly destroyed in their infancy. But with regard to sons, the poorest father is ready to respond to the Psalmist's exclamation,

"Happy is the man that hath his quiver full of them." A large family occasions a native none of the anxieties experienced by most Europeans, in looking forward to their establishment in life. The Hindu, as a matter of course, follows the occupation of his father and shares his possessions. The property seems to pertain not so much to the father as to the family, whence no testamentary powers are recognised. On the death of the father the eldest son succeeds to the administration (with some superior benefit), and the proceeds are shared as before among all the sons, the daughters receiving portions from the shares of their brothers. In the poorer classes the necessary expenses of living are too low to admit of much anxiety on account of a few additional mouths. On the contrary, the family tie is so strong, that the larger the number the greater appears to be each individual's chance of advancement in life. Still the preference for males over females is such, that a nephew is often more esteemed than a daughter. A poor widow will leave her own female child to the charity of strangers, while she installs her sister's boy into the place of an eldest son, and starves herself to find him ornaments and pleasures.

This undue depreciation of the woman is, no doubt, the natural result of a state of society, in which all the business of life is transacted by men, leaving neither taste nor room for female graces and accomplishments. With the Hindus, religion itself throws its weight into the same scale. An important part of its ceremonial are the funeral obsequies, which can only be discharged by a male heir. Where none is provided by nature, every Hindu makes it a point to adopt one of his relations or caste to perform these essential rites of his faith. Mussulman women, however, appear to derive but little benefit from the absence of these religious peculiarities. They are excluded from the mosques, as well as from the social intercourse of the men; and the general tone of Mohammedan feeling is more derogatory to the sex than those of the Hindu.

The birth of a child is observed with a variety of superstitious ceremonies among the natives of both religions. The Shastras prescribe a drop of honey to be given to the infant immediately on its birth, and this ancient usage appears to be practised also by Mussulmans. Other rites take place at the naming of the child, which Hindus perform on the twelfth day, and the Moslems either on the day of its birth or on that day week.

Both classes resort to the aid of astrology in the selection of the name, and the lucky hour for imposing it. Among the Hindus the Brahmans, of course, have the direction of this important ceremonial. The names have usually a signification, such as *Light*, *Peace*, *Health*, or words of some agreeable meaning. The Rajpoots, Mahrattas, and some others who value themselves on caste, use family or *surnames*, of which they are not a little vain. These names not unfrequently designate a sort of clan, or caste within the caste, the members of which decline to intermarry with other families. To the bulk of Hindus, however, and especially among the lower orders, the use of surnames is still unknown.

The Mohammedan names are more numerous and expressive. The first invariably denotes the father's tribe or class; as *Syed* or *Meer*, which indicate descent from the prophet, through Ali and Fatima his favourite daughter; *Sheikh*, the name of the prophet's own tribe in Arabia; *Bey*, a title conferred by the prophet on one of his Mogul followers, and retained by all of that race; and, lastly, *Khan*, a word of similar import, bestowed on a Patan* chief, and now used as the designation of the Affghan Mussulmans. This tribe-name, however, is generally dropped in common usage. Two or three additional names are usually given, the choice of which is regulated to some extent by the parentage of the child. Syeds and Sheikhs unite in the use of *Khooja*, *Golam*, *Mohammed*, *Deen*, *Bukhs*, *Ali*, *Sheikh*, *Abd*, or *Allah*, etc. Moguls employ *Imja*, *Bey*, *Aga*, etc. *Shurreez* denotes the son of a Sheikh father and a Syed mother. The daughters of Syed families are called *Begum*, *Beebee or Bee*, *Nissa*, and *Shah*. Sheikh girls have the words, *Ma* or *Bee*, added to their names: Moguls use *Khanum*, and Patans *Khatoon* or *Bano*. *Baee* denotes an illegitimate daughter, or an adopted slave, and sometimes a dancing-girl.

The other names of children are usually borrowed from members of the family, but *not* from the father or mother. Sometimes they are selected by dipping into the Koran, or by casting lots, or from reference to the horoscope, or the day of the child's birth. Thus, a boy born on a *Sunday* is called Ibrahim, Suleiman, Dâood, Moosa, etc.; on *Monday*, Mohammed, Ahmud, Qazin, etc.; on *Tuesday*, Imael, Ishag, etc.; on *Wednesday*, Oosman, Ali, Haroun, Hussein, etc.; on *Thursday*, Jusoof, Mustapha, etc.; on *Friday*, Salayh, Eesa, Adum, Sooltan, etc.; and, on *Saturday*, Abd-ul-Gadir,

* Mussulman writers say that the Patans are descended from Jacob, and that the name was originally *Futt'han* (or victorious), with which Mohammed saluted Khalid, whom he also honoured as Khan. In process of time, *Futt'han* was corrupted into Patan. See Qanoon-e-Islam, p. 12.

Shums-oo-Deen, Nizam-oo-Deen, etc. Mohammedans often prefix the father's name with the word *bin* (like the Norman *fitz* and the British *ap*), signifying "son of," as *Mohammed-bin-Abdallah*, *Khalid-bin-Walud*, etc.

On the fortieth day after the birth, Mussulman women observe a ceremony of "purification," attended, among those who can afford it, with a sacrifice of two he-goats for a boy and one for a girl. This ceremony, as before observed, is quite inconsistent with the spirit of Islam, which acknowledges no doctrine of atonement or substitution. On this occasion the boy's head is shaved, and an offering made of the hair. Hindus also shave the heads of their sons, but defer the ceremony to the age of three years.

At four years of age the Mussulman child is solemnly taught the *Bismillah*, or Name of God, which gives occasion to another religious ceremony; and at some time between the seventh and fourteenth year the rite of circumcision* is performed. Soon after twelve he undertakes the whole five duties of Islam; confession of faith, prayer, fasting, almsgiving, and pilgrimage. This early age is usually accounted the time of maturity in India. The Hindu boy then receives the sacred string of his caste, and is initiated into the ceremonial of idolatry. Marriage quickly follows with both, and before time has been allowed for their own education, these lads become the parents and guardians of other responsible and immortal creatures.

* It has been observed, that the Koran never once mentions this rite, nor is it deemed essential to *adult* proselytes. All Mussulmans, however, initiate their children in the sign of the covenant with Abraham, but they observe the age of their father Ishmael in preference to that of Isaac.

The native funeral rites are burdensome and expensive. As a general rule Hindus burn, and Mussulmans bury, their dead; but many of the poorer sort of Hindus also bury, from not being able to meet the expense of burning. On the banks of the Ganges and other rivers it is common for Hindus to commit the corpse to the stream. To die in the sacred waters, or with a portion of them in the mouth, is deemed the happiest termination of life. For this purpose sick and aged persons are hurried from great distances to the banks of the Ganges, where they often lie for days expecting their last hour. It is the duty of their attendant relatives, when the moment arrives, to pour the holy water into the mouth of the dying, that his latest breath may be mingled with the purifying element. There is reason to fear that, tired of waiting, the attendants not unfrequently hasten their release, by covering the mouth and nostrils of their helpless charge with mud, and launching him into the torrent. When the dying are not taken to the water, it is deemed essential that they should expire on the earth. They are accordingly dragged from their beds and laid on the ground as the last moment approaches.

The funeral obsequies are performed as soon as possible after death. The pyre is erected near a river or tank; and must be fired by the eldest son of the deceased or his adopted substitute. Great importance is attached to this duty by all the upper castes, and the person who discharges it inherits the property of the deceased like a legitimate son. The family and near relations are considered unclean, for a period longer or shorter according to circumstances, after which they assemble by the water-side to perform the ceremonies called *shradh*, which are supposed (like masses) to benefit the departed spirit. On this occasion a large assemblage of Brahmans and devotees are usually present, and as all are entitled to presents, the cost is often considerable. A monthly *shradh* is performed for a parent during the first year, and an annual one (at least) in honour of all the ancestral manes. No religious ceremonies are accounted more essential or meritorious than these.

Mohammedans are exhorted, four or five days previous to death, to make their wills and appoint an executor. At the hour of dissolution, a man learned in the Koran being sent for repeats with a loud voice the 36th chapter, called *Soora-e-ya-sin*, the sound of which is declared to be as music to the soul.* The *kulma*, or creed, should be repeated by a sick man; if he expire without it, after being called upon to do so, his faith is considered dubious, and the person who so called upon him incurs a reproach. It is thought better, therefore, for some of the company to repeat the creed, and leave it to the sick person to follow, either aloud or in his own mind. At the point of death a little sherbet is poured down the throat to facilitate the exit of the vital spark. Some great persons procure water from the well *Zemzem* for this purpose.

The corpse is bathed, shrouded, and buried, if possible, the same day, or the next at latest. This haste is fully justified by necessity in a tropical climate; but the Mussulmans assign the further reason, that, if a good man, he may the sooner reach heaven, and, if a bad one, his doom may not linger in the house. As India lies to

* This chapter receives its name from the letters *ya* and *sin*; it contains a description of the unity of the godhead, and is one of the earliest lessons taught to children.

the eastward of Mecca, the Mussulman *Kebla*, the feet of the corpse are turned to the west. The winding-sheet is written over with extracts from the Koran, and by religious men is often prepared in their lifetime. Before interment, the wife of the deceased, if she has not previously remitted her dowry, is desired formally to discharge the corpse of that debt, so to complete its acquittance from earthly demands. The mother, also, is accustomed in India to release the dead body from the obligation of the milk bestowed in infancy.

The corpse is carried by the relatives on a *doola*, or bier, enclosed (if there are means) in a coffin, which however is not interred with it: the kulma and other scriptures are repeated as they proceed. On arriving at the cemetery, which is always outside the town, the body is taken out of the coffin and exposed to view, while the funeral service is read by the cazee, or by any learned person appointed by the relatives. After laying the corpse in the grave (with the feet to the *Kebla*), the by-standers gently cast earth upon it, having first repeated the verse from the Koran, "We created you out of the earth, and we return you to the earth, and we shall raise you out of the earth on the day of resurrection." The grave is vaulted or roofed over, at about a yard above the body, and water is poured upon the earth on the top to form it into clay. Wealthy persons have a mausoleum built in their life-time, or a grave surrounded by a square wall, and some fill the grave with sand or grain, as being less oppressive to the deceased than earth. The wheat or paddy so employed is annually changed, and the old grain given to the poor.

After the interment, *fateeha* is offered at the grave,

in the name of the deceased; and again, at about forty paces off, in the name of all that lie in the same cemetery. At this juncture it is believed the two angels, Monkir and Nakir, visit the corpse; and having recalled the soul into it, compel it to sit up and undergo the ordeal called the examination or beating of the dead. This absurd superstition appears to be firmly impressed on the minds of the Indian Mussulmans, and must encompass the prospect of death with new terrors. Rice, salt, and other articles of food, are then distributed to the *faquirs*, and on returning to the house the *fateeha* is finally offered in the name of the family, and they are exhorted to patience and resignation.

To follow a bier on foot to the grave is one of the five obligations incumbent on good Mussulmans. When the corpse even of a Jew, or other sect, is borne past them, the more particular stand up and accompany it at least forty paces. No one presumes to walk *in front* of the corpse; that space being left for the *angels* to escort it to its resting-place. It is usual to build tombs of brick or stone over the grave, the women's not being so high as the men's; and the name of the deceased, with the date of death, is inscribed on the north side. But extracts from the Koran and the name of God are strictly prohibited.

Three days after the interment a ceremonial, called *teeja* or *zeaarut*, is observed in India, which is acknowledged to be inconsistent with the laws of Mohammed, and is doubtless imitated from the Hindu *shradh*. The relatives visit the grave with fruits, flowers, and incense, offering *fateeha*, and making supplication for the remission of the sins of the deceased. The most extraordinary part of this ritual is the *Khutum-e-Koran*, consisting of the repetition of the *whole Koran* over the grave, by which all the benefits of the sacred book are supposed to be transferred to its occupant. For this purpose wealthy Mussulmans engage fifty or a hundred moollahs, who, sitting down, and dividing the task among them by sections, read all together and as rapidly as they can, getting through it sometimes twice, or oftener if desired; of course with so much additional benefit to the departed believer.

Independently of the prescribed duties of their respective religions, all classes of the natives are addicted to a variety of superstitious observances. The fatalism common to Hindus and Mohammedans does not interfere with an universal belief in lucky and unlucky days and hours. Recourse is had to the art of the astrologer and to various kinds of divinations, in order to discover the auspicious moment for every undertaking. Believing also in the power of ghosts, goblins, demons, phantoms, and fiends, the trades of the sorcerer and the exorcist are extensively practised. Offenders are detected by means of various ordeals, and any evil that befalls is as often attributed to the malice of a wizard, as to the wrath of the god.

In this respect the Mohammedan theology has little to boast over the Hindu. The Koran itself teaches the existence of genii, who can be employed in human affairs; and the Mussulman writer, Jaffeer Shurreez, to whom we are indebted for the fullest account of his people in India, devotes nine whole chapters to the science of *exorcism*, which he had carefully studied. He informs us that this science is had recourse to for seven objects:—1. To command the presence of genii and demons for any service required; 2, to establish friendship or enmity between persons; 3, to cause the death of one's enemy; 4, to increase one's salary or subsistence; 5, to obtain victory in battle; 6, to procure an income gratuitously or mysteriously; and 7, to secure the accomplishment of one's wishes, both temporal and spiritual. Truly, if the "science" were to be relied upon, little other religion or instruction would be requisite. Our author, however, admits that after associating much with divines and devotees, exorcists and travellers, both from Arabia and Ujjum,* all the knowledge and advantage he has derived may be summed up in the proverb (common to the Oriental and the classical poet), "Dig up a mountain to find a mouse." He adds with some simplicity, that "*when* an exorcist has once commanded the presence of genii and demons, he may, through their means, cause whatever he pleases to be effected." These invisible beings he divides into *jins*, or good genii, and *shytans*, or devils; but these names, he tells us, are assigned according to the character of the action performed, since there is no real difference in the nature of the spirits, who always do what is commanded by the exorcist.

The natives all believe in possession by evil spirits, and many maladies are attributed to this cause, such as the loss of speech, palsy, madness, and general indifference to the duties of life. The sorcerer is then called in to cast out the devil. Jaffeer Shurreez has given diagrams of the magic circles, squares, and other figures, used with divers incantations in this process. His sketches of the demons are certainly hideous enough to make the patient's "liver melt

* All countries except Arabia, the holy land of the Mussulman, are included under this designation.

away" on being shown to him; and in some cases we may well believe what he says of the foolish people that resorted to him for assistance, "Whether, owing to my reading supplications, tying on an amulet, or burning a charm, or to *the force of their belief*, or to *some wise contrivance of my own which I put in practice*, they have been cured." Love philters, amulets, and spells of all descriptions, are compounded and vended by these impostors, and a very general belief exists in their potency.

The knowledge of medicine and surgery must, of course, have fallen to a very low ebb, since their practice is hardly ever unmixed with some of these fooleries. In ancient times a truer science seems to have been realized; but the art of healing never occupied its due position, and the British rule is greatly sustained in native estimation, by the extensive and important benefits diffused by our surgeons and hospitals.

Astronomy, too, was once pursued in India for higher ends than those of the modern astrologer. The Greeks appear to have been much indebted to the Hindus in this branch of science. Correct views were entertained of the solar system; and the tables composed for calculating eclipses, and making the almanack, are used at this day by astronomers who are ignorant of the principles on which they were framed. The common people know nothing of these scientific truths, but, adopting the wild notions of their mythological legends, fancy an eclipse to be occasioned by a dragon, called Ketu, endeavouring to destroy the sun or the moon. On such occasions the Brahmans proclaim a fast, and the natives offer earnest petitions to the gods to interpose their aid, or to the dragon to spare the orb of day.

In adding a brief sketch of such customs and manners of the natives as have not yet been noticed, it must be remembered that considerable diversity exists in appearance, habits, and civilization, between the several portions and classes of so vast a population. As a general rule, the natives of Hindustan and the north are a fairer race, taller and stronger than those of the south of India. They are also better clothed, and more independent in spirit and action. In the Deccan, the Mahrattas and Guzerattees are more manly than the Tamilers, Telugus, or Canarese. Almost every shade of complexion is to be met with, from the European to the negro's, but (save perhaps among some of the aboriginals) the peculiar features of the African are altogether wanting. The Hindu visage is oval, the hair black and straight, the eyes dark, the lips thin, the figure slender and graceful, and the general appearance pleasing.

Men of all classes (except the aborigines, religious Brahmans, and mendicants) shave the head and wear turbans. The Moslems cultivate a flowing beard, but the Hindus retain the hair only on the upper lip. The remainder of the common Hindu dress consists of two cotton cloths, one wrapped round the middle and descending to the calf of the leg, and the other thrown about the shoulders like a mantle. There is but a slight difference in the female dress; the lower cloth descends a little nearer to the feet, and the upper one is frequently drawn over the head, which has no other covering. The Mohammedan dress is a long robe with loose trousers, both which have been adopted by the better classes of Hindus in Bengal and the north. In the Deccan, respectable Hindus, and such as mix much with

Europeans, wear a jacket or open tunic as low as the knee, with the upper cloth thrown loosely over it. Women of the same description wear a close jacket over the bosom, with short sleeves. Both sexes wear sandals, which are carefully put off on entering a place of worship, or the presence of a superior. The Parsees, and some others of the more Europeanized natives, have adopted shoes and stockings.

The clothing is mostly made of white calico of various degrees of fineness. Gaily coloured cloths, however, are often worn by the Hindu women; the Mohammedans, also, and natives of rank, exhibit, on great occasions, rich garments of silk and brocade glowing with brilliant colours. Valuable shawls are worn by distinguished persons, and a shawl or sash round the waist is usual in Bengal, and among Mohammedans. Secular Brahmans indulge in fine apparel as freely as any other natives; but the more religious members of the caste affect the old Hindu fashion, and wear but little clothing of any kind. It is common for Hindus of all kinds to strip themselves almost to a state of nudity when within their own houses, a custom which Cæsar observed among the ancient Britons. Arms are commonly worn in the north and in the disturbed districts. The ploughman in Oude and Hyderabad goes to the field furnished with sword and buckler; and Mohammedans, Rajpoots, and Mahrattas, seldom appear without *tulwar* and dagger in their belts.

All classes take an extraordinary delight in ornaments. Bracelets, necklaces, and ear-rings of gold, silver, and jewellery, are common to men and women. The latter are further ornamented with rings in the nose, and *bangles*, or heavy gold or silver circlets, round the ankles. Rings on the great toe are often added, and gold coins are lavished plentifully over the hair. These ornaments are worn at marriages, holidays, and other festive occasions; children of both sexes are sometimes loaded with them. The passion extends to the poorest classes; and infants, whose whole clothing besides is not worth two or three rupees, will be seen decked out in trinkets to the value of two hundred. A vast quantity of precious metals and jewellery is thus locked up in ornaments, ready at any time to be converted into money; but the convenience is dearly purchased by the personal insecurity attendant on their possession. Women and children are often kidnapped or murdered for the sake of their ornaments, and thefts and robberies are continually taking place on the same account.

The native habitations are small and inconvenient. They have seldom any glass windows, or other flooring than the earth. The furniture is scanty; chairs and tables are seldom used, as the natives sit on mats or cushions, and eat with their fingers. Porcelain and plate are equally unknown, save among the very wealthiest classes. The common people are content with a few brass or earthen vessels, and plates neatly fashioned of leaves. The bed is seldom more than a mat or mattress, spread on the ground, or elevated on a rude rattan frame. Little change is made in the apparel at night, beyond loosening the tighter portions. Both men and women sleep as they walk about, making their ablutions and change of garments at intervals, according to their means. The heat and closeness of the rooms often occasion the men to sleep in the open air, where, stretched on the ground, with the cloth drawn over the whole figure to keep off the musquitoes, the slumberer not a little resembles a corpse laid out under a winding-sheet.

The *ryot*, or husbandman, rises with the earliest dawn, and, after washing and saying a prayer, sets out with his cattle to the distant field. After an hour or two he eats some remnants of his yesterday's fare for breakfast, and goes on with his labour till noon, when his wife brings out his hot dinner. He eats it by a brook or under a tree, talks and sleeps till two o'clock, while his cattle also feed and repose. From two till sunset he labours again; then drives his cattle home, feeds them, bathes, eats some supper, smokes, and spends the rest of the evening in amusement with his wife and children, or among his neighbours. The women fetch the water, grind the corn, cook, and do the household work, besides spinning and such occupations. Such is the daily round of village life.

In towns it is varied only by the diversity of occupations required by the extent of the populations, each within itself being equally subject to a monotonous routine. With the break of day the male inhabitants sally out into the fields, to perform their ablutions and summary toilet. The shops are then opened by the simple expedient of lifting the bamboo screen which forms a shutter by night, and converting it into a *pandal*, or sun-blind, for the day. The front apartment is thus laid open to the street; and the tradesman takes his seat cross-legged on the floor, which is raised some two or three feet above the road in front, surrounded by the articles for sale. The counting-houses of native merchants and bankers exhibit but little superiority over common shops: the owner is better clothed, perhaps, and seated on a richer carpet. Money-lenders, or shroffs, abound in every native community, and extend their dealings from the prince to the ryot. Under native rule they were ready to farm, or accept a mortgage of, all the revenues of a kingdom; and they are still as influential in their several circles as the Rothschilds in Europe. The rate of interest is exorbitant; and, whether from the extent of their dealings, or the general poverty, or the national love of money, it is a common proverb, that if two natives be seen in earnest conversation, the subject is sure to be "rupees."

The streets (or more often street) of a village are usually broad, and lined with trees. One or more such thoroughfares are also to be found in most towns; but the cross streets are crooked and narrow, seldom broad enough for a carriage, even if the road were in a condition to allow the passage of wheels. Carriages, however, are still in a very primitive condition among the natives. Goods are carried in *bandies*, or carts drawn by bullocks, which are little more than two solid circles of wood joined by an axle, across which a few timbers and boards are roughly nailed. The *hackery*, for the conveyance of men and women, boasts a pair of wheels with spokes, some approach to springs, and a cushioned seat, shaded by a canopy with curtains. The bullocks which draw it are occasionally urged into a trot. No superior kind of vehicle seems to be yet naturalized, though carriages of the European fashion, with horses and harness complete, are common in the presidency towns, and among the most wealthy natives.

The bulk of the population travel on foot, sometimes accomplishing extraordinary journeys in that primitive fashion. A sepoy going on leave has been known to walk sixty miles in a day. Women and elderly men are generally mounted on bullocks or small ponies. The richer classes ride horses or camels, elephants being reserved for princes and the highest ranks.

The most common conveyance for both men and women is the *palanquin*, which is a box about six feet long and three wide, thickly roofed against the sun, and fitted with sliding doors at the sides. A stout pole projects in front and behind, by means of which it is borne on the shoulders of four or six bearers in single rank, while an equal number run by the side, ready to take their turn under the pole. A relief takes place about every five minutes. A *mussalchee*, or torch-bearer, completes the set: *coolies* are hired to run with the baggage as may be needed. The bearers form a trade or caste of their own, which is much in vogue with the Telugu nation. They are to be met with all over India, and will readily contract to carry a traveller for almost any distance. If the palanquin be not too heavily loaded, they will carry a European gentleman at a speed of four or five miles an hour, and accomplish thirty miles in the night; this rate they can sustain for months, if relieved by a halt every fourth night.

The bearers keep up a continued cry while under the pole, which serves at once to amuse themselves, and give notice of their approach to others. The traveller, stretched on his pallet within, finds it not altogether without melody, while the wild beast is warned to retire into a deeper part of the forest. The *mussal*, or torch, consists of a large roll of cotton cloth, somewhat thicker than one's wrist, one end of which is saturated with oil, and set on fire. The flame, being constantly fed from a vessel of oil which the bearer carries in the other hand, sheds a wild, picturesque lustre over the party, which the state of the roads renders indispensable. Quitting the common track, the bearers often strike across ground as yet unploughed by the bandies. In the dry weather they descend into the beds of rivers, winding along the banks and shoals, and casting a lurid gleam over the scanty waters. When the channels are full, some preparation is necessary to cross the turgid stream. Boats of a primitive construction are hastily framed to float the palanquin, while the bearers wade or swim. Sometimes baskets, covered with hides or rafts, supported on empty earthen jars, form the frail supports of the traveller's person and property. At every halt it is important to examine the flask of oil, and not unfrequently the bearers rouse the merchant in some village bazaar, in the dead of night, in order to replenish their stock. On such occasions one is forcibly reminded of the parable of the ten virgins, whose "lamps" were very probably torches of the description still used in India, for the replenishment of which the wise had taken care to bring oil enough in their vessels, while the foolish had to seek more in the bazaar.

The food of all the native population is simple, and the drink almost uniformly water. Brahmans and Jains eat no animal food, from considerations of religion or caste. Even eggs are rejected, as containing the germ of life. Mohammedans, like Jews, abominate *pork*, and Hindus of all classes abstain from *beef*. Some classes eat no meat but fish. With these exceptions, animal food appears to be acceptable to all, though, in point of fact, it is sparingly used. The rural population do not indulge in it perhaps once in a week; and this arises not altogether from poverty, since fowls and eggs seem attainable by all, and a sheep can be got for a rupee. The forests also abound in game, and the open country is covered with birds; yet the natives seem to make but little use of them for food.

Tobacco is both chewed and smoked in various ways; but its quality is not so strong as the American plant. All classes of society chew the leaf of the areka nut, called *betel*, mixed with some pungent spices. A lump of this mixture, called *pawn*, is invariably offered to every guest. It seems to possess a narcotic effect, but is not intoxicating. Opium is both eaten and smoked, as also a cheaper substitute, made from the Indian hemp, called *bang*, and the lower classes often intoxicate or stupify themselves with these preparations. A spirituous liquor is distilled from rice, called arrack; *toddy*, also, or the juice of the palm tree, when fermented acquires an intoxicating property. But the use of strong liquors in any degree is highly disreputable; and drunkenness is almost confined to Europeans, and those of the natives whom their example and intercourse have infected with this destructive vice. Wine is not made in any part of India, though the grape is by no means uncommon.

The native amusements are few and trivial. No manly sports adorn the village green. In most parts athletic games are precluded by the climate and low physical development of the inhabitants. Yachting, boating, and angling, are as little practised as cricket and foot-ball. The intercourse of society is deprived of charm and variety by the exclusion of the females, and by the restrictions of caste. The excitement of politics is wanting, and neither literature, arts, nor science, exist to supply the deficiency. Reading and writing are rare accomplishments. Drawing, singing, and music are only learned as professional attainments. The press is a thing of foreign and recent introduction, and its productions are still utterly unknown to the masses.

The chief entertainments are *nautches*, or exhibitions of dancing-girls (natives of either sex never dancing for their own amusement), puppet dramas, illuminations, and fireworks. Wandering jugglers and story-tellers amuse the occasional audience. Cock-fighting, quail-fighting, cards, and gambling, with a game resembling chess, are diversions of the lower and middle classes. The higher orders indulge in hunting beasts of prey, and in fights between the captured animals. Visits of ceremony afford occasions for the display of jewels and fine clothes. Dinners and suppers are limited to family or caste connexions. Marriage ceremonies consume a good deal of time; and the festivals of the gods supply the principal occasions of excitement. Beyond, all is low and sensual debauchery. The labouring classes seek the oblivion of sleep with a relish, which induces it to be called among the English, "black man's fun." The higher are consumed with indolence and sensuality, or only roused by longings for an impossible pre-eminence, vainly plotting against the civilization which has destroyed their ascendancy. On the whole, native life appears to the European observer insupportably dull, monotonous, and insipid.

CHAPTER VIII.

STATE OF KNOWLEDGE AND EDUCATION.

Profession of the native religions—Popular ignorance—Old-world knowledge—Division of classes—Injury to science, philosophy and religion—Decay of literature—Superiority of modern civilization—Impotence of Brahmanism—Former attainments—Caste—Decline of learning—General ignorance—Female sex—Want of history and geography—Mathematics—Fine arts—Agriculture—Implements—Productions—State of rural population—Manufactures—Want of capital—Tariff—Education—Early measures—Oriental literature—Vernacular teaching—English—Missionary education—Caste—Distinctions—Popular-preference—Enlarged scheme of native education—Universities—Colleges—Anglo-vernacular schools—Vernacular—Different plans—Normal schools—Female education—Grants in aid—Mission schools—Opposition of "old Indians"—Reply—Quality of the education—Defects—Caste—Inconsistency of its recognition—Brahman admissions—Exclusion of the Bible—Excessive caution—All education subversive of idolatry—Native testimony—Reform of the Shastras—New worship—Infidelity—Hindu bigotry—Dharma Sobha—Necessary agitation of thought—ONWARD—Duty of government—Need of the Bible.

THE Shastras and the Koran are both eloquent in the praises of knowledge: both attribute the misfortunes of mankind to ignorance, and connect the hopes of religion with the cultivation of reason. The Hindu system devotes its sacred caste to the pursuit of learning; the schoolmaster is incorporated into the village community, and the scholar is traditionally entitled to the companionship of princes. The Mussulman theology, with lower pretensions to philosophy, still boasts of its rational and reflecting character. Its appeal is made to the written word, which every one who can read is at liberty to expound. Tradition is restrained to fixed authentic records, and *kias*, or "reasoning," is recognised as one of the foundations of Islam. Its favourite appellation, in a word, is the religion of the *Book*: it unites learning with piety, and makes the instruction of the young an obligation of the faith. Neither creed has admitted the unworthy maxim that "ignorance is the mother of devotion." It might have been expected, therefore, that their united influence would have disseminated a considerable amount of useful knowledge among the natives of India. The fact, however, is that, in no country pretending to a character for civilization is the population so absolutely uneducated, or the state of knowledge more deplorable in all the departments of practical life.

At no time, indeed, was the Brahmanical learning deserving of the encomiums lavished upon it by some European scholars; nor was any practical system of popular education in existence in India, till it began to be attempted by the British government. Hindu knowledge, like that of the old world in general, was confined to a literary class; between which and the bulk of the population extended a gulf, bridged neither by compassion nor inquiry. The philosopher left the common people undisturbed in their ignorance, or even encouraged their worst errors, rather than share with them the treasures of learning. The working-classes, on the other hand, accepted the lot that was cast for them, without a suspicion that the knowledge so jealously removed above their reach contained the means of alleviating their daily toils. Science was deprived of its proper action on the necessities of humanity: and being at the same time excluded from the larger inductions of general observation and experience,—became limited within itself. Many a branch of learning was thus arrested in its infancy, which a freer social intercourse could not have failed to develop.*

Still more injurious were the effects of the literary monopoly on the progress of moral and religious truth. The condition of the human soul and its aspirations for the future, being regarded as parts of philosophy, were withdrawn into the domains of the learned, leaving the outer world as void of spiritual guidance as of temporal improvement. Teachers, who, among the initiated, could discourse not unworthily of the Divine attributes and the immortality of the soul, joined without remorse in the obscene idolatries which stood the masses in place of a religion. Hence, instead of raising and refining the lower, each higher form of truth only debased itself by the contact. The coarser and more earnest polytheism of the multitude prevailed over the unreal speculations of the *literati*. The path of knowledge, unillumined by love, instead of "shining more and more unto the perfect day," was seen narrowing and growing faint, till it was ultimately swallowed up in the overgrowth of the world's ignorance.

Such was the fate of the old classic learning of the west. The gospel introduced a truer theory of society,

* A striking illustration of this remark may be found in the very recent rise of the interesting study of *geology*. The facts must have been known to the miners and diggers of ancient times as well as our own. The *strata* and the *fossils* would secure the attention and awaken the curiosity of many an intelligent workman; while, on the other hand, there were always minds that could have arranged and classified the facts, so as to arrive at rational conclusions. The misfortune was, that the facts lay on one side of the gulf, and the knowledge to investigate them on the other. The science, which arises out of their *union*, was consequently deferred to a period of more general information.

and the invention of printing has diffused an enlightened literature through all its parts. Hence the superiority of modern European civilization; while the east, removed from both, has continued to sink deeper and deeper in ignorance.

The impotence of an unsanctified philosophy to educate the masses has nowhere been more conspicuous than in India. The Brahmans were emphatically a race of philosophers. They very early attained some considerable progress in scientific, moral, and religious speculations; the acquisition of truth was declared to be the great object of life, and a large part of each man's existence was devoted to its study. To read and to teach the Shastras conferred a nobility which looked down upon monarchs. The influence of this race extended itself over all the populations of India. From north to south were accepted the civil and religious institutions, which make the schoolmaster a member of every society, as indispensable as the accountant and the watchman.

Here was an organization framed apparently for the education of India; and the existing remains of Sanscrit literature exhibit no deficiency in taste or power. Vicramaditya, who reigned in Oude fifty-seven years before the birth of Christ, and has left an æra of his own still extensively used in Hindustan, was associated with eight literary friends, under the complimentary appellation of the "Nine Gems of Hindustan." One of them, named Kalidas, has even been designated the Hindu Shakspeare. The following is a specimen of the style and sentiments cultivated by this Hindu poet at a time when the Celts roamed the forests of Britain in primitive barbarism. It is translated from the *Cloud Messenger*, a simple drama, in which a *yaksha*, or inferior divinity, being exiled to a sacred forest, sends his love to his mortal wife by a cloud which he invokes for the purpose.

> "I view her now; long weeping swells her eyes,
> And those dear lips are dried by parting sighs;
> Sad on her hand her pallid cheek declines,
> And half unseen through veiling tresses shines,
> As, when a darkling night the moon enshrouds,
> A few faint rays break straggling through the clouds.
> Now at thy sight I mark fresh sorrows flow,
> And sacred sacrifice augments her woe.
> I mark her now with fancy's aid retrace
> This wasted figure and this haggard face.
> Now from her favourite bird she seeks relief,
> And tells the tuneful Sarika her grief;
> Mourns o'er the feather'd prisoner's kindred fate,
> And fondly questions of its absent mate.
> In vain the lute for harmony is strung,
> And round the robe-neglected shoulder slung;
> And faltering accents strive to catch in vain
> Our race's old commemorative strain;
> The faltering tear that from reflection springs,
> Bedews incessantly the silvery strings;
> Recurring woe still pressing on the heart,
> The skilful hand forgets its grateful art,
> And idly wandering, strikes no measured tone,
> But makes a sad, wild, warbling of its own."

A glimpse of the state of arts, also, in Ayodhya, the capital of this ancient kingdom, is afforded by a passage in the "Ramayana," which, after every allowance for Oriental exaggeration, undoubtedly attests a civilization of no ordinary occurrence in that age of the world. The city is said to have been founded by Manu himself:—

"Its streets, well arranged, were refreshed with ceaseless streams of water; its walls, variously ornamented, resembled the checkered surface of a chessboard. It was filled with merchants, dramatists, elephants, horses, and chariots. The cloud of fragrant incense darkened the sun at noon-day; but the *glowing radiance of the resplendent diamonds and* *jewels that adorned the persons of the ladies, relieved the gloom.* The city was decorated with precious stones, filled with riches, furnished with abundance of provisions, adorned with magnificent temples, whose towers like the gods dwelt in the heavens—such was their height—palaces whose lofty summits were in perpetual conflict with the soft clouds, baths, and gardens. It was inhabited by the twin-born, the regenerate, profoundly instructed in the Vedas, adorned with every good quality, full of sincerity, zeal, and compassion, and like the venerated sages."*

These examples certainly evince a considerable amount of knowledge among the ancient Hindus. All was neutralized, however, by the operation of *caste*. In refusing the Shastras to the Sudras, and other inferior classes, the Brahmans dug the fatal gulf, between their learning and the people whom it might, perhaps, have raised and civilized. The secluded treasure rusted and grew stagnant, like every human gift when denied its circulation among men. The Brahman schoolmaster is still found in every Hindu village; but all the lore he imparts consists of the names of the false gods, and a few legends from a mythology which primitive Brahmanism would reject with abhorrence. The guardian of the Vedas and the student of Manu is degraded into a reciter of the Puranas. Sanscrit, the dialect of the gods, which disdained to impart its treasures to the vernacular speech, is become a dead language, indebted to the patronage of *Mlechas* for its elucidation and study. Philosophy and science have fled from the colleges of the pundits. Astrology takes the place of astronomy, and witchcraft of medicine. The graces of poetry no longer

* Percival's "Land of the Veda."

impart refinement or kindle aspiration. The ambition of the modern student is stimulated by the prospect of a place under government, or the hope of becoming a *moonshee* to European officers.

The population generally lies in the densest and most degrading ignorance. One-half—the whole female sex—the mothers and early trainers of the men—is excluded in the mass from all kinds of instruction. They neither read, nor write, nor sew, nor, except for professional and dishonourable pursuits, are instructed in the accomplishments of drawing, music, or dancing. The lower orders are the mere drudges of household or field; the higher are condemned to mental and bodily chains, not less oppressive though a little more gilded. Of the men, the immense majority can neither read nor write. A little arithmetic, and the customary rules of agriculture, constitute all the knowledge of the rural population. Some legends from the Puranas, with the dumb rites of idolatry, make up the popular religion. The customs of the village, or the caste, prescribe the entire circle for thought and debate.

The inefficiency of Brahman literature to any useful education is apparent in the entire absence both of *history* and *geography*. While other nations have taken delight in recording the progress of the institutions under which they lived, the Hindus have laboured only to involve antiquity in impenetrable obscurity. Their chronology is fabulous; the real personages who figure in their mythology seem to be purposely and hopelessly removed from historical associations; and it is a singular fact that, for many centuries after the cultivation of letters, no Sanscrit author condescended to record the history of his own nation or tribe.

This strange indifference on the subject most interesting to other men, may possibly be connected with the tenet of *transmigration*, so early and universally prevalent in India. To the metempsychosist, the transactions of this life must appear like an odd volume in the biography of the soul. Having passed through many existences before it reaches the human form, and being destined to many others after "this mortal coil is shuffled off," the events of one brief phase of its being seem undeserving of record; and the more so, since men only suffer here the predetermined consequences of former deeds, and are incapable of changing their destiny, by any reflections drawn from the virtues or errors of those who preceded them. Whatever be the cause, it is certain that history was always a blank among the Hindus; and Europeans are indebted to the less literary Mohammedans for the little knowledge they possess of the course of events in India.

In geography, also, the Brahmans have been content to circulate and hand down ridiculous fables, without an attempt at explanation or system. The rotation of the earth on its axis was known to their philosophers in the fifth century of the Christian æra; it was, perhaps, approximated at a much earlier period; yet they have acquiesced in the popular figments of the Puranas, which represent the earth as a flat surface, the centre of which is occupied by Mount Meru, surrounded by seven concentric belts or circles of land, with as many intervening seas. In the innermost of these circles India is placed, encompassed by a sea of salt water; the other portions of the world are separated by fabulous oceans of milk, wine, sugar-juice, etc.; and the whole is sustained by an elephant, who stands upon a tortoise, which again rests upon another creature. How inferior must have been the state of intellect, which could accept these puerile imaginations, from that of the patriarch of Uz, who could exclaim, "He stretches out the north over the empty place, and *hangeth the earth upon nothing*." *

Almost every other department of knowledge exhibits a condition of equal ignorance or decline. In *mathematics* alone the Brahmanical attainments lay claim to respect: their systems of geometry, arithmetic, and algebra are admitted to be superior to those of Europe; and, though involved in the general decline, these branches of science are still cultivated with marked success. In arithmetic especially, all classes of Hindus exhibit a skill which excites the surprise of European inquirers.

In the *fine arts*, if the native accounts could be trusted, no less proficiency was formerly attained. To judge from such descriptions as that of the city Ayodhya, architecture flourished at an antiquity, and to a degree of excellence, unparalleled in any other country. Even so late as the first Mohammedan inroad, it commanded the admiration of the invaders; and Mahmoud of Ghizni adorned his capital with the spoils of Hindu cities, and the productions of Hindu workmen. The houses of the natives were indeed, as they still are, mean and contemptible; but stone edifices adorned with colonnades were erected for public purposes; and the number, size, and occasionally imposing appearance, of temples still in existence support the traditionary claim to former magnificence. Still there is no reason to think that Hindu art ever approached the beauty and

* Job xxvi. 7.

dignity of the classical orders of architecture, or even equalled the florid but elegant structures subsequently produced by the Mohammedans. In the present day both races are utterly destitute of design and practical skill. The few edifices now attempted are copied from European works; and a native architecture can hardly be said to exist. Native music, painting, and sculpture are at a still lower ebb, and in all probability were never in the least to be compared with those of Europe.

The more important operations of daily labour display an ignorance and want of cultivation yet more deplorable. *Agriculture*, the employment of the bulk of the people, and in all ages the main-stay of the public revenue, remains, after three thousand years, in a condition hardly removed from barbarism. The Dasyus, so despised by the victorious Aryans, could not have cultivated their fields on a more primitive system than still obtains in the greater part of India.

The crooked-stick, with which the ryot scratches the surface of the ground, would not be recognised for a plough in any part of Europe or America. A kind of drill not less primitive, with a rude harrow, mattock, and sickle, complete the list of agricultural implements. The grain is trodden out by cattle, brought home in carts, and stored in pits under ground. The cultivators seem pretty well acquainted with the quality of their soils, and the kind of grain best adapted to each. In some parts, also, the rotation of crops is understood; but whether from indolence or want of capital, the same kind of grain is commonly reproduced, or only varied by the slovenly practice of mixing different seeds in one sowing, to come up together, or in succession, till the land is exhausted and lies fallow for years. Little or nothing seems to be known of the value of manure. From this imperfect state of cultivation, several acres of ground in India scarcely equal the yield of one in the best parts of Europe. Cotton and sugar are indigenous, and have been cultivated from the earliest periods, but it is only by the application of European skill that either can compete with the products of America and the West Indies. Indigo, also, which is produced in large quantities, owes its value as an article of commerce to similar foreign assistance.

The natives of India, in a word, have never attained a thorough knowledge of any branch of agriculture, though in possession of magnificent soils lying under an ever-fertilizing sun, and ruled from time immemorial by governments which drew their chief revenue from the land. The rural population is accordingly sunk to the lowest stage of existence. They are generally densely ignorant, depressed in spirit, and involved in debt; nor does golden hope visit them with any dreams of amelioration. Dull and callous, they plod the weary round of their scanty, coarse, hard-earned existence, and leave their children to the same fate without emulation or concern.

An equally low state of knowledge is apparent in the *manufactures* of India. No improvements in machinery have been invented to lighten the toil or increase the productions of the workman. Naturally ingenious and artistic, their fabrics of cotton, silk, and brocade, with the exquisite work of their goldsmiths, early challenged the admiration of the civilized world. They have never been surpassed, nor perhaps equalled, by the workmen of any other land. Yet the implements of these delicate crafts continue to be of the rudest description, while the progress of knowledge in Europe has reversed the stream of commerce, and well nigh extinguished native manufactures. The cotton goods, once the pride and wealth of India, and never equalled in fineness and delicacy of texture, are almost superseded by the products of English steam mills. The looms of India, from which the East India Company a few years back imported six or seven millions of pieces annually, do not furnish a single venture in the year, and the consequent suffering among numerous classes of the natives is unparalleled in the history of commerce.

No doubt the native workman lies under other disadvantages, besides ignorance, in this competition. Without capital to purchase European machinery, he is to a great extent denied the means of constructing any indigenous equivalent. The rivers seldom furnish an efficient water-power, and coal is too far off to render steam generally available. The want of roads, too, is an impediment insurmountable to native resources; while great injustice is inflicted by the unequal tariff, to which India has been compelled to submit for the advantage of the British manufacturer. Still, if native learning and thought had occupied itself on the real wants and interests of the country, it seems unlikely that such improvements should not have been continually going on in the cultivation of her indigenous productions, and in the instruments of daily labour, as would at least have saved her from the shock she has actually sustained. Looking to the abundance and cheapness of the raw material, with the low price of native labour, it does not seem improbable that a wider diffusion of practical knowledge, aided by the development of Indian resources from the construction of railroads, and the further application of European skill and capital, might yet repair these losses and render India again the seat of manufactures for a large portion of the world. For these, however, as for all other elements of national prosperity, the natives must look to the progress of an education prompted by higher motives, and conducted on more expansive views than has ever pertained to Brahman philosophy.

The British government has long been anxious to raise the condition of its native subjects, by removing the wide-spread ignorance which deprives them of social power and consideration. Viewing with respect the hereditary claims of the Brahmans as national teachers, it first sought to revive the expiring flames of ancient learning, and unite it with some portions of European intelligence, in the hope that education would so descend in a natural order to the uninstructed masses. With this object in view, much encouragement was bestowed on the study of Sanscrit and other branches of Oriental literature. Government colleges were established for their pursuit, and they were further stimulated by promises of public employ. Experience, however, has demonstrated the inadequacy of Oriental literature to meet the wants of the case. Its systems of science and philosophy were found disfigured by incurable absurdities. Wholly void of history and geography, it was impenetrable to the light of modern researches and travel. The exposition of Hindu and Mohammedan law was doubtless aided by a knowledge of Sanscrit, Arabic, and Persian; but neither language could help to any just conception of the great wants of the country.

They could not teach the right employment of labour and capital, the benefits of commerce and manufactures, the laws of wealth, the development of internal resources, or the conditions of physical and social health. The attempt to graft on the Oriental systems some germs of a sounder science of morals, proved tardy and discouraging in the extreme; while to those who desired the spiritual illumination of the deluded idolaters, it seemed intolerable to keep the masses waiting, till the learned classes should have found time to appropriate and dispense the information demanded for the general good. It was soon acknowledged by all practical men that European knowledge, not Asiatic, is the great requisite to native education; that the bulk of the population can only be educated in their own tongue; and that for students of a higher order, *English* supplies a far better medium than the decaying and polluted Sanscrit.

Attention has been thus recalled to the indigenous schools scattered throughout the country. It was resolved to infuse new life into these institutions, and so, at a comparatively small expense, without offence to caste or creed, imbue the native mind with the lower elements of European knowledge. At the same time colleges were established in the presidency towns to impart a superior English education, and academical degrees were proposed to be bestowed for its encouragement. These endeavours of the government were long uncertain and experimental. Its measures were of partial and very limited application; urged in some parts, by the zeal of local agents, perhaps further than was feasible, they were in others restrained by unnecessary scruples.

Meanwhile an education definite in aim, and direct

and practical in operation, came into notice from another quarter. The Christian missionaries of various denominations opened schools for the instruction of their children, as a matter of course. It was soon found that the heathen youth were willing to attend, and that no invincible objection existed on the part of their parents. Large numbers of both sexes came quietly and unostentatiously under instruction. The missionaries proceeded to extend their schools and improve the quality of the teaching; each denomination erected its college or seminary of a higher description, and with their circles of vernacular schools attached to every station, began to enter on an honourable rivalry with the government in the education of the natives.

The object of the missionaries was simple and avowed; they were in the country for the sole purpose of persuading its inhabitants to receive the gospel of Christ. The government, on the other hand, were chiefly anxious to avoid interference with the native creeds; it was harassed with a perpetual fear of exciting religious prejudice. The distinctions of caste were carefully respected in their schools, all Christian teaching was excluded, and declarations of neutrality were reiterated with a zeal which almost seemed to deprecate conversion. The result affords a striking instance of the inapplicability of such notions to the native mind. The mission schools are so much better attended than the government ones, that the latter acknowledge that they have no chance in any station which enjoys the teaching of a missionary. This preference in the very quarter where repugnance was prophesied, is a marked illustration of the superior blessing attending on a single-minded effort after the highest good of our fellow-creatures. It deserves the most careful consideration from all who are still hampered in their views of native education by the fear of offending prejudices and awakening opposition.

The character and progress of these educational efforts having been earnestly discussed at the renewal of the East India Company's charter in 1853-4; one of the first measures of the newly-appointed Court of Directors was to review the state of government education, and lay down a scheme for its future direction. The despatch sent to India on this occasion, dated July 19th 1854, abounds in sentiments of an advanced and liberal character. It recognises as one of the great duties of government "the extending far more widely the means of acquiring general European knowledge, of such a character as may be practically useful to the people of India in their different spheres of life." With this object in view, they are to be "made familiar with the works of European authors, and with the results of the thought and labour of Europeans, on the subjects of every description upon which knowledge is to be imparted to them." The English language is directed to be taught wherever there is a demand for it, not as the end or object of the pupil's education, but as the most perfect medium of conveying the higher order of instruction. At the same time the vernacular languages are to be employed in teaching the far larger class who are ignorant of English.

In execution of these instructions, the government of each presidency has established a "Department of Education," under a high civil officer, with the title of "Director of Instruction," assisted by a competent staff of inspectors and sub-inspectors. Universities have been constituted at Calcutta, Madras, and Bombay, on the model of the University of London; and all existing educational agencies, with such additions as may be requisite, are sought to be comprehended in one great plan of native education.

The Universities are not themselves places of instruction, but *examining* bodies, whose office is to test the instruction acquired elsewhere, and fix the standard of education, by granting degrees in arts, medicine, law, and civil engineering. The instruction which is to qualify for these honours is to be attained in one of the affiliated *Colleges*. These include the various government Institutions opened for professional studies, such as medicine and engineering; the old Sanscrit, and Madrissa colleges, established for the cultivation of Hindu and Mohammedan learning respectively; and the later Institutions of general instruction. Of the latter description the Bengal presidency contains the "Presidency College" at Calcutta, and the colleges at Berhampore, Dacca, Hooghly, and Kishnagur. In the North-western province, government colleges exist at Agra, Delhi, Benares, and Bareilly. In Madras, the old "University," now styled University College, is the only government Institution for an advanced education. In Bombay are the Elphinstone Institution at the presidency, and the College at Poona. All these are superintended by English principals, with English and native professors of high qualifications.

Below these higher Institutions the scheme provides for classes of *schools* in regular gradation, to be placed in connexion with the colleges and each other, by means of scholarships conducting from the lower to the superior Institution. These have not been formed in all the presidencies on precisely the same plan. The class next in order to the colleges consists of Institutions, bearing the various designations of Provincial Schools, Collegiate Schools, High Schools, Zillah Schools, and Government Anglo-vernacular Schools. They exhibit no little difference also in their degrees of efficiency.

The lowest are the *vernacular schools* designed for the mass of the population unacquainted with English. It was in this department that native education received its greatest impulse from the scheme of 1854. The late Mr. Thomason, when lieutenant-governor of the North-western provinces, had introduced a system for the improvement of the indigenous schools, by means of inspection and the communication of better systems of teaching, which was attended with much success. He even prevailed on the landowners to contribute to their support. In Bengal, also, a number of vernacular schools existed, but with little superintendence, and consequently a low degree of qualification in the teachers. These naturally failed to obtain popularity, and were in course of being abandoned. A similar decay had overtaken the vernacular schools established by sir Thomas Munro in Madras.

Mr. Thomason's plans have now again been taken up on a larger scale in Bengal and the North-western provinces. In the former an attempt was made to augment the number of schools by making "grants in aid" to local managers; but this system has been judged inapplicable, in that part of India, from the great difficulties experienced in obtaining local support. The plan has been adopted of forming the existing indigenous schools into groups of from three to five, appointing a qualified teacher paid by government to each group, whose duty is to go from school to school, instructing the village schoolmasters in their duties, and teaching some of the higher subjects to the best pupils. In the North-western provinces the system includes schools established at the chief native towns, denominated *Tehseel*, and also "circle schools," called *Hulkabundee*, for the benefit of the rural population. These are planted in central situations to receive the youth of the surrounding villages within two miles. For the support of these schools the consent of the landowners was asked to appropriate one per cent. on the government assessment, half of which was to be paid by themselves, and the other half by the government. The required consent had been obtained in many districts, when the rebellion of 1857 interrupted the measure. It is intended, in the re-settlement of the land-revenue, to introduce this plan throughout the provinces. The sum so appropriated to the Hulkabundee schools will eventually amount to £40,000 per annum, of which one moiety will be contributed by the native proprietors.

A plan of popular education resembling the Hulkabundee has been introduced in some of the districts of the Madras presidency; but it is thought to be inapplicable to the revenue system generally prevailing there. The authorities have accordingly sanctioned an experiment of the nature of that approved in Bengal. In Bombay the vernacular schools are partly on a self-supporting plan, though still constituted as government institutions. Circle schools of a superior class are also in contemplation.

In all the presidencies, normal schools or classes

have been established for the instruction of vernacular *teachers*. Four such schools are in operation in Bengal, attended by more than two hundred and fifty pupils. In Madras the normal school is further constituted to supply masters for the Anglo-vernacular schools. The college at Benares, and the principal Institutions in Bombay, have opened normal *classes*, and regular training schools were sanctioned at Agra and two other places at the time of the recent outbreak.

The scheme of 1854 did not omit the great subject of female education, which the Court of Directors had previously desired should be comprehended in all the efforts of government, equally with other branches of education. The actual progress, however, is but little. A school at Calcutta for Hindu girls of the higher classes, seems to be the only government establishment for this especial object. Female schools exist at Dacca and Howrah, for which grants in aid have been sanctioned, and a considerable number of girls have been induced to attend some of the vernacular schools. Nineteen Brahmanee girls of good parentage are reported at one school in Bengal, and nearly five thousand were computed in 1857 to be in attendance on the schools of the Agra district, where a committee of native gentlemen had been induced to undertake the visiting and general superintendence. A female school in Mynpoorie contained thirty-two Mohammedan girls of respectable parentage. A few girls' schools have been opened by native efforts in the presidency of Bombay. An inspector reports from the Deccan that "the prejudices against female education are fast disappearing," and it seems now that, by proper exertions, female schools would flourish, as well as boys', in all parts of India. The action of government, however, is indispensable, as the people generally are opposed to any decided elevation of the female sex in mind or position.

Such were the means contemplated by the late Court of Directors for the advancement of native education through the direct action of the government. Their liberality took a still wider scope, in recognising and inviting the co-operation of the natives themselves, with all other labourers in the same great cause. The despatch of 1854, expressing a conviction that government was unable to effect all that was requisite for native education, acknowledged the liberality shown by some of the natives in the support of educational institutions, and further redeemed the long neglect and indifference of government to evangelical efforts, by handsomely recognising "the noble exertions of societies of Christians of all denominations to guide the natives of India in the way of religious truth."

To add efficiency to these exertions, and to call out local efforts in other ways for the advancement of education, a system of *grants in aid* was authorized, to be "based on an entire abstinence from interference with the religious instruction conveyed in the schools assisted," and to be extended, within certain limits, to all schools imparting a good secular education, "provided they enjoy an adequate local management, are duly open to government inspection, and are subjected to any other rules which may be prescribed by the government notifications." Regulations were accordingly published in India, under which some most important additions have been made to the educational establishments.

In some of the Bengal districts, advantage has been

taken of these rules by native promoters of vernacular schools; but generally speaking, the value of education is too little appreciated, and the wealthier classes are too indifferent to the improvement of their inferiors, to make it likely that any extensive results will ensue from that quarter. It is even feared that the endeavours of the educational officers to awaken native interest, and procure a proportionate amount of local support, may create a prejudice against education altogether, and render the government itself unpopular. On this account her Majesty's government have lately expressed an opinion, that the system "is unsuited to the supply of vernacular education to the masses of the population," and that "the means of elementary education should be provided by the direct instrumentality of the officers of government." The establishment of an *education rate* on the land is suggested in preference to making grants in aid.*

Education of a higher order awakens somewhat more interest in portions of the native community: accordingly grants in aid have been applied for, to some extent, by native associations and individuals, for the establishment or improvement of *Anglo-vernacular* schools. In some cases, too, proposals have been made by natives for the formation of still higher, or collegiate, schools, with the English language as the medium of instruction.

The most effectual result, however, of the system of grants in aid is found in the assistance afforded to the mission schools of the various Christian denominations. Few other private schools exist in India, at

* Lord Stanley's despatch to the government of India, dated April 7, 1859.

which a liberal English education can be obtained, and none are conducted with so large and comprehensive a benevolence towards all classes of the natives. Most of the denominations having established Institutions of a superior order for the training of catechists and missionaries, these were ready at once, as affiliated colleges under the several universities. The missions were supplied, also, with middle and elementary schools, teaching both English and the vernacular languages, and enjoying a large amount of popularity. The secular instruction imparted in these several schools is acknowledged to be equal or superior to that of the government Institutions: and it would be strange if, in inviting private co-operation, a Christian government should repudiate the most valuable class of assistance, merely because those who offer it aim at the further object of disseminating the Christian faith.

Yet this outrageous demand has not failed to be made by the "Old Indian" party, who for sixty years have been prophesying dangers from Christianity which never ensued, and do not even yet perceive that the government was never in so much peril, as when conducted upon their way in the Bengal native army. All that used to be said against the admission of missionaries, the building of churches, ecclesiastical establishments, and the freedom of the press, is now charged anew on "the grants in aid" to missionary schools. It is making the government a party to aggressions on the religion of the natives; it is applying the money derived from taxing Hindus and Mohammedans to subvert the most cherished convictions of the taxpayer. The objectors omit that grants in aid are offered on the same conditions to schools under native management,* while the Sanscrit College and the Madrissa are maintained at the public charge, for the exclusive benefit of Hindus and Mohammedans.

The two last-named Institutions are, in fact, inconsistent with the principle of neutrality laid down by the government, since they teach and *impose* a particular creed, excluding pupils of any other faith. But the mission schools are open to all; heathen pupils attend them without hesitation, and in most instances, unhappily, remain unimpressed by the Christian instruction. If others are persuaded to embrace the gospel, it is of their own free will; no deception is practised to procure their attendance, no undue influence is brought to bear on their conversion. Unless "the principle of neutrality" require the natives to be *precluded* from the opportunity of learning Christian truth *when they will*, it is impossible to sustain this objection.

After late events, it is really too much to suppose that the natives are so languid in vindicating their prejudices as to need the over-anxious protection of European champions. When they discover or surmise any evil in the mission schools, they have the remedy in their own hands by ceasing to attend them. The fact, however, is on the other side; the

* The grants in aid up to the 30th of April, 1857, amounted to the following sums:—

In Bengal.	Rs.
To missionary schools	9,828
To other schools	68,604
	Rs. 78,432
In Madras.	
To missionary schools	28,597
To other schools	5,613
	Rs. 34,210

Altogether the missionaries dispense but a small proportion of the public expenditure on education.

mission schools are *preferred* to those of the government. To deprive them of their share in the public grant would be to sacrifice the best education to the worst; to overrule the liberality of the larger number of scholars by the prejudices of those who would reject education altogether. Still, it appears that an influence has been exerted at the India House sufficient to induce the Queen's minister, while exposing the unfounded nature of the objection itself, to require the opinion of the Indian government on the operation of the system, and the feeling with which it is regarded by the native community in general.

In regard to the *quality* of the education contemplated in these Institutions, it ranges from the most elementary instruction up to the branches inculcated in the best schools of England, with the addition of some Indian and professional teaching. Reading, writing, arithmetic, geography, and history, and "common things," are taught in the lowest schools, and the government is about to add instruction in practical agriculture, one of the greatest boons that could be conferred on the vast rural population.

On the whole, there can be no doubt that the scheme of native education is sagaciously and liberally designed, and calculated to produce the most beneficial effects on the population. It is true that as yet its operation has been too recent and limited to have effected much practical improvement; and, owing to the recent mutiny, the reports are too imperfect to exhibit the statistical results. It seems but too probable, however, that they who relied upon the assistance of the natives were too sanguine in their expectations; and there can be little doubt that the government and the missionaries will, for some time to come, be the only educators of the masses. Their success, especially among the large rural population, will be slow in comparison with the results which are aimed at, and the zeal embarked in the undertaking; but if measured by the experience of past, and the state of native feeling and opinion, the progress may already be accounted surprisingly rapid. Probably more new ideas have been imparted to the native mind by the educational efforts of Great Britain, including the administration of government, legislation, and the press, during the last thirty years, than in as many previous centuries.

It is to be deeply regretted, then, that so wise and liberal a plan of education should be narrowed in its field of operation by the unnecessary recognition of caste distinctions. Of all places, the school is the last in which concessions should be made to the false and wicked assertion, that God has created men of different natures, and endowed them with unequal rights. The government does not scruple, in its schools of medicine, to teach and demonstrate the unity of the human species; in its legislation it affirms the perfect equality of all its subjects in the eye of the law. It is singularly inconsistent, then, to allow the pretensions of caste to find a recognition in the place devoted to the instruction of youth, which is denied in the leading transactions of public life. The true character of these distinctions, and the incompatibility of maintaining them in any sound system of general education, were forcibly pointed out by a distinguished Brahman at a meeting held in Madras to consider of the formation of a university at that presidency. A gentleman present on the occasion, and who took the most prominent part in the design, has related the discussion which arose on the difficulty of mixing youths of all castes promiscuously with Christians and Pariahs in the same school-room and on the same benches, without any difference or distinction whatever. Some were ready to concede; others desired impossible regulations; several were averse altogether to such a violation of feelings which they held sacred. All parties had been gradually won over but one distinguished Brahman, who at last slowly rose, and in very good English delivered himself pretty much as follows: "It is well for you, gentlemen, to consent in common, to do for the good of others what is hateful to your own feelings, and odious in the sight of all your connexions. You are not of my caste, and some of you yield little, and some nothing. But when I am pressed to join you, I am asked not only to violate my religious duties, but to degrade myself and my family from the highest station in our community. We all know the value of rank in society, what it is to hold an honoured and exalted station. Our friend Mr. Norton, and others like him, would hardly endure to mix on equal terms with the lowest of his own countrymen; and we are aware that the English nobility are a privileged class, to whom every honour and deference is paid as if they were a superior race. *What the nobility is to the English people, that is my caste to myself, my family, and my brethren;* and it is much more. But I know that something must be done, and is now doing, for the advancement of the rising generations of my countrymen, and it can only be effected through education. I have heartily united with my friends in promoting this object, and I feel that the welfare of my country is at stake. I also yield. But it is fit you should feel what sacrifice I make. I shall now co-operate with you all cordially in overcoming every caste obstacle to the cause of native education; and to prove my sincerity, I shall send my own child as one of the first pupils of the intended High School."

The result of these, and many previous consultations with the heads of the native society of Madras, was a petition to government, signed by upwards of seventy thousand Hindus, for the establishment of educational seminaries for the superior classes of every denomination.*

Surely, there can be no occasion for a Christian government to show itself more fastidious in the support of caste than this closely calculating Brahman. His unambiguous confession that caste is a social distinction, like nobility, and that its so-called "religious duties" may be surrendered to higher considerations of the general good, should be allowed to decide the question for ever. That which seventy thousand Hindus, "wise in their generation," could concede to the design of a "superior instruction" for their own benefit, a paternal government may justly insist upon for the general education of the people.

Another cause of complaint arises from the restrictions imposed on the use of the Holy Scriptures in the schools maintained by the government. On this point the views of the Court of Directors were expressed in the following words:—

"The Bible is, we understand, placed in the libraries of the colleges and schools, and the pupils are

* Letter to sir G. Clerk, by George Norton, M.A., late advocate-general at Madras. London: 1859.

able freely to consult it. This is as it should be; and, moreover, we have no desire to prevent or discourage any explanations which the pupils may, of their own freewill, ask from their masters upon the subject of the Christian religion, provided that such information be given out of school hours." But when it was proposed, in 1847, to introduce a Bible class into a school at Madras, the measure was positively forbidden by the Court, though the attendance was to be purely voluntary, and though the proposition emanated from the Council of Education, comprising the governor, with nine other distinguished government officers and two native gentlemen, one a Hindu and the other a Mussulman.

The anxiety of the Court to avoid "the slightest suspicion of proselytizing," would appear to be little shared by the natives themselves, who not only send their children to the mission schools, where the Bible is the most prominent element in the instruction, but introduce it into their own schools, and freely discourse of its contents. The rajas of Mysore and Travancore, both Hindu princes, have personally desired the Christian Scriptures to be read and taught in schools founded and supported by themselves. It is common also to hear educated natives boast of their acquaintance with the sacred volume, and express their admiration of its contents. Nor is it apparent why its presence in a school should incur the "suspicion of proselytizing" any more than the Vedas or the Koran. These works are freely studied by Christians without awakening any alarm for their faith in themselves or others. The Hindu would appear even less liable to such apprehensions, since his religion is so much more a matter of inheritance and custom than of doctrinal conviction. A Roman Catholic might object to a Protestant version of the Bible, as tending to undermine his children's belief in the dogmas of his church; but to a Hindu it is comparatively of little consequence what he *thinks;* his religion and his caste depend upon what he *does;* and, so long as the external rules are observed, their requisitions appear to be satisfied. At all events, it is not the part of a Christian government to anticipate an objection which does not naturally arise from the natives, nor to disclaim so eagerly the "suspicion" of a zeal for their religion. Such disclaimers are often the very way to awaken suspicion; and recent events have shown that government was not, with all its anxiety, acquitted of designs upon the native religions, which a more open circulation of the Scriptures would have shown to be impossible.

If this restriction then be uncalled for, the friends of the Bible are entitled, on that ground alone, to object to it as injurious and dishonouring to the holy volume. Its perusal should be left as free as any other work. Its introduction into the government schools might be safely confided to the local authorities, subject to the general security for the enjoyment of religious liberty. No one desires the Bible to be forced upon a reluctant reader; but, on the other hand, no prohibition ought to be intruded which may have the effect of intercepting a voluntary resort to it. The "libraries of colleges and schools" are not always the most accessible places to the pupils; and it is not a vague, *amateur* discussion of its pages, "out of school hours," between heathen pupils and some unqualified, perhaps unbelieving masters, that can be admitted as dispensing with the duty of imparting the most sacred instruction with all possible efficiency, wherever a class can be formed for its free and voluntary reception.

The question is altogether misconceived when it is spoken of as a means of proselytizing. No one acquainted with missionary operations would look for "proselytes" through the aid of government schoolmasters, when the much shorter course is open of direct missionary teaching and preaching. Nor would the removal of the restrictions complained of have any immediately extensive operation, on account of the paucity of the schools where a Bible class could be expected, and a competent teacher be procured. The Bible is not needed to refute the Shastras, or to destroy the convictions which rest upon their authority. This is effectually accomplished by the education actually introduced. It is well understood that English education, apart from all religious teaching, is surely subversive of the Hindu creed and worship. This has been its invariable effect hitherto. The editor of a native paper in Calcutta, speaking for himself and others, declares that "no missionary ever taught them to forsake the religion of their fathers; it was government that did them that service."* Another demands whether "all the efforts of the missionaries have given one tithe of that shock to the superstitions of the people which has been given by the Hindu College?" It is simply impossible that a belief in the Puranas, and the absurd idolatries of the Hindu system, should co-exist in the same mind with the truths of science, or even a moderate acquaintance with the facts of nature and history.

It is idle then to attempt to "improve the moral

* Land of the Veda, by Dr. Percival.

and intellectual condition of the natives without in the least infringing on their religious convictions." Religion, true or false, will invariably challenge the subjection of the intellect and heart; to transfer these to another master is at once to subvert the empire of religion. This effect has already been experienced in India, not only as the result of direct education, but of the still wider action of British government, legislation, language, and literature. Hinduism finds itself as much threatened by the very law and equity of a Christian nation as by the gospel itself. There is, consequently, an angry and wide-spread effort, on the part of the bigoted Hindus, to sustain their tottering institutions. The *Dharma Sobha* (or Holy Alliance), a native association at Calcutta, was established to withstand the progress of the new knowledge; and there can be little doubt that the recent mutiny was largely due to its instigations, repeated in the native press, and circulated by means of the numerous religious mendicants.

The Bible, then, is not required to overthrow the native religions; but it is unfortunate that, so far as government education has hitherto gone, its results have been simply *destructive.* Limited, for the most part, to the colleges of superior instruction in the principal towns, it has raised up a class of educated natives who have discarded their own religion without obtaining a better. Discovering, by the light of science, the falsehood of their own Scriptures, they are apt to jump to the same conclusion as to all others; and this error is likely to be confirmed when they see the government exclude the Scriptures of its own faith from the schools of the country. It has become most important to show this class that a revelation exists which commands the intellect and the reverence of the highest minds among their instructors and guides. The education which displaces a mistaken confidence ought to point at least a silent finger to the repository where the grounds of a true faith are contained. The teacher who controverts the long-cherished convictions of millions, is bound to declare the source from which his light has been derived, and to help all who will seek it to a full enjoyment of its rays. There are many branches of secular instruction, also, which are directly founded on the Scriptures. Books are read in the schools such as works on moral philosophy, poetry, and history, which cannot be thoroughly understood without the sacred volume. It is possible even that false and injurious ideas might result from such a book as "Paradise Lost," if the reader be precluded from access to the Bible.

These convictions have acquired strength from the testimony recently borne by sir John Lawrence and other distinguished officers in the Punjab, that the sacred volume might be safely admitted into the government schools in the manner contended for. Unfortunately, however, the prejudices of the Court of Directors seem to have descended in even greater force on the minister who succeeded to their authority. Lord Stanley, in his despatch of the 7th of April, goes so far as to pronounce the desired liberty "objectionable and dangerous in a political point of view, as tending to shake the confidence of the native community in the assurances of a strict adherence to past policy in respect to religious neutrality, which her Majesty has been pleased to put forth."

The proclamation here referred to declares "her

Majesty's firm reliance on the truth of Christianity;" and the proposal to admit the Bible, which is the authentic record of Christianity, into the schools for voluntary study, seems to be only a practical method of asserting the same fact. The minister's interpretation, therefore, has been naturally appealed against to his successor. A deputation of seventy noblemen and gentlemen, headed by the archbishop of Canterbury, waited on lord Palmerston and sir Charles Wood, on the 30th July 1859, "to request a removal of the authoritative exclusion of the word of God from the system of education in the government schools in India, so that none, who may be so disposed, be interdicted from the hearing or the reading of the Bible in school hours, provided always that such safeguards be adopted against undue interference with the religions of the natives, as may appear just and proper to the local authorities in the several governments of India." Upon this occasion a written paper was submitted, in which, after stating the case, and "repudiating the notion that a voluntary Bible class can be considered, or would be considered, a proselytizing act," the following unhappy results, which flow from the maintenance of the interdict, were pointed out:—

"1. The interdict of the Bible in government teaching is regarded by the natives generally as antagonistic to Christianity. Hence a general impression has prevailed that the rulers of India desire their native subjects to remain ignorant of the sacred books of the Christian religion. Innumerable instances might be cited in which the exclusion of the Bible from school teaching has been publicly alleged as a proof of this. Thus the continuance of the interdict cannot be characterized even by the term 'neutrality.' It is a positive disadvantage to Christianity.

"2. The exclusion of the Bible necessitates the employment of a variety of secondary modes of inculcating moral truth. Smith's 'Moral Sentiments' was long a standard work. Whewell's 'Moral Philosophy,' and other works, are taught in the government schools. But the Bible is withheld, which is the standard of all moral truth for all mankind, and which has been universally found to carry with it an authority and power to which no human composition can pretend.

"The exclusion of the Bible is equally disadvantageous in respect of a correct knowledge of Christian truth; for Milton's 'Paradise Lost,' and various other works, are taught, which, without the Bible, tend only to confuse the native mind in respect of Christian truth.

"The effect of an education without the true standard of moral and religious truth has been pronounced by many of the most intelligent observers of native character to tend to the formation of a dangerous class of society, more hopelessly opposed to the Christian religion and to the British rule than all other classes.

"3. It is an injustice to India to withhold the Bible from the system of education which the government provides for its native subjects. The British government has taken upon itself the well ordering of populations ignorant of the true principles of right and wrong. Its tribunals of justice have superseded native tribunals; its legislation has made many things criminal which native codes of law enjoin, and which native religions sanction. The people have, therefore, a just claim to have the true standard of right and wrong set before them, in the moral instruction which the government system of education provides.

"4. The exclusion of the Bible from the national system of education lays the government open to the unfair suspicion of an intention to proselytize by underhand and indirect means. That such a suspicion is widely spread the late mutiny testifies. The only valid argument against such suspicions is that the Christian religious books repudiate all such means, however sanctioned by the Koran and other religious books with which the natives are familiar. But the British government cannot urge this argument without an obvious retort against our fidelity to our own principles."

To the apprehension of danger which affects the minds of some Indian officials, especially of those who resided in India before the mutiny, the deputation opposed the following memorable words of sir John Lawrence:—

"'Sir J. Lawrence has been led, in common with others, since the occurrence of the awful events of 1857, to ponder deeply on what may be the faults and shortcomings of the British as a Christian nation in India. In considering such topics he would solely endeavour to ascertain what is our Christian duty. Having ascertained that, according to our erring lights and conscience, he would follow it out to the uttermost, undeterred by any consideration. If we address ourselves to this task, it may, with the blessing of Providence, not prove too difficult for us. Sir John Lawrence entertains the earnest belief that all those measures which are really and truly Christian can be carried out in India, not only without danger to

British rule, but, on the contrary, with every advantage to its stability. Christian things done in a Christian way will never, the chief commissioner is convinced, alienate the heathen. About such things there are qualities which do not provoke nor excite distrust, nor harden to resistance.'"

This remonstrance elicited no more satisfactory reply than a reference to a previous despatch, under which it was stated that a Bible class may be formed *out* of school hours, and that the Bible itself may be read as an *historical* book, without teaching its *doctrines, in* school hours. These distinctions can satisfy no one; it must still be considered as a national reproach that the fountain of all our knowledge and greatness should, by the act of government, and from motives of supposed worldly policy, be subjected to restrictions not imposed on any other book.

The justice of the demand for its enfranchisement may further appear from the efforts of the educated natives themselves to supply the void, occasioned by the abandonment of their former superstitions, through a reform of the Hindu Shastras. This was the object of the celebrated Ram Mohun Roy. Fixing on those portions of the Vedas which enunciate the doctrine of one God, he declared this dogma to be the true religion of their fathers, and so rejected the Puranas, with the whole existing idolatry, as corruptions of later date. He translated the Upanishads, also, into some of the vernacular languages, and circulated them along with a work called "The Precepts of Jesus," compiled by himself. The deism thus eliminated by an arbitrary selection from the sacred books of Hindus and Christians, was embodied in a society, meeting at Calcutta, for the worship of *Brahm* (the divine essence) with praise and prayer. Ram Mohun Roy visited England in 1830, where he naturally associated himself with the Socinians, whose views and principles bore the closest resemblance to his own.

The society, which had declined on his departure, was revived, in 1839, under the name of the Tattwabodhini Sobha. Branches have been since established, and schools opened in Sanscrit, Bengali, and English, and great exertions are being made to propagate the principles and increase the numbers of this sect. Its system is simply one of natural religion, sheltered under a few texts from the Vedas. Disclaiming idolatry for themselves, these philosophers (like those of ancient times) find an excuse for it in others, by teaching that they who cannot turn their minds to God in spirit, from ignorance and want of learning, may worship him through the medium of matter. The sect is said to number about five hundred members in Calcutta, where a weekly meeting is held every Wednesday evening, after the model of Christian assemblies, the services being selected from the Vedas, and closed with a discourse on some portion of natural theology. Such a system, resting on no historical foundation, and contradicted by the actual worship of every age of Hinduism, appeals to the Vedas only in appearance. It can never engage the affections, or direct the lives, of the millions of India.

Another class of educated natives, discarding the Shastras altogether, have had recourse to the deistical and atheistical writers of Europe, as teachers of moral and social philosophy. The works of infidel authors of the last century are imported from England and France, and eagerly studied by these blind followers of the blind. All these classes preserve their caste, notwithstanding their defection from Hindu creed, so long as they keep themselves free from external pollutions; indeed, the "educated" high-caste men are often as jealous of the distinction, and as arrogant and intolerant towards their inferiors, as those who confidently believe themselves to be made of a different kind of clay. Such men are usually among the bitterest enemies of the gospel: their education serves to illustrate the apostle's maxim, "Knowledge puffeth up, but charity edifieth."

Amid all this fermentation of knowledge it may be hoped that a few are being secretly guided to the true Light and Teacher of men. It is certain that many educated Hindus speak with respect of the Christian Scriptures; some even avow a conviction of their truth, and profess to expect that one day all will be Christians. They decline, however, to take a step by themselves, entailing sacrifices which they are not prepared to endure.

These wild efforts of the unassisted intellect call loudly for the true Guide of mankind. It is impossible to withdraw the light already introduced, and restore the reign of ignorance. The more that knowledge of any kind is diffused, the more will the heterogeneous elements of native opinion be separated and tested. One result must of necessity be the unloosing of many odious and discordant spirits. The long-imprisoned powers of thought will fly abroad in all directions. The feeble organs, on their first illumination, will be liable to an imperfect and distorted action: they will "see men, as trees, walking." Forms of error, hitherto unknown, may attend the outflow of truth, while those which have already appeared will doubtless acquire a larger development. All will add to the rage and resistance of the votaries of the decaying superstitions, and the conflict already waged must be expected to grow and enlarge itself between the adherents of the old and the new knowledge.

With such expectations, there is but one course for the rulers, and one remedy for the evil in view. The course is ONWARD! The remedy lies in the diffusion of *more light*. The foundations already laid must be deepened and widened; the edifice we have commenced must be carried on to completion. Yet, in view of the tempests already shaking its walls, it may be deeply pondered whether all available supports have been provided for their security. The Christian church recognises in this agitation of the native mind a stronger incentive to proclaim that saving truth which alone can effectually rebuke the winds and the waves, and say to the sea, "Peace, be still." This is not the province of the civil government, nor could the church consent to devolve her trust upon another. But it is a question for the gravest consideration of those who bear the responsibility of diffusing secular knowledge, whether they are in fact using all the safeguards in their power against the ebullitions and eccentricities which may attend its course. In deliberately uprooting the convictions of centuries, unchaining thought, and placing the light of reason and conscience in the inexperienced hands of an enormous population, they seem imperatively called on to place within reach of all the most effectual guide that human reason has received from the hands of its Maker. If that guide be found in the pages of the inspired Scripture, then assuredly it is demanded for the *education*, apart from all considerations of the *evangelization*, of India.

The more this great question is considered, the more it will be seen that, not only is it not right to embarrass the holy volume with derogatory prohibitions, but that the course of education, already entered upon, demands its free circulation as a measure of *prudence*. It is the only safeguard against the evils of an imperfect, unsanctified knowledge. That the government should undertake the circulation of the Bible is not desired. The missionaries can do this more effectually. What is asked is, that they should not *exclude* it from a system of instruction which professes to embrace the elements of genuine education; that they should not compromise its character before the natives in order to conciliate prejudices adverse to the truth. The friends of religious education cannot be satisfied when representations, resting on principle and experience in many parts of India, are met by apprehensions of political dangers which have always proved unfounded. Nor is it just to the sovereign or people of Great Britain, to insinuate that the abrogation of a gratuitous and offensive restriction, imposed by the officious anxiety of Europeans, would be an interference with the religion of the natives, contrary to the proclamation of her Majesty on assuming the government.

CHAPTER IX.

CHRISTIANITY—EARLY EFFORTS.

Review of leading agencies in India—Indirect influence of Christianity—Foreseen by Wilberforce—Direct evangelization twice failed—*Syrian churches*—Lack of missionary zeal—Disputes with Portuguese—Numbers and condition—Tenets—Relations with English church—Rupture—Present state—Morals—*Church of Rome*—Portuguese missions—Inquisition—Xavier—Numerous conversions—Retention of caste—Feasts, etc.—Assimilation to heathen—Spiritual condition—Recent efforts from Rome—Schism of Portuguese clergy—Numbers—*British government*—"Traditional policy"—Early favourable indications—Services—Churches—Chaplains—Missionaries—Ecclesiastical establishments—*First Protestant Mission* at Tranquebar—Translation of Scriptures—Assistance in England—British missions at Madras and Cuddalore—Increase and effect of the missions—Swartz's plans—Native agents—Schools—Conversations—Funds—Simple living—Results—Native ministry—Letter of a convert—Bengal—Kiernander—Mission Church, Calcutta—Liberal views.

In the foregoing chapters some attempt has been made to review the leading agencies, which have conduced to the present condition of the natives of India. Greatly diversified in race and language, they have for centuries been subjected in common to the action of the Hindu religion and castes, to the sword of Mohammedanism, and to government institutions of a despotic type. The effect has been to superinduce a certain uniformity of social and domestic life, with a general want, or low condition, of knowledge; modified, however, by numerous national and local distinctions. It is only in respect of the resemblance so impressed on the surface, that any general view can be taken of the heterogeneous masses. In all practical dealing with the natives, it is indispensable to study the distinctive characteristics of the particular nation or tribe to be affected.

Since the rise of the British government, influences have been brought to bear of an entirely new description. While professing to maintain the established laws and usages of the natives, the administration has been, more or less directly, influenced by the antagonist principles of Christianity. The legislation, jurisprudence, and general policy, of Great Britain are confessedly moulded by the spirit of the gospel. All her knowledge and principles of education found themselves on the same basis. In whatever degree, then, British views and principles have been imported into the government of India, to the same extent has the latter been subjected to the indirect influences of the gospel. In the amelioration of barbarous laws, in the equal administration of justice between man and man, in the observance of public faith, and in every endeavour to extend the blessings of knowledge and liberty, the government has in fact been walking by a light, the source of which it has often sought to conceal. What Christian nations call the dictates of humanity and justice are really the improved views of moral duty, which result from the regenerating power of Christ's holy religion; and in the providence of God many a ruler, "howbeit he meant not so, neither did his heart think it,"* has been unconsciously preparing the way of the Lord, while he reckoned only on advancing the political or intellectual welfare of his charge.

Remarkably has this result ensued in India from the means adopted for the diffusion of knowledge, and

* Isaiah x. 7.

the improved education of the natives. The effect was foreseen by Mr. Wilberforce, when, in the debates of 1813, he expressed himself as follows:—"After much reflection I do not hesitate to declare, that from enlightening and informing them, in other words, from education and instruction, from the diffusion of knowledge, from the progress of science, and more especially from all these, combined with the circulation of the Scriptures in the native languages, I ultimately expect even more than from the direct labour of missionaries properly so called." These indirect influences of Christianity are important to be noted, in estimating the means for the evangelization of India. They constitute the most widely-spread advantage she has hitherto enjoyed from her connexion with Great Britain, and the foundation of what is most hopeful in the policy adopted for her improvement.

The more direct preaching of the gospel has been either mixed with serious error, or confined within a comparatively narrow extent. Twice before the period of British intercourse, the seed of Christianity was sown upon the shores of India; and twice, being uprooted by enemies from without, or corrupted and decaying within, it failed to bring forth fruit to perfection. The origin of the first attempt is lost in obscurity. All that remained of it at the commencement of European intercourse, were the Syrian churches on the coast of Malabar, claiming descent from the apostle Thomas, but really founded about the fourth century by another Thomas, a Syrian monk, and placed under the jurisdiction of the patriarch of Antioch, and afterwards of Mosul. The early condition of this Christian community can now only be conjectured.

If its first preachers and converts were ever in danger of the pains of martyrdom, the heathen must have soon relaxed their persecutions, or the church her aggressive efforts. In the ninth century, the Christians had become a recognised community on the coast of Malabar, enjoying privileges from the native powers, and living under a chief of their own, who was honoured with the appellation of *raja*. Their condition, perhaps, in some degree, resembled that of the Greek churches now under the dominion of Turkey, save that the Malabar princes seem to have been more tolerant than the sultans of Constantinople.

The Syrian Christians appear to have enjoyed a high rank in the state and in society. They are still accounted next in precedence to the Nairs. Before the arrival of the Portuguese, they were distinguished, also, by a scrupulous regard to truth, and a general manliness and independence of character. It may be feared, however, that the Syrians had purchased their social *status* by abandoning all attempts on the surrounding heathenism. The church dwelt among idolaters without vexing her soul with their unrighteous doings, or making any systematic effort for their conversion. The consequence was the same as in the early churches of Africa, and in the British churches in England; suffering the missionary spirit to languish and die within, she proved unequal to maintain her own position when the evil hour came upon her from without.

The Syrian churches were in possession of an episcopal government and Oriental ritual, when the Portuguese landed in their neighbourhood. The new comers were surprised to meet with Christians who had never heard of the Roman pontiff, and were ignorant of the language in which he promulgated his decrees. The Syrians were not less astonished to find that ignorance on these important points more than overbalanced all the claims of a common Christianity. They were required to acknowledge the supremacy of the pope, and submit their ritual to emendations designed to effect a conformity with the doctrines of Rome. On declining, they were subjected to ecclesiastical intrusion, and as soon as temporal power was acquired, to active persecution. The Portuguese ecclesiastics engaged with ardour in the conquest of heretics, more odious in their eyes than the heathen themselves. A schism was brought about among the Syrians; their bishops were seized and carried prisoners to Goa, where a provincial synod fulminated decrees against their doctrines. At length archbishop Menezes, convoking a council at Diamper, committed their ecclesiastical books to the flames, and, with the aid of the Jesuits, succeeded in reducing a portion of their number to obedience to Roman jurisdiction.

These Syro-Roman congregations were indulged in the use of the Syrian language, after their ritual had been expurgated and altered to suit the views of the papacy. The remainder, flying to the hills, preserved an independent episcopacy, which continues to the present day; but their numbers are few, and diminishing. At the close of the eighteenth century Gibbon estimated the whole Syrian population at 200,000. The abbé Dubois reduces the total to 100,000, of whom he supposes two-thirds to be Romanists. A more recent calculation gives 100,000 as the number of the Syro-Romanists, and about half that as the sum of the "Christians of St. Thomas."

The discovery of the last-named body by Dr. Claudius Buchanan, when he visited the mountains of Malabar in 1806, was hailed with much satisfaction in the Church of England. Bishops Middleton and Heber entered into a cordial intercourse with the metran (or bishop), and concerted measures for reviving the knowledge and moral purity of his decaying congregations. They were found (unlike the Indo-Portuguese) to retain none of the distinctions of caste. While rejecting the papal supremacy, they maintained a firm acknowledgment of the authority of Holy Scripture, their canon also agreeing with our own. They cordially accepted the offer of being supplied from England with copies of the Bible in Syriac, to be freely circulated and taught among the people. It was agreed, too, that schools should be opened, and a college established for the education of the clergy.

The low state of learning among the latter was the occasion of some corruptions, such as the acknowledgment of seven sacraments; though archbishop Menezes could never induce them to extend that name to more than three, baptism, holy orders, and the communion. It was satisfactory, however, that, like other Oriental churches, they had *not* adopted the celibacy of the clergy, the doctrine of purgatory, nor the worship of images. *Paintings* were allowed in their churches (as among the Greeks); but when a Jesuit priest, at the close of the 16th century, exhibited an image of the virgin Mary, the whole congregation rose up, and cried out, "Away with the idol, we are Christians."*

* Bishop Wilson's Charge, 1843. App. iv. This protest stands in honourable contrast to the reply of a Romish priest to Mr. Hough when reproved for his imitation of heathen ceremonies: "If we come among dogs we must do as the dogs do."

With these favourable auguries a college and a printing-press were erected at Cottyam in 1817, by the Church Missionary Society; and the English missionaries laboured for a series of years, with the full approbation of the metran, in multiplying copies of the Syriac Scriptures and translating them into the vernacular Malayalam, establishing schools, improving the education of the clergy, and preaching in the vernacular. The prospect, however, became clouded by the discovery of superstitions and corruptions in discipline among the Syrian clergy, which had not been anticipated. A new metran proved impatient of the remonstrances, perhaps jealous of the superior attainments, of the English missionaries. At last, in 1835 the metran not only summarily rejected a string of reforms suggested by bishop Wilson, but imposed an oath upon his clergy to hold no further intercourse with the English.

Since the separation thus effected, the missionaries have become still more convinced of the corrupt condition of the Syrians generally. Though no canons, or articles of faith or communion, have been formally adopted inconsistent with the admitted supremacy of the Scripture, it is stated that the majority now practically hold the grievous errors of transubstantiation, the sacrifice of the mass, purgatory, worship of the Virgin, adoration of the saints, extreme unction, and others of a similar tendency. As they retain all their ancient dislike of the Church of Rome, it is little probable that these corruptions have been imported from that quarter: it would rather appear that there is a natural tendency in the human heart to engraft them on the Christian system, when not continually irradiated with the light of God's word. It may still be not impossible, if the Syrian clergy could be raised from their depressed condition, and persuaded to embrace the means of education, that their teaching should be reduced to a more scriptural standard, without any disturbance of their ecclesiastical system. The moral character of their people is still admitted to present many points of superiority over other natives. A simplicity of manner, accompanied by no small degree of honesty and plain dealing, distinguishes their intercourse with others, and renders it the more to be regretted that designs undertaken for their spiritual improvement should for the present be so unhappily interrupted.

The Church of Rome has exhibited in India, as in other parts of the world, a missionary spirit of unquestionable ardour and perseverance. The Portuguese conquests were avowedly devoted to the conversion of the heathen. Missionaries of various orders sailed with all their expeditions, and colonies were planted among the natives, who were encouraged to intermarry, on condition of embracing the Christian religion. On taking possession of Goa, a church was dedicated to St. Catherine, then solemnly chosen to be patroness of the city, and protectress of the Portuguese in India. The Inquisition was soon added, to guard against heresies and relapses; and though the zeal of the holy fathers was often diverted to repress the enormities of Judaism and Syro-Christianity, it is but fair to confess that, according to their light, they laboured much and steadily for the extension and defence of the church among the heathen. In Hindustan the Jesuits penetrated to the court of Akbar, while in the further south they appeared in the disguise of white Brahmans, come to instruct their brethren in a new Veda. Some efforts of a more evangelical character were undertaken by Xavier and a few other single-minded, if misguided, missionaries. Nothing was omitted, which persuasion, force, or fraud could supply; and the exertions of the church were backed by all the resources of the state. Bishoprics were founded; churches and monasteries rose in succession to the demolished pagodas; and money was freely lavished on a cause which never ceased to command the expenditure of willing and devoted lives. Exertions of this description, steadily maintained for two hundred years, could hardly fail to make an impression on the native population. Xavier reports ten thousand baptisms by his own hand in a month; nay, not unfrequently, he declares that a populous village was baptized in a single day.

Such a statement seems incredible; but similar wholesale conversions are not entirely unknown at the present time. The village authorities in Tinnevelly have not unfrequently applied to the missionaries, to receive the whole community under Christian instruction; and doubtless all would have readily submitted to baptism, had it been consistent with the principles of the new teachers to dispense that rite so indiscriminately. The constitution of Hindu society, indeed, renders it far easier to take possession of a community than of an individual. A general change of religion would entail less individual sacrifice or reproach. The distribution of castes and families might remain unaffected; the business and recreations of daily life would proceed as before; and no disturbance would ensue in the complicated system of property and succession. Hence, it is not uncommon to hear the natives prophesy, that "they shall all be Christians some day." Doubtless, numbers would embrace the gospel to-morrow, if all their friends would go with them, and no change of position resulted in society.

There need be no question, then, of the large numbers admitted into the Romish communion. Care was taken to make the change as little burdensome as possible. The rules of caste were retained so rigorously, that churches are still found in the south of India, divided into compartments, and provided with separate entrances, for the respective orders of worshippers. The feasts and ceremonies of the new religion were purposely assimilated to the old one, so that while acquiring many substantial advantages of a temporal character, the neophytes should be scarcely conscious of parting with a single rite of superstition. The Jesuit father Martin thus reports to his superior at Paris his device for obliterating the distinctions between heathenism and Christianity:—

"On Saturday evening I got ready a small triumphal chariot, which we adorned with pieces of silk, flowers, and fruits. On it was placed an image representing our Saviour risen from the dead; and the chariot was drawn in triumph round the church, several instruments playing at the same time. The festival was greatly heightened by illuminations, lustres, skyrockets, and several other fireworks, in which the Indians excel; then verses were spoken or chanted by the Christians, in honour of our Saviour's triumphing over death and hell. The chief personage of the settlement, his whole family, and the *rest of the heathens who assisted in the procession,* fell prostrate thrice before the image of our Saviour risen from the dead, and worshipped him *in such a manner as very happily* *blended them indiscriminately with the most fervent Christians!*"*

While heathen rites were thus openly imported into the church, it does not appear that any portion of the Scripture was ever published by the Church of Rome in the vernacular languages; and it may be inferred that few of the truly evangelical doctrines and precepts were urged on the native conscience. The darling object of that church, to keep the word of God from the knowledge of the laity, was never so effectually carried out as in India. The power of the church, and the observance of its ritual, were proposed without a rival; and the native mind accepted them with implicit, unreasoning submission. For the kind of religion so imparted, we have the witness of a "prophet of their own." The abbé Dubois declares that in a long ministry, during which his flock was numbered by thousands, he never met with *a single sincere Christian.* He affirms that sixty thousand native Christians in Mysore repudiated the gospel and embraced the creed of Mohammedanism, at one time, on the order of Tippoo Sultan. And although the majority of these afterwards returned to their nominal Christianity, their pastor bitterly declares his conviction that any similar trial would result in the same "tame submission and general apostasy."

Dr. Allen, an experienced American missionary, who takes a somewhat more favourable view than many Protestants of the present state of Romish Christianity, writes as follows:—

"In the southern part of India I was several times in company with a large number of natives, who, I

* Lettres Edifiantes et Curieuses.

supposed, from their dress and appearance, were heathens and idolaters, but found, on inquiry, that most of them were Roman Catholics. I learned, in answer to my inquiries, that in their marriage connexions, their eating and drinking, and in all their social and religious intercourse, they observed the rules of caste as much as the Hindus did. I asked them how they could all participate in the same sacraments, and yet preserve their rules of caste. They replied that 'their *padre* (priest) put his hands upon what was to be eaten, and consecrated it, and then it became *prusad*, and could be taken and eaten by persons of different castes without their losing caste.' This word, '*prusad*,' is the name given to food cooked in heathen temples and then offered to the idols, and consecrated with such rites that people of different castes can handle it and eat it, and yet preserve their caste.

"In other matters, also, they retain much of their former heathen customs. The Hindus are very fond of show and noise in their religion; and it is a frequent custom, in some districts, to put the idols of their gods on a car or carriage of some kind, on festival days, and then draw it about in procession. This usage has been retained by the Roman Catholics, only substituting the images of their saints for the idols of the gods. *In some places the same car is used on Hindu festival days for the idols of the gods, and on Romish festivals for the images of the saints.*"*

The abbé Dubois, also, describing how Roman Catholics imitated the heathen in such things, says:—

"This Hindu pageantry is chiefly seen in the

* Allen's India, p. 529.

festivals celebrated by the native Christians. Their processions in the streets, always performed in the night time, have indeed been to me at all times a subject of shame. Accompanied with hundreds of tom-toms (small drums), trumpets, and all the discordant, noisy music of the country, with numberless torches and fireworks; the statue of the saint placed on a car which is charged with garlands of flowers, and other gaudy ornaments, according to the taste of the country; the car slowly dragged by a multitude, shouting all along the march; the congregation surrounding the car all in confusion, several among them dancing or playing with small sticks, or with naked swords; some wrestling, some playing the fool, all shouting or conversing with each other, without any one exhibiting the least sign of respect or devotion: such is the mode in which the Hindu Christians in the inland country celebrate their festivals. They are celebrated, however, with a little more decency on the coast. They are all exceedingly pleased with such a mode of worship; and anything short of such pageantry, such confusion, and such disorder, would not be liked by them. I at several times strove to make those within my range sensible of the unreasonableness of so extravagant a worship, and how opposite it was to true piety; but my admonitions proving everywhere a subject of scandal rather than of edification among my hearers, who in several instances went so far as to suspect the sincerity of my faith, and to look upon me as a kind of free-thinker and a dangerous innovator, merely on account of my free remarks on the subject, I judged it more prudent to drop the matter, and to overlook abuses it was out of my power to suppress."

The present author is always loth to undervalue any profession or form of Christianity; but truth requires it to be stated that, in his own little mission in the Mysore territory, when Roman Catholic natives sought admission, they were generally found as ignorant of the Scriptures and of the gospel as the heathen themselves. In fact no distinction was made in their instruction or reception, save that the so-called Christian was not again baptized. The author has now before him two rosaries given up to him by natives so received into his congregation. They are made of what are commonly termed Brahmanee beads, being the same as the Brahmans use in the construction of their sacred string. To one of them is appended a small crucifix, having the figure of the Virgin on the reverse; and also a medal, one side of which presents a full-length figure of the Virgin, and the other her monogram, surmounted by a cross, with two flaming hearts below, one of them being transfixed by a sword. These were worn as amulets or charms (in which all natives repose great confidence), and were delivered up, as a matter of conscience, on adopting the evangelical faith.

Dr. Allen states that the great and besetting sin of the Roman Catholic population is *intemperance*, a vice for which they are often reproached by the Hindus and Mohammedans. "Still (he adds) there is more domestic happiness among them than among the Hindu or Mohammedan population in corresponding circumstances. Polygamy is never allowed; the women dress more decently, and have more their appropriate place in their families. More of them are educated, and they generally appear with more propriety and better manners in their intercourse with strangers and among their own people."

This writer adds, of the Roman Catholic population of India, that "even in their present ignorant and degraded state, they present a very interesting view to the Christian and the philanthropist. They are nearly a million in number; and though the greater part of them live in the peninsula, yet there are small communities of them scattered over all the country, from Cape Comorin to Cashmere, and from the Indus to the Burma frontier. These communities are made up of all the different nations, and some of them using all the different languages of India. They have been all baptized; they all bear the Christian name; they have some knowledge of the Christian doctrines, as the Trinity, the crucifixion of Christ, a future resurrection and judgment; and they hope for salvation through Christ, though with only vague and indefinite views of his work and character. This profession and this knowledge, vague and obscure as it is, yet put them on a very different ground from the Hindus and the Mohammedans. Should a reformation, like what occurred in Germany in the sixteenth century, take place among the Roman Catholics in India, should many of the priests and of the people be truly converted to God, the Scriptures in their own language be freely supplied to them, and they all be stirred up to read, great indeed would be the effect, not only through the 1,000,000 Roman Catholics, but through the 150,000,000 of the Hindus and Mohammedans. And how soon in this way might hundreds of native missionaries be raised up to preach, each in his own language, the wonderful works, and the yet more wonderful love, of God. In this view of the Roman Catholic population of India, I believe they have not received the attention from Protestants which their number, their circumstances, their character, and their relation to the native population of the country generally require." These impartial reflections are entitled to the candid attention of the dispassionate inquirer. Roman Catholics must admit that they present a more favourable judgment than is given by their own missionary, the abbé Dubois, who proclaims his conviction that India has rejected the appointed day of its salvation, and is now consigned to irremediable reprobation!

Of late years the see of Rome has exerted itself to improve the moral condition of its native congregations in India, but hitherto the results are not favourable. Differences with the crown of Portugal, whose supremacy is still acknowledged by the archbishop of Goa, led to the sending out vicars apostolic to the Indian dioceses, and these were received with great jealousy by the Portuguese clergy, who not unnaturally suspected a design on the endowments which remain in their possession.* The delegates of the Holy See, on the other hand, treated with disdain the pretensions of the Indian primate and his subordinates. The result was a complete schism, in which the archbishop of Goa retains three bishops and episcopal governors, with about one hundred priests, under his authority, while the papal obedience comprehends six bishops, ten vicars

* When the author was at Madras in 1837, a furious war was waged between the vicar apostolic (an Irish monk) and the bishop elect of the see of Meliapore. The former having received consecration as a bishop *in partibus infidelium,* pressed the Portuguese hard with his episcopal and apostolical powers; while the latter, though rightfully elected by the chapter of Goa, and in possession of the temporalities, remained without papal confirmation, and was consequently unable to obtain episcopal consecration. The dispute came at last into the British courts, which, strangely enough, were employed in adjudicating on the rival pretensions of *two* foreign potentates to exercise jurisdiction within the dominions of the English crown.

apostolic, and above three hundred priests in different parts of India. The former body is not likely to maintain itself long against the power and influence of Rome, reinforced by missionaries from Europe (English, Irish, and Italian) gifted with far higher powers both of body and mind. It remains to be proved, however, what effect the new European influence will produce on the native Roman Catholic population. It may well be doubted by those who know the depravity of human nature, and recognise the one means of its renewal in evangelical truth, whether the papal system can, under any development, really extirpate the idolatries of India, or elevate its inhabitants to the moral and spiritual standard indispensable to national improvement.

The British government has acted from the first on an opposite principle to the Portuguese; but it is a mistake to ascribe to its earlier authorities that indifference to Christianity, and encouragement of idolatry, which have lately been dignified with the singular appellation of the "East India Company's traditional policy." The fact is, that the first Company, though purely a mercantile corporation, were, like other London companies, neither unmindful of religion themselves, nor indisposed to assist in its extension in India. Their ships usually carried chaplains, and in the preface to a farewell sermon preached on the despatch of a fleet in 1618, the author, Dr. Wood, distinctly asserts that the Company were "seeking to honour His (Christ's) name among the heathen."* About the same time the Company's factor at Agra was writing to them to send out "solid and sufficient divines to encounter with the arch enemies of our religion," the Jesuit missionaries.†

* Kaye's Christianity in India, p. 40. † Ibid, p. 41.

Divine service was held twice *daily* in the president's house, and three times on Sunday. Sir George Oxenden asked for the erection of a church at Bombay, that "the natives might observe the purity and gravity of our devotions;" and in 1681, Teynsham Master, the governor of Madras, laid the foundation stone of a church, which is still standing, in Fort St. George. Chaplains were always sent to the chief factories by the Company from England; and in the charter granted by king William III. (5th September, 1698), there is a clause enjoining them to maintain a minister in every garrison and superior factory; and such ministers are expressly required to "apply themselves to the native language of the country where they shall reside, the better to enable them to instruct the Gentoos, that shall be servants or slaves of the same Company or of their agents, in the Protestant religion."

It is true that these extracts do not evidence a fixed design of preaching the gospel to the heathen; but neither do they exhibit these early traders as basely hiding their religion from motives of commercial gain. On the contrary, it is clear that they provided for the open celebration of Christian worship among themselves, and distinctly contemplated the conversion of, at least, their own households. The subsequent neglect arose from another source; it can be traced to the crooked policy of statesmen, rather than the inordinate covetousness of merchants. The latter drew up a set of regulations for their servants in India, "with a view to render the religion we profess amiable in the sight of those heathens among whom they reside;"* and the president at Madras was wont to walk to the new church every

* Kaye's Christianity in India, p. 59.

Sunday, at the head of the English residents, through a street of sepoys.

These outward demonstrations of religion were doubtless accompanied, as they often are in all countries, with much profligacy and immorality of life. Vice and infidelity overspread all classes in Europe at the age of the French revolution, and were reproduced in greater enormity on the distant shores of India. These were the faults of the community and of the times, not the effects of any "policy" on the part of the authorities at home or abroad. By the latter, even direct missionary work was not regarded as beyond the province of government. The early Danish and German missionaries in the south continually received recognition and support from the government of the day. Kiernander, the first Protestant missionary in Bengal, was invited thither from Cuddalore by lord Clive, who placed a house at his disposal. Schultze, on coming to open the first "British mission in Fort St. George," in 1728, was received with much cordiality by the governor, who himself attended on his preaching. The directors also frequently furnished the missionaries with a free passage from Europe. The unhappy jealousy evinced on some other occasions was a plant—or a *fungus*—of later growth, for which not any definite "policy" of government, but the unbelieving views of the persons temporarily in authority, are responsible.

Even after this jealousy prevailed, the Company's ecclesiastical establishments were maintained as enjoined by the charter; and though, in conformity with the new ideas, their numbers were proportioned to the amount of English duties; and some individuals were occasionally heard to assert that, as officers of the government, the chaplains had no right to "interfere with the religion of the natives," yet no restriction was laid on the many exemplary members of those establishments, whose zeal prompted them to undertake the translation of the Scriptures, or the conversion of the natives. Brown, Buchanan, Martyn, Corrie, were all government chaplains; and many others of later date have both personally engaged in mission work, and actively befriended those who were exclusively devoted to such labours.

The episcopal superintendence, also, added by the Act of 1813, was designed to assist, in some degree, the extension of Christianity among the natives. The plan was proposed, indeed, by lord Castlereagh, as a measure to enable British subjects resident in India to exercise their national religion; but the design had been conceived by Buchanan, as a means of enlightening the Hindus, and it was supported in Parliament by the champions of Christian missions, in connexion with the clauses for facilitating the despatch of missionaries. There can be no question, in short, that the ecclesiastical establishments, augmented as they have been from time to time, and now numbering three bishops with above one hundred and twenty chaplains, officiating at the principal stations in India, are not only a source of strength to the missions of the Church of England, but largely contribute by their labours towards the impressions of Christianity made on the native mind, and so to the missionary influence in general.

Still the honour of first offering Protestant truth to the direct acceptance of the native population is not the distinction of the British government or of the British nation. It belongs to an inferior state, and a people of far less advantages. It was at Tranquebar, a Danish settlement on the coast of Coromandel, that this honourable undertaking was commenced. The first labourers were two Lutheran divines, commissioned by Frederick IV. of Denmark, to be not only his royal chaplains for the spiritual benefit of his own officers and subjects, but especially as missionaries to the idolatrous heathen inhabiting and adjacent to the settlement.

The missionaries, who bore the memorable names of Bartholomew Ziegenbalg and Henry Plutscho, landed at Tranquebar on the 9th July 1706, a day that was afterwards remembered with jubilees, as the beginning of a new life. Applying themselves at once to the study of the Tamil language, under a common native schoolmaster who taught them to trace the characters on the sand, they made such astonishing progress as to preach and baptize in the vernacular the following year. The first converts were only a few slaves, but in a short time, in spite of the total want of dictionaries, grammars, and all the appliances which now facilitate the acquisition of native languages, the new preachers had excited the alarm of the Brahmans, and the jealousy of the Romish priests. The New Testament was translated into Tamil by Ziegenbalg: to this he added the books of the Old Testament as far as Ruth. Fabricius completed the whole Bible, and his production is still regarded as the authorized version of the Protestant missions in the south.

These promising openings were threatened by a calamity which, in the good providence of God, was converted into the means of a far greater expansion. The war in Europe by separating the Danish settlements from their resources at home, seemed to menace the missionaries with the loss of all their hopes; but the Tranquebar mission had become an object of no little interest in England, where king George II. had received Ziegenbalg with marked cordiality, and the Society for Promoting Christian Knowledge had opened a subscription in aid of his designs. This society's committee at Madras now gladly stood forward to supply the mission with material supports; by their encouragement it was enabled to plant an offshoot at Madras in 1728, and a second at Cuddalore in 1737. The Danish and British missions were all conducted by Lutheran ministers, mostly educated in the university of Halle under the good professor Franke: they were managed on a uniform plan and in the strictest bonds of unity. About 1734 the British missionaries at Fort St. George completed a translation of the Bible into the Gentoo or Telugu language; this was written on *cadjans*, or palm leaves, with an iron style, and widely circulated, but it would seem not to have been printed. Soon after, the society having sent out a press from England, translations from the Scriptures and Prayer-book, with tracts and hymns, were issued in considerable numbers.

Among this band of labourers appear the honoured names of Fabricius, Swartz, and Gericke, all in the service of the society as "British" missionaries; each of whom received many marks of encouragement from the government of Madras. A considerable portion of the Carnatic was affected by these missions. Swartz after journeying and preaching in Tanjore fixed his residence in Trichinopoly, from which Palamcottah and Tinnevelly were reached by him and his assistants. Fabricius and after him Gericke were at Vepery in Madras; Kohloff and Gericke at Tanjore; John and Cammerer at Tranquebar. Pulicat, Sadras, Vellore, Negapatam, Madura, Dindigul, Ramnad, Tuticoreen, Manapur, Kanandagoodi, Adanjour, Lenhoor, Poodapett, Cumbagonum, Buddaloor, were the stations of schools, and many of them of churches or chapels in connexion with the missions.

The plan of proceeding was that which has since been generally followed in the Protestant missions. The missionaries conducted divine service publicly every day, both in their own and in the native languages. At their principal place of residence a church was usually erected, either by government assistance or by local subscriptions. Preaching in the streets or other places of public resort appears to have been little resorted to; but, following the example of St. Paul at Athens, they sought opportunities for conversation and discussion with the learned men, and, like the same apostle at Rome, "received all who came to them in their own houses." The first-fruits of their labours were trained to be catechists, readers, or schoolmasters. Six native catechists were in daily attendance upon Swartz, three of whom went abroad in the forenoon to converse with the heathen; a fourth was set to instruct the children, while the other two assisted the missionary in preparing inquirers for baptism. In the afternoon, the whole party went out to visit the Christian congregation, and to call on the heathen at their homes.

Every month two of the catechists were despatched into the country to extend the knowledge of the gospel, and at intervals the missionary also made his circuits to the out-stations, examining the schools, talking to the people by the wayside, and seeking every opportunity to ingratiate themselves into their confidence. Resting in a *choultry* during the heat of the day, they would begin after this fashion: "I can see that you are people that do not know the true God, because the marks on your foreheads show that some of you are worshippers of Vishnu, and others of Siva." Meeting a little party on the road, they would accost them with, "Stop a little, I pray, we will tell you something of God, whom you do not know." Or, on finding persons sitting down to rest by the roadside, they would join them, and begin the history of Adam and Eve, and their expulsion from the garden of Eden.

These addresses were listened to with eagerness; they were always concluded by a simple statement of the way of salvation through Christ, and the distribution of some missionary publications. Fabricius composed for this purpose a letter to the heathen, expressed in the most friendly and compassionate terms. Particular attention was paid, also, to the education of the children; by establishing boarding-schools for orphans of both sexes, the missionaries had soon a little flock under their exclusive training. It must be borne in mind that these pioneers of the gospel had none of the present committees and societies to apply to for their expenses. The whole cost was defrayed by their own exertions, and not a little was contributed out of their scanty stipends, or from donations awarded them by the government for public services.*

* Swartz was allowed £100 per annum by the Madras government for the spiritual care of the garrison at Trichinopoly. On taking leave of Hyder Ali, that prince bestowed on him "a bag of rupees," which he delivered over to the governor at Fort St. George; but the latter urging him to keep it for his trouble, he appropriated it to found a fund for an English charity school at Tanjore.

Their method of life was simple in the extreme: their food was as coarse and scanty as that of the lowest natives, while they abounded in good works, which invested them with an extraordinary influence over all classes of society. Swartz was often admitted to preach in the palace at Tanjore, and before the raja himself. His reputation among the natives generally was so great, that when the forces of Hyder Ali ravaged the Carnatic, he was selected, as the only European that could venture to pass through the enemy, to execute a mission of considerable importance from the government. At Tanjore, when the country people had lost all confidence, both in the British authorities and their own raja, they were induced to bring in supplies on the simple promise of the "Christian." To the same proved integrity the raja, on his death-bed, confided the guardianship of his youthful son Serfojee. The charge was transferred for awhile, for reasons of state, to the young prince's uncle who was appointed regent; but the latter abusing his trust, Swartz obtained the youth's release from captivity, and continued after his accession to the *musnud* his familiar adviser and friend. Serfojee was, in fact, "almost persuaded to be a Christian." On the death of his "father Swartz" (as he loved to call him), he caused a monument to be erected to his memory in the mission church at Tanjore, on which the venerable features were carved in marble by Flaxman. A similar memorial was erected in the fort church at Madras, by order of the Court of Directors.

Circumstances have occasioned the name of Swartz to be better known in Europe than those of his brethren in the work to which his life was devoted; but he would himself have repudiated any invidious superiority; and in the field of their common labours the memories of all are still cherished with an impartial affection.

The success which attended these exertions was astonishing. Within fifty years from the landing of Ziegenbalg and Plutscho, the number of converts amounted to six thousand; and when, on the 9th July 1706, a centenary jubilee was kept throughout the missions in commemoration of the gospel advent, upwards of *ten thousand* disciples were found to rejoice before the Lord, in addition to the cloud of witnesses who during the century had been gathered into his rest. The author may be permitted here to transcribe the expressions with which, when fresh from the scene of these exertions, he reviewed the labours now adverted to.

"The pen which has hastily traced this sketch of our Protestant missionaries, in the first century of their labours, has been employed for many years in correspondence and reports, connected with similar designs in the present day. I have visited many of the places named in this paper, perused the manuscript registers and deeds of these departed champions of the cross, and ministered in spiritual things to the descendants of their converts. I have been personally acquainted, also, with some principal missionaries now employed in the same country, not only by the Society for the Propagation of the Gospel, and the Church Missionary Society, but by the London and Wesleyan Societies also. There are men among them as faithful and laborious as any upon record; but I know not that I have ever been more deeply impressed with the manifestation of a truly missionary spirit, than in perusing the records from which this sketch is compiled. For patience, integrity, learning, self-denial, zeal, love, and the simplicity of the gospel, I know of no missionaries to be set above those of the last century; and when we consider the difficulties inseparable from first enterprises, the labour attendant on translations, grammars, and dictionaries of languages wholly unknown, with the disordered state of India from the constant wars that prevailed throughout that period, the success with which God was pleased to crown their endeavours is no less astonishing. Surely it is a far greater triumph to have won these thirteen thousand out of unbroken idolatry than, after the first successes achieved, to have increased the number to fifty thousand, enjoying, as the English now do, peace, safety, and mighty influence among the natives, with a more perfect ecclesiastical establishment abroad, and a more generous missionary spirit at home. Surely we cannot but think of the text, 'Other men laboured, and ye are entered into their labours.'" *

That nothing might be wanting to the example set by these apostles of Protestant Christianity, it was granted to them to devolve a portion of their spirit and ministry on the choicest of their converts. On the 26th of December 1790, the first† native missionary was ordained in the person of Sattianaden, one of the catechists whom the brethren had judged worthy of the ministry. On this occasion the new minister delivered a sermon in Tamil, a translation of which was published in England by the Society for Promoting Christian Knowledge. It was joyfully received, "not only as a curiosity, but as an evidence

* Brief Sketch of Missions to the Heathen. York, 1848.

† That is, the first in the missions of the Society for Promoting Christian Knowledge; but we observe in their reports, at an earlier date, the names of pastors Aaron and Diego, native ministers in the *Tranquebar* Mission, the former of whom died in 1745. There is no account of their ordination.

that the work of God is advancing in India, and the light of the gospel spreading through those regions of darkness and idolatry."*

The mode in which the early missionaries dealt with the standing difficulty of *caste* has already been noticed.† Among the converts at Cuddalore, in 1765, was a Pandaram priest of Siva, whose defection filled the Brahmans with anger and alarm. A letter of warning was sent him from the sacred college, his reply to which bears witness at once to the sincerity of his convictions and the real nature of the Hindu distinctions:—

"Answer of Arrunasalum Pandaram, now called Aralunaden, which is the same as Johannes. The grace of Parabara Wastu, who is Jehovah, the living God, the very blessed Creator and Preserver of the universe, fill the souls of all Pandarams at Tarmaburam. I have received your letter, and read the contents with true compassion: will you know the reason? It is this:—You have unaccountably forsaken the living God, the eternal Creator of all that exists, and have given the honour due to him to the creature. You think yourselves wise, though fallen into the most dreadful foolishness. You worship the arch enemy of all that is good, the devil. You give divine honours to men who were born of father and mother, and who during their lives have been notorious fornicators, adulterers, rogues, and murderers. Fourteen years have I been witness of your infamous worship in your pagodas, and I am convinced in my conscience you are in the road that leads directly to hell and eternal ruin.

"How holy, how majestic is God as described in

* Reports, p. 324.

† Chapter iv.

the Vedam of the Christians! You call them a base and ignorant people, but this is owing to your pride, which cometh from that proud spirit, Satan. Be not deceived to expiate your sin by washing and sacrifice of Lingam. The Christians alòne have an expiatory sacrifice worthy of God. You know the integrity of my life, and you never heard scandal of me; could you, then, think that I should renounce the religion of my fathers without conviction of its falsehoods and dreadful tendency? The God of infinite compassion has delivered me, wretched sinner, out of Satan's captivity. Your promises of riches and honour touch me not. I have the hope of an everlasting kingdom; you can also inherit it when you repent.

"I have changed my religion, but not my caste. By becoming a Christian I did not turn an Englishman. I am yet a Tondaman. Never did the priest of this place desire of me anything contrary to my caste. Never did he bid me eat cow-flesh or beef; neither have I seen him eat it, or any of the Tamilian Christians, though such a thing be not sinful in itself. 'Turn to the living God;' so writeth Aralunaden, formerly a Pandaram, but now a disciple of the blessed Jesus."

While the gospel was thus rooting itself on the shores of Coromandel, an opening was gladly accepted for throwing out an offshoot in Bengal. Mr. Kiernander proceeded from Cuddalore to Calcutta in 1758, and was warmly welcomed both by the governor-general (lord Clive) and the Company's chaplains (Butler and Cape), by whose influence large subscriptions were obtained in aid of the mission.

Having married a wealthy widow,* this missionary

* Kaye's Christianity, p. 91.

was less straitened than many others in the means of worldly support. He erected a church, mainly at his own expense, in the room of that which had been destroyed on the capture of Calcutta by Surajah Dowlah. Schools, too, were planted at his charge. The mission, however, did not extend beyond Calcutta, and its converts were mostly from among the Portuguese Romanists of the lower orders. A priest of that church, born of European parents at Goa, embraced his teaching and became his assistant. A few heathen and Mohammedans were also baptized; but in 1787, Mr. Kiernander having become old and falling into difficulties, his property was sold by the sheriffs of Calcutta, to satisfy his creditors. The church, school, and burying-ground were purchased for ten thousand rupees by Mr. Charles Grant, and conveyed to trustees, on whose application the Society for Promoting Christian Knowledge sent out to its charge the first English clergyman who undertook the missionary's office in India. Unhappily, being the same year appointed to the more lucrative post of a chaplain, this clergyman proceeded up the country, leaving the mission to the care of David Brown and John Owen, then chaplains at Calcutta. A German missionary was found for it some years later; but he, too, abandoned his post and returned to Europe; after which the trustees made arrangements with the Court of Directors to appoint two chaplains to the "old," or "mission" church, and from that time nothing but the name has remained to perpetuate the memory of an attempt, which once gave good promise of success.

In tracing these notices of the early Protestant missions, it is refreshing to notice the large and liberal spirit in which they were conducted. The Society for Promoting Christian Knowledge, by which so large a portion of the missionaries were provided and paid, was then, as it is now, a Church of England society. It was presided over by the bishops, and all its members were clergymen, or devoted members of the episcopal communion. Yet this society cheerfully accepted candidates for employ from the colleges of Copenhagen and Halle, and gladly contributed to the support of missions conducted by Lutheran ministers on a Presbyterian model. No question of that kind seems for a moment to have disturbed their unanimity. The Lutheran missionary attends before the episcopal committee to receive the farewell address, and reciprocate the brotherly regards of the dignitary in the chair. He is received, on landing, with open arms by episcopal clergymen, the Company's chaplains. He baptizes, catechises, and ordains in his mission, no man gainsaying his authority or the value of the ordinances so dispensed among the natives. The Society at home expresses its joy at every door that is opened, and prays that multitudes may enter by it. Nay, in Calcutta, an episcopal missionary succeeded, and was succeeded by, a Lutheran in the same charge, and no apprehension was expressed on the score of order and ecclesiastical discipline.

It may be granted that the age referred to was somewhat too indifferent to questions affecting the constitution of a church, and that, in the natural progress of thought, points which have been neglected at one time assume an exaggerated importance at another. The case, too, had not then arisen of different denominations of Protestant Christianity appearing side by side in the missionary field. It is by no means intended to censure any, who may now think that a judicious zeal for the propagation of the truth requires more attention to the local system which is to conserve and extend it. It may be true that the ancient unanimity has, from various causes, become more difficult of attainment; still it is pleasant to linger over a scene where it was both feasible and actual—when the exclamation was heard as of old, "Christ is preached, and I therein do rejoice." The members of the Established Church may be reminded that this kindly spirit had its reward in the quiet adoption of her own order and liturgy, as soon as she found herself able to undertake the care of these missions. Others will be consoled by observing that the district, so planted and watered in love, is still the part of India where the gospel has realized the most abundant first-fruits, and enjoys the brightest prospect of a further harvest.

CHAPTER X.

CHRISTIANITY.—EXISTING MISSIONS.

New era—Change of feeling in India and at home—Government connexion with idolatry—Declarations against missionaries—Home feelings—Baptist ministers—Carey—Difficulties at Calcutta—Ward and Marshman—Serampore mission—Translations—Preaching—Repudiation of caste—London Missionary Society—Resistance in Calcutta—American missionaries ordered to return—Fly to Bombay—Captured—Permitted to remain—Movement in Parliament—Act of emancipation—Ecclesiastical establishments—Society for the Propagation of the Gospel—Tinnevelly missions—Happy contrast—Contradistinguished from Rome—Madras—Bishop's College, Calcutta—Church Missionary Society—Kishnagur—Company's chaplains—General Baptist Society—Orissa—Victims rescued from Khonds—Preaching mission—Wesleyan Missionary Society—Madras and Mysore—Scottish Missionary Society—Free Church—Educational character—American and German missions—General results—Masses not reached—Idolatry powerful—Arduous struggle—Believer's hope—Instruments—Diversity of aspect—Practical union—Question submitted—Political and ecclesiastical peculiarities—Church of India—Foundation-stone—Acts of the Apostles—Faith required—Witness of false creeds—CHRIST the personal Saviour.

A NEW era of Protestant missions opened with the early part of the nineteenth century, and India became the field of employment to an increased number of agencies. The Court of Directors in transmitting the monument to the memory of Swartz, which they ordered to be placed in the church of Fort St. George, expressed their "unanimous and anxious desire to excite in others an emulation of his great example." But a spirit was fermenting among some of their servants, which soon infused itself into their own councils, and when the emulation was exhibited, the government was found anxious to suppress it.

The growth of the British empire in India had developed a political expediency which regarded evangelical zeal with distrust and apprehension. The pagodas and mosques having been taken under the patronage of the state, regulations were enacted which declared it to be the duty of the government officers to see that their endowments were duly appropriated to the purposes for which they were made.* Nor was it only a general superintendence and patronage of idolatry that was required from British officers: an active participation in its rites, shamefully inconsistent with Christian integrity, was demanded by government, and conceded by their unreflecting or unresisting inferiors. To this state of things the presence and labours of missionaries were of course highly distasteful; efforts were made to alarm the public at home for the danger that might ensue from their exertions; it was declared by numbers who claimed to be listened to with deference, that India itself would be lost if missionaries were allowed to "interfere with the religion of the natives." Some even protested that the native creeds were entitled to respect for their moral and philosophical tendencies, and better suited to the condition of India than the gospel of eternal life.

Happily, a spirit of another kind had been gaining ground in England, and was found ready to encounter and put to flight the new champions of idolatry. Both within and without the pale of the Established Church, there was now a growing sense of the respon-

* Reg. xix. of 1810, Bengal Code. Reg. vii. of 1817, Madras Code.

sibilities of the gospel, with a fixed determination to labour for its dissemination among the heathen. India, with its millions of idolaters brought by Providence into immediate connexion with Protestant England, presented the first and loudest demand, and her cry was no longer to be neglected. The first association to take the field originated in 1784, with a few ministers of the Baptist persuasion assembling for prayer at Kettering, in Northamptonshire. One of them, who has been called "the inspired cobbler," was Mr. William Carey. He had prepared for a mission to Tahiti, when the arrival in England of a Mr. Thomas, formerly a surgeon, who had been employed by Mr. Grant, after the retirement of Kiernander, in an endeavour to found a mission at Malda, determined his course to Bengal.

The Court of Directors regarded this design with far less favour than had been shown to the German missionaries. Not only was no free passage granted, but a license of embarkation was refused, and the adventurers were obliged to proceed in a Danish ship. On arriving at Calcutta, sir John Shore, then governor-general, having granted them permission to reside, they betook themselves to secular employment, in order to provide the means of support. Thomas was in evil repute on account of former misdoings, and no welcome was extended by Brown and the friends of missions in Calcutta. Carey, after retreating to the Sunderbunds, where he lived on the produce of the jungle, obtained the charge of an indigo factory in Malda, and a few years later was enabled to purchase a small concern for himself, which he proposed to make the nucleus of a missionary institution.

He was followed, however, by Mr. William Ward,

formerly a printer in Derby, and Mr. Joshua Marshman, a schoolmaster, and these having passed Calcutta, in order to avoid detention by the British authorities, found a welcome at the Danish settlement of Serampore, sixteen miles further up the Hooghly. Here Carey joined them early in 1800; and as in the south of India so in the north, the first permanent mission of Protestant Christianity was opened under the protection of the Danish flag.

The first object of the missionaries, as of their predecessors in the south, was the translation of the Bible, a work for which Carey had been diligently studying the native languages since his arrival. In March 1800, the printing of the New Testament in Bengali was commenced, and in little more than a year two thousand entire copies were struck off. A translation of the Old Testament was finished the same year, and in 1809 the whole Bible was revised and sent to press in five large volumes. A version of the New Testament in Sanscrit next appeared, and so high was now the reputation of the missionaries for Oriental learning, that Carey was appointed one of the professors in lord Wellesley's college at Fort William. These early versions were regarded by their authors as merely "tentative," and they have received many improvements in subsequent revisions. They served to fix the leading features of the Serampore mission as a seat of biblical literature. Translations have since been completed there in no fewer than forty-three dialects of India, Ceylon, Malacca, Burmah, Java, and China, while above a million of copies have issued from the press at Calcutta in the principal languages of Northern India. Grammars, dictionaries, and other valuable contributions to Indian literature, general and religious, have issued from the same source, and the first native newspaper was the production of the zeal of the Baptist missionaries.*

While thus efficient in literary labours, the mission was not inattentive to the more direct preaching of the gospel. Carey laid down his pen to preach in the highways, while his colleagues were setting up the press; Marshman and his wife presided over boarding-schools, which obtained an extended reputation; and Ward, the author of the most accurate account we still possess of the Hindu superstitions, was animated by the purest zeal for their conversion. Their first disciple was baptized on 28th December 1800, in the river Hooghly, in the presence of the governor of Serampore; and in 1803 the little flock was increased by the accession of a Brahman. The views of these missionaries, social as well as religious, had been formed in a different school from those of their German predecessors in the south. They decided at once to hold no terms with *caste*. Their maxim was that "Christianity is but of one caste." The Brahman joined his fellow-Christians, renouncing all privilege of natural birth; and so thoroughly was the new doctrine

* The summary of Scriptures printed at Calcutta, up to March, 1856, includes:—

	Copies.
Armenian	2,990
Bengali	718,417
Mussulman do.	33,000
Hindi (Deva Nagri)	57,500
Hindi (Kaithi)	182,500
Sanscrit	76,580
Sanscrit Bengali	7,500
Hindustani	155,530
Persian	38,500
Kassia	1,000
Nepalese	2,500
Lepcha	1,500
Sontal	800

imbibed, that he actually married the daughter of the carpenter who had been the first-fruits of the mission and its first native evangelist. The educational repute of this mission is still sustained by the Serampore College, founded in 1818 and lately affiliated on the Calcutta University, while its mission stations have extended to Calcutta and to seven other large native cities on the Ganges.

The Baptist Missionary Society was not long to enjoy the field to itself. The closing days of the year 1798 witnessed the arrival in Calcutta of a missionary despatched by the "London Missionary Society," then newly formed on a plan intended to comprehend all orthodox and evangelical denominations. The conception, however, proving more liberal than feasible, the members of the Church of England mostly withdrew from the association, and established another under the title of the "Church Missionary Society to Africa and the East." The London Society continued for awhile to afford a common ground to Presbyterians and Congregationalists, but eventually lapsed to the latter denomination, to which it now exclusively appertains. Its earliest station was the Dutch settlement of Chinsurah, on the Hooghly in Bengal. A mission to the Telugus was next opened at Vizagapatam, and another in the native state of Travancore. After establishing itself at Madras, the society extended its operations to the Southern Mahratta country and to Guzerat. Its missionaries have laboured in translating the Scriptures into Bengali, Urdu, Telugu, Canarese, Tamil, Malayalam, and Guzerathi. It has mission stations in each of the three presidencies, and in the native state of Travancore; and a valuable college for the training of a native ministry is in operation at Bangalore.

The increased exhibition of missionary zeal seems to have only added force to the resistance determined on at Calcutta. The Vellore massacre, in July 1806, produced from the Court of Directors no more than an injunction to guard against "any imprudent or injudicious attempts" on the part of the missionaries which might "irritate and alarm the religious prejudices of the natives." The caution was accompanied by a distinct intimation that "the Court was very far from being averse to the introduction of Christianity into India, or indifferent to the benefits which would result from a general diffusion of its doctrines." * Nothing would appear to be more explicit than these instructions, and nothing could well be more directly in opposition to their spirit and letter than the proceedings of lord Minto's government in 1812.

Actuated by a zeal to partake the labours and honour of their transatlantic brethren in Christ, the American Board of Missions despatched five missionaries to Calcutta. The experiment proved highly distasteful to the authorities, whose objections were, possibly, political as well as religious. The little party was informed that, having arrived in the Company's dominions without a license, they must immediately return in the ship that brought them out. With some difficulty one of them obtained leave to proceed to the Isle of France. Two others (Judson and Rice), having embraced the Baptist persuasion, determined to find a new field for themselves, and sailed for Burmah, then altogether unevan-

* Despatch, 7th Sept., 1858.

gelized. The others took shipping for Bombay, but being anticipated by orders from the supreme government, were again commanded to leave the country. They had sailed for Cochin; but intelligence having been received of the breaking out of hostilities between England and the United States, an armed courier was despatched to bring them back to Bombay. There they were under orders for England, when the governor was prevailed on to make another reference to Calcutta. Lord Moira, who was now in authority, proved to be animated by a more generous spirit: he allowed the missionaries to remain till the Court of Directors had been consulted; and the latter body having finally left the decision to the Bombay government, the desired permission was readily granted. This first Protestant mission in Bombay was enabled to commence its labours in 1814-15.

The intolerant spirit displayed by the authorities at Calcutta only added force to a determination, already taken at home, to impose a Parliamentary restraint on their caprices for the future. The state of Christianity was made the subject of inquiry in committee, and of earnest debate in both Houses of Parliament. It was resolved to establish an episcopal see at Calcutta, with archdeaconries at Madras and Bombay, in order at once to add efficiency to the ecclesiastical establishments of government, and to give expression and dignity to Christianity in the eyes of the natives. To this enactment was added another, directing the Company (in the cautious language still deemed essential to success) to "afford facilities to persons desirous of going to and remaining in India, for the purpose of introducing useful knowledge and religious and moral improvement."

The new law was hailed by the friends of missions as an "act of emancipation," and immediate measures were adopted to take full advantage of its provisions. The erection of ecclesiastical dignities incited the Established Church to a fresh arrangement of its missions. The Christian Knowledge Society transferred their charge in the south to the care of the Society for the Propagation of the Gospel, by whom the congregations were organized in closer connexion with the Church, and gradually supplied with missionaries of episcopal ordination. The Book of Common-prayer, already extensively used, became as in England the sole authorized ritual; but it was accompanied by a valuable inheritance from the German missionaries in a copious hymn-book, which is still the delight of the Tamil congregations.

The Tanjore, Tranquebar, and Tinnevelly missions, have greatly prospered and extended themselves under the new organization. The Church Missionary Society, being attracted to the same promising field in 1814, further enlarged the area of operations; and these united labours drew from bishop Heber a declaration that "the missions in the south were the strength of the Christian cause in India." Since then it seems as if the prophecy of Gericke on first visiting Tinnevelly in 1792, were about to receive a speedy fulfilment—"There is every reason to hope that at a future period Christianity will prevail in the Tinnevelly country."

In many of the villages, demonolatry and idolatry are already extirpated. The devil temples have been thrown down or converted to Christian uses, the idols are destroyed, and the whole community have embraced the profession of Christianity. Most of these villages have now their modest houses of prayer, where "supplications, prayers, intercessions, and giving of thanks," are daily offered to the true God in the name of Jesus Christ. In some, churches of larger dimensions receive overflowing congregations on the Christian festivals, in happy exchange for the forsaken rites of heathenism. The improvement thus effected is strikingly contrasted with the former condition of these villages. "Picture to yourself," writes an eye-witness, and labourer in the field, "the frantic rites with which the heathen Shanar worships his devils. The stillness of the night is broken by the din of the drum and the harsh bray of the horn, announcing the commencement of a devil-dance in a neighbouring village. Follow the sound through the tortuous prickly-pear lanes, and witness the performance from a distance by the help of the flickering torch-light. Observe in everything the combination of the ludicrous and the sanguinary; the grotesque insignia of office worn by the officiating priest, his truculent, devilish stare, the blood-bespattered garlands on the temple and altar, the row of boiling pots on one side, and the row of energetic musicians on the other, the promiscuous heap of offerings, and the characteristic union of finery and filth everywhere visible. Watch the excitement of the admiring crowd rising higher and higher with every new contortion and shriek of the devil-dancer, and with the rising vehemence of the musical uproar; and hear ever and anon the long vibratory shout of delight and wild devotion into which the assembled crowd breaks out. Then, as you turn away from these debasing orgies, contrast with them the worship of God in spirit and in truth, the reasonable service with which Christians worship their holy and beneficent Creator through their Mediator's merits, the renunciation of the devil and all his works, to which Christ's followers are pledged, the stillness of the Christian sabbath, the "sound of the church-going bell," the soothing, cheering voice of psalms and prayers, the instructions, the persuasions, the devout earnestness of the Christian preacher, the healing balm of sacraments;—institute this comparison and you will not only be impressed with the greatness of the difference between Divine worship and the worship of devils, but will also be stimulated to use every means in your power for the diffusion of the knowledge of the better way."*

The evangelical character of Protestant missions, as contrasted with Romish ones in the same neighbourhood, is attested by the appellations, bestowed on them by the heathen, of *Mary* churches and *God* churches respectively. When the bishop of Madras visited Tinnevelly in 1845, a petition was presented to him from 150 heathens, complaining that whereas "the Mohammedans, the Hindus, *and the Papists* abide by their own religions, and never consent to force over persons of other religions into theirs, the missionaries who come out to teach *Christianity* make congregations of Shanars, Pullars, and Pariahs, who have always been our slaves, and shoemakers, basketmakers, and other low-caste persons, and teach them the gospel, the ten commandments, and the other things."†

The first "British mission" in India is still continued at Vepery, near Madras, under the Society for

* Shanars of Tinnevelly, by Rev. R. Caldwell.
† Bishop of Madras's Visitation Journal, 1845.

the Propagation of the Gospel. A valuable seminary for catechists, and a grammar school for general instruction, are combined with this mission. Another institution in the native town, called Bishop Corrie's Grammar School, is under the care of the Church Missionary Society.

In Bengal the introduction of the episcopate was followed by the foundation of an important missionary institution, erected by the Society for the Propagation of the Gospel with the assistance of other Church societies, under the supervision of the first bishop. Situated on the opposite bank of the Hooghly, about four miles below Calcutta, "Bishop's College" is designed both for the education of missionaries, and the translation of Christian literature into the native languages. Its system of instruction includes a good English collegiate education, modified to the peculiar wants of India. Sanscrit, Bengali, Hindustani, Persian, Arabic, Tamil, and Cingalese, are taught by native pundits and moonshees, under the direction of a principal and two professors from home. Several missionaries and catechists—European, country-born, and native—have been trained in this institution, and its literary reputation is deservedly high. Some flourishing missions, also, have been opened in connexion with Bishop's College, in the neighbourhood of Calcutta. The Society for the Propagation of the Gospel has further planted missions at Delhi and Cawnpore, which, though apparently extinguished in the blood of the martyrs slaughtered during the recent mutiny, are about to be re-established on a larger scale.

A still wider field in Bengal is occupied by the Church Missionary Society, which sustains a greater number of missionaries in India than any other Protestant Association. A signal measure of success has attended the exertions of its agents in Kishnagur. It has established stations at Calcutta and seven or eight other places along the course of the Ganges, in Himalaya, the Punjab, Peshawur, and recently at Lucknow. This indefatigable society is labouring also at Bombay, and at Nasik, Junir, Mulhjam, and Sindh.

The missions of the Established Church are assisted in various ways by the clergymen on the ecclesiastical establishments of the government, some of whom have been always actuated by the purest missionary zeal.* Most of the chaplains superintend schools and assist more or less in the Christian education of the natives. Many of them are engaged in active missionary efforts. All contribute to enlarge the rising cloud of witnesses who testify in India to the existence and the nature of England's religion; and if their personal labours are directed chiefly towards raising the standard of practical Christianity among the European residents, no one who knows the course of evangelization, and the impediments to its progress, will refuse on that account to include them among the missionaries of India.

While the Church of England was thus enlarging its efforts, the Nonconformist bodies were increasingly pressing into the field. The New Connexion of General Baptists organized in 1816 a missionary society, which has concentrated its labours on the province of Orissa. Renowned among Hindus as the peculiar abode of the gods, no part of India seems to a Christian in a more

* To the honoured names of Brown, Buchanan, Martyn, Thomason, and Corrie, may now be added that of Jennings, the late chaplain at Delhi, founder and director of the mission which he has watered with his blood.

barbarous and pitiable condition. Juggernath holds his bloody and obscene orgies at Pooree, annually drinking the blood of some hundreds of victims, who perish in the fatal pilgrimage to his altars. The sanguinary rite of Meriah pollutes the neighbouring Khonds, and hardly any of the influences of Hindu or Mohammedan civilization seems to have descended on this uncultivated province. In choosing this dismal quarter for its field of labour, the society was guided by the apostolic principle, "not to boast in another man's line." Its founders resolved to select a sphere which should be at once wide and unoccupied. And as they did to others, so it has been done to them. No other society (save its kindred association in America) has invaded the honourable monopoly.

Guided by Mr. Ward of Serampore, the first mission was planted at Cuttack in 1816. Stations have been since occupied in Piplee, half way to Pooree, and at Berhampore. Notwithstanding some vehement opposition from the high-caste men, here as in other parts of India even the Brạhman has been persuaded to receive the yoke of Christ. Land is cheap, and when cleared of the jungle villages have been formed for the native Christians, where the means of obtaining a respectable livelihood are offered to all that will embrace the apostolic injunction to *work*. These Christian villages, with the houses embowered in trees, the little sanctuary in the midst, the Christian sabbath, and the evangelical pastor (once a heathen himself), form a refreshing contrast to the jungle out of which they have been rescued, and to the spiritual wilderness, still more dreary, from which their inhabitants have been translated by grace.

The asylums established for orphan children have

afforded a home to several of the victims rescued from the Khonds. More than two hundred boys and girls, intended for the dreadful sacrifice, have been trained in godliness, and instances have occurred in which children newly arrived were recognised as the brothers or sisters of others already in the schools.

This mission has been distinguished by the honourable appellation of the great *preaching* mission of the Bengal presidency. All other plans are regarded as subordinate to the oral promulgation of the gospel in the vernacular language. For this purpose many thousand miles are annually gone over, and frequent visits are paid to Pooree, when the festival of Juggernath is attracting its enormous concourse of pilgrims from all parts of India during the burning month of June. The pilgrim-tax having been discontinued since 1840, no official account is now kept of the numbers who flock to see this hideous idol drawn on its rude car in unmeaning triumph: they are estimated at nearly a hundred thousand, three-quarters of whom are *women!* The practice of self-immolation under the wheels of the car is now prohibited, but six or seven hundred deaths from disease and other causes still appease the monster's thirst for blood.

The Wesleyan Missionary Society has some missionaries in Madras, Trichinopoly, and two or three other stations in the Southern Carnatic. A still larger number have commenced a great work in certain districts of Mysore, their labours being directed to portions of the Tamil and Canarese nations. A considerable share of their labour has been spent on publications in those two languages, which are issued in great numbers from a very efficient press at Bangalore. Their educational institution at Royapettah in Madras is among the colleges affiliated on the university of that place.

The Scottish Missionary Society, having turned its attention to India about 1822, selected the western coast as least provided with preachers of the gospel. Their first missionary reached Bombay in 1823, when the Church of England mission had been in operation for three years, and the American for eight or nine. These were then the only labourers in the Mahratta language, which extends from Nagpore to Goa, and is spoken by one of the proudest and most intractable of the native races. The predominant feeling of this people, smarting under the recent humiliation and deposition of the Peishwa, was one of intense hostility to the British, religiously and politically. Being on this account refused permission to settle at Poona, the Scottish missionaries receded into the Southern Konkan, a province which enjoyed the bad distinction of retaining the practice of suttee after it had been abolished throughout the rest of British India.* Two of the missionaries obtained permission to remove to Poona in 1829, and a third was established at Bombay in the same year. Much pains having been taken in acquiring the language, discussions were held with the Brahmans, which resulted, as usual, in exposing the folly of their traditions, and the solidity and purity of the Scripture doctrines. The missionaries, also, early took a prominent share in the educational work for which the western presidency was distinguished, till it was outstripped by the broader plans of Mr. Thomason in the North-west provinces.

* It was not till 1830 that this barbarous practice was finally suppressed throughout the Bombay presidency.

This mission was adopted by the Established Church of Scotland in 1835; thence it passed to the Free Church, and the work of native education has been subsequently prosecuted as a special object of pursuit. The policy of this body is to appoint missionaries of superior attainments, who shall open institutions of a high order of education, with a view (in addition to their general influence) of training up natives well qualified for every department of the evangelical work. The preaching of the gospel from class to class in the school or college, and the thorough indoctrination of educated natives to bear the word of life to their countrymen, is considered as a strictly missionary employment, and one which is peculiarly suited to the wants of a large portion of the Indian community.

On these principles a mission was opened at Calcutta in 1830, at Madras in 1837, and at Nagpore in 1844. The leading feature in all is the offer of a sound Christian education to all classes of society, Hindu and Mohammedan, accompanied by the uniform adoption of the Bible as a class-book, and a resolute rejection of the pretensions of *caste*. Brahmans and Pariahs sit side by side in the same class, and are practically made to feel the unity of human nature, even while clinging to the empty theory of a difference of species. Many battles have been fought with the caste men on this question, and the schools have been repeatedly emptied of their students; but the missionaries remaining inexorable, the advantages of the education imparted are so well appreciated, that the natives have always yielded in the end, and returned to seek admission for their children in greater numbers. The Scottish schools have not unfrequently yielded fruit in the conversion of some of the elder youths to Christianity. Several of these being of the higher castes have occasioned no little excitement among the natives. One of them, Krishnu Mohun Banerjea, a Brahman of high descent, is now professor of Sanscrit in Bishop's College, Calcutta, and an ordained missionary of the Society for the Propagation of the Gospel. Another, Gopanâth Nandi, has been ordained in the American Presbyterian Mission at Futtehpore; and a third, Rajendra C. Chanda, having embraced the medical profession, came to England, carried off the highest honours in the London University, and received an appointment as assistant surgeon in the Company's service.

At Bombay the Scottish mission schools have been attended, in addition to the ordinary classes of native youth, by Parsees and Jews; though the former have almost all withdrawn in alarm at the recent baptism of one of their race. The moral and religious improvement effected among the Ben Israel is said to be of a promising character.

In all the presidencies great attention has been paid to female education. At Calcutta, besides an orphan asylum, a school has been opened for Armenian and Jewish girls, and more recently another for high-caste females, which is already attended by seventy pupils. The other presidencies, being more free from prejudice on this subject, the numbers of girls are considerably higher. At Nagpore (the only mission station in the newly annexed kingdom of Berar) the results are as yet comparatively few.

These exertions of British Christianity have been ably responded to from Protestant America and Germany. Missions have been planted by the American Board, the American Presbyterian Board, and the

American Baptist Union. The Berlin and Leipsic Missionary Societies are also in the field.

The exertions of these agencies have been crowned with a tolerable amount of success at each of the presidency towns and in the southern portion of the peninsula. Missions also exist at some of the chief European stations, at several points on the coast, and at one or two large native cities of the interior, such as Benares, Delhi, Mysore, Nagpore, and Lahore. They extend by isolated and widely separated points from Cape Comorin to Peshawur, but many of these are recently planted and feebly manned, while the intervening territories are vast, and the population may be counted by millions, among whom no vestige of evangelical labour as yet exists. The "harvest truly is great;" and we may trust that the labourers have at least begun to be sent forth into it. In many districts the natives are generally acquainted with the existence and character of evangelical Christianity; in some they have learned to hold it in high admiration. The increased communication to be expected from railways and other internal improvements, the efforts of the press, and the general diffusion of knowledge, will give a wonderful extension to these impressions, and possibly within a very few years a spirit of inquiry may be awakened which will largely affect, and be affected by, the government schools.

Still it must be borne in mind that the missionary agencies have as yet *hardly reached* the mass of native society. The vast agricultural population, the martial races, the aboriginal tribes, and the whole female sex, are as yet almost untouched. It is only in the southern extremity of the peninsula that any real impression has been made on the villages. The large provinces, or rather kingdoms, of the Punjab, Sindh, Rajpootana, Oude, Hindustan, the Mahratta country, Guzerat, and the dominions of the Nizam of Hyderabad, are scarcely, if at all, entered upon.

On the other hand, idolatry, though evincing many symptoms of decay, is established through the length and breadth of the land, and rooted in the affections of millions. The struggle for its overthrow must be arduous and protracted, and it would be a ruinous delusion to expect any extensive assistance from the recent change in the government of the country. The province of government is to afford an open field for the church. The ministers of the crown are not likely to be more favourable to missionary efforts than the defunct East India Company. Symptoms have even appeared of an indisposition to give full effect to principles already agreed upon. *The gospel and the Lord of the gospel must be the believer's hope for the evangelization of India.*

In regard to the instrumentality to be employed, no better can be suggested than that which is actually in operation. The great work at present is to increase the number and qualifications of the missionaries. Those who exercise a conscientious discrimination will, of course, give a preference to the associations of their own religious communion; yet all may be assured that in contributing to *any* they are directly assisting in the civilization of the natives, the circulation of the Scriptures, and the lively preaching of that truth which maketh "wise unto salvation."

It is a subject of regret with many that Protestant Christianity should exhibit itself to the Hindu inquirer under so many aspects; and where the different denominations are found in the same place some confusion may possibly arise. But the evil is by no means so great as some would represent. The native mind is familiar with the existence of sects and schools, more discordant far, in their own religions; while the missionaries, being removed from the political and polemical dissensions of the mother land, are powerfully attracted to each other by the common necessities and aspirations of their all-important work. The degree of practical union is great and apparent, and the day is far distant when the numbers of their converts, and the disappearance of idolatry, will leave them at liberty to scan their distinctive features more closely.*

Still in anticipation of such a day, a question may be submitted, whether the lines which separate Christians in Europe must of necessity be perpetuated among the natives of India. The different denominations owe their peculiarities, in some degree, to the local incidents, political and ecclesiastical, which contributed to their rise and progress. It may be impossible or undesirable to attempt any extensive alteration in the views which have been permitted to gain predominance among themselves; but it is another question how far it is necessary to imprint such views on the rising church of India, which, in the providence of God, will have its own history, and stand in circumstances widely differing from that of Europe. The work of the European missionary seems

* The author recalls with thankfulness that at a meeting of missionaries of various denominations, held for the formation of a Christian School-book Society at Bangalore, he was himself placed in the chair, as the government chaplain of the station, and continued to hold the presidency for seven years in perfect amity, every other minister on the committee being a Nonconformist. He can never remember their labours and spirit without admiration and respect.

to be to lay the foundations of that coming church: the fabric will be shaped and edified by the native pastors who are to succeed them.

May it, therefore, be permitted humbly to suggest to missionaries of every communion to concentrate their labours more and more on preaching and teaching Christ, the true Foundation-stone? Such a course might abridge the time for which inquirers are too often kept under instruction prior to baptism. The object of this delay, no doubt, is to protect the gospel from false adherents, but the effect in some cases may be to impose a heavier burden than the newly-born faith can sustain. During this interval the disciple is exposed to a mingled torrent of entreaties, reproaches, and threats, from heathen connexions seeking to avert his purpose. In this moment it is that the influence of the women and the power of caste are most prejudicial. Once baptized, he is relinquished to his fate, and in the communion of his Christian brethren finds a new home and a better *caste*.

In the Acts of the Apostles—that great repertory of missionary principles—we see little of our modern precautions. The first preachers of Christianity were not afraid to baptize on a simple profession of faith, though the Epistles show us with how much of imperfection and sin the faith of the baptized was still polluted. If we inquire, then, into the nature of the faith so accepted, we shall find that it was not a clear, connected assent to a number of theological propositions, but the surrender of the heart's affection and trust *to a Divine Person.* "I believe that Jesus Christ is the Son of God:" this was the sum and substance, the glory and strength, of apostolical Christianity.

The personality of God and the genuine manhood of the Redeemer are the pillars of such a trust. The Hindu and the Mussulman seem to be feeling after it in their misplaced attachment to Krishna and Mohammed. What these can never truly be JESUS CHRIST may be to both, and with that higher adoration and love which belong to his superior nature and grace. Let the gospel missionary then never cease to "teach and preach JESUS CHRIST." Let his catechumens "learn CHRIST." The Hindu will here find the very Sacrificial Male, the only Incarnation of the Godhead, the Substance of all that is vainly grasped at in his incoherent legends. The Moslem will hail the true Messenger and Well Beloved of the High and Holy One, the Human Person who is the centre and joy of man's heart, and the Divine Regenerator of his nature. In this "Second Adam, the LORD from heaven," the many tongues and races of India are to own the long-expected Restorer of Unity, the Desire of all nations, the Saviour of mankind. Be it ours to present him to their acceptance in the majesty and goodness of his Divine Person; and when the door of their hearts shall be opened to his reception, when the cleansing streams of his blood are secretly shed abroad in their souls, and the dew of his Spirit descends upon the creature which he hath fashioned anew to his glory, the CHRIST who will be so formed in them will reproduce himself in the outward life, and "supply all their need according to his riches in glory." *

* Phil. iv. 19.

INDEX.